# OVER THE SUMMIT

# OVER THE SUMMIT

## *How Britain's railways crossed the high hills*

Christopher Awdry

Silver Link Publishing Ltd

# ACKNOWLEDGEMENTS

Many people have contributed to this book, and my sincere thanks go to the following:

Public Record Office, Kew
Scottish Record Office, Edinburgh
Essex Record Office, Chelmsford
Clwyd County Record Office, Mold
Royal Commission on Ancient & Historical
   Monuments in Wales
Cambridge University Library
National Railway Museum Library
Public Libraries in Bath, Buxton, Chester, Gloucester,
   Leamington Spa, Stamford, Peterborough,
   Plymouth and Winchester
Chester Cathedral

Michael Baker, Colin Caddy, Frank Cossey, Robert Humm, John James, Gwyn Briwnant-Jones, Steve Machell (Cumbrian Railway Assoc) and John Norris The photographers who have allowed me to use their work, and are individually credited, and Allan Mott for printing photographic material and for his expertise in other allied matters.

Finally, but by no means least importantly, to Will Adams of Silver Link for suggesting the idea, to the Rev W. V. Awdry whose 'library' I have frequently raided, and to my wife Diana, who has kept the word processor on the rails and provided plentiful supplies of encouragement and black coffee.

First published in August 1993

British Library Cataloguing in Publication Data

A catalogue record for the book is available from the British Library

ISBN 1 85794 001 6

Maps drawn by Ian Body

The gradient profiles, from *Gradients of British Main-line Railways*, published in 1947 by The Railway Publishing Co Ltd, are reproduced by kind permission of Ian Allan Ltd.

The negatives of photographs credited to E. D. Bruton are held by the National Railway Museum, York.

Silver Link Publishing Ltd
Unit 5
Home Farm Close
Church Street
Wadenhoe
Peterborough
PE8 5TE

Printed and bound in Great Britain

# CONTENTS

Introduction 7
Bibliography 8

1 South and West
Hemerdon and Rattery 9
Dainton 12
Meldon 14
Mortehoe 16
Whiteball 18
Semley, Milborne Port, Hewish
and Honiton 20
Evershot and Bincombe 23
Micheldever 27
Sole Street 29
Guston 31

2 London, Midlands and East
Victoria (Grosvenor) 33
Liverpool Street (Bethnal Green) 34
Brentwood 36
Elsenham 38
King's Cross (Holloway) 40
The 'Northern Heights' (1):
Potters Bar and Woolmer Green 42
Stoke 45
The 'Northern Heights' (2):
Elstree and Sandridge 48
Sharnbrook 49
Euston (Camden) 53
Marylebone 54
Amersham 55
Saunderton 56

3 Cotswold Country
Masbury 58
Sapperton 61
Box and Dauntsey 64
Severn Tunnel, Patchway and
Badminton 66
Chipping Camden 68
Hatton 70
Notgrove 72
Lickey 74

4 Cambrian Mountains
Drws-y-Nant 77
Talerddig 79
Llandre 83
Trawscoed 84
Llangunllo and Sugar Loaf 85
Torpantau (Seven-Mile Bank) 88
Llanvihangel 90
Church Stretton 92
Gresford 94

5 Across the Pennines
Hopton 97
Peak Forest 99
Cowburn 102
Woodhead 104
Standedge 107
Werneth 109
Summit 110
Stainmore 112
Goathland 114

6 Borders and Galloway
Grayrigg and Shap 116
Ais Gill 120
Cockburnspath 123
Whitrope 127
Falahill 130
Beattock 133
Polquhap 136
Cowlairs 138

7 North of Forth
Glenoglehead 141
County March (West Higland) and Corrour 143
Druimuachdar 146
Dava Moor 150
Slochd Mhuic 151
Raven's Rock, Corriemuillie and Luib 154
Lairg 156
County March 158

Index 159

The line over Shap summit is perhaps the best-known and most celebrated of all Britain's great railway climbs. Here 'Britannia' 'Pacific' No 70024 *Vulcan* storms northwards with a down freight assisted in the rear by a Standard Class '4' 4-6-0 in June 1967. *Les Nixon*

# INTRODUCTION

I suppose it would be true to say that this book owes its origin to a combination of a car journey and Dr Beeching. The latter, I grant, may be an immediate turn-off for some, but perhaps they can be reassured by the fact that the connection is fairly tenuous. It happened this way.

Some years ago my wife and I were driving in Yorkshire - or rather, she was driving and I had the map on my knees.

'There's a closed railway somewhere over there,' I remarked, pointing to the left. This was a waste of time since she, quite properly, kept her eyes on the road.

A quick study of the landscape on that side quickly showed where the old line must have run, and my wife demanded how I could tell. I didn't know, really, until I had thought about it, and I then decided that because nature creates very few straight or level planes, those that are must stand a fair chance of being man-made. Ergo, a railway. Could this not, I wondered over the next few days, be a theme for a book about how man used (and still uses) the landscape in building railways, and the geographical reasons for their running where they do.

The idea simmered for some time. I made a few notes, and set them aside. Then Will Adams, Editor at Silver Link, became a catalyst by being kind enough to ask what I wanted to do for my next book. I propounded the lines/landscape idea. He was sympathetic, though with hindsight I fancy that he could already foresee some of the pitfalls.

'All right,' he suggested. 'Go away and see if you can work up a preliminary draft, rationale and so on.'

Well, an 8,000-word draft dealing with East Anglia alone barely scratched the surface, so clearly complete coverage of the country would be not only impractical in one book, but would take years to do even in several volumes. Will, generously refraining from saying 'I told you so', suggested that perhaps we could concentrate on a single aspect of the problem - the big banks, say. And here we are.

Earlier writers have shown that while something is known of the men who actually built the lines, the men with the picks and barrows, rather less is known about the jobs they did. More space seems to have been devoted to the squalor in which they lived - true at least in some cases, but by no means all, and in some instances probably no worse than they would have had at home - rather than to their work. Many - no, most - of these men could not write, so they can hardly be expected to have kept diaries. In addition, contemporary newspapers (like today's) seemed to regard good behaviour as non-news, so that what got reported were the accidents, the thefts, the riots and the incidents outside the pub on payday when Joe Bloggs imbibed too well and thumped an innocent passer-by. No wonder the navvies got a bad reputation.

Railway company half-yearly reports, though generally fascinating, were of limited use too, at least so far as progress and life on the line was concerned. Mostly Chairmen were at pains to deliver anodynes to shareholders along the lines of 'the work is proceeding satisfactorily', and while these may have kept the shareholders happy, they are not much help to the poor historian. Some newspapers, notably the *Stamford Mercury*, were very good at providing progress reports on the work in their area, but others ignored it completely apart from noting the half-yearly meetings. But many sources *have* helped in my task and are listed elsewhere - I am most grateful to all, and any errors herein are, of course, nothing to do with them, but entirely my own responsibility.

Yet there are stories to be unearthed from among the big banks and the bare hills, and it has been a fascinating exercise to delve into the records and try and dig them out. It is my hope that readers will enjoy the experience as much as I did.

# BIBLIOGRAPHY

Atthill, Robin: *The Somerset & Dorset Railway* (David & Charles/Pan, 1967)

Baker, S. K.: *Rail Atlas of Gt Britain & Ireland* (OPC, 1988)

Biddle, G. and Nock O. S.: *The Railway Heritage of Britain* (Michael Joseph, 1983)

Blower, Alan: *British Railway Tunnels* (Ian Allan, 1964)

Borley, H. V.: *Chronology of London's Railways*, and Supplement
(RCHS, 1982)

Briwnant-Jones, G.: *Railway Through Talerddig* (Gomer Press, 1990)

Brooke, David: *The Railway Navvy* (David & Charles, 1983)

Carter, E. F.: *The Railway Encyclopaedia* (Harold Starke Ltd, 1963)

Casserley, H. C.: *The Lickey Incline* (Oakwood Press, 1976)

Chapman, W. G.: *Track Topics* (GWR, 1935)

Christiansen and Miller: *The Cambrian Railways* (David & Charles, 1967)

Clinker, C. R.: *Register of Closed Stations* (AvonAnglia, 1978)

Course, E.: *Railways of Southern England; Main Lines* (Batsford, 1973)

Daniels and Dench: *Passengers No More* (Ian Allan, 1974 edn)

Dow, George: *The Great Central Railway, Vols 1 & 2* (Loco Publishing Co, 1959-62)
*The First Railway Across the Border* (LNER) 1946
*The First Railway between Manchester and Sheffield* (LNER, 1945)

Fellows, R. B.: *Railways to Cambridge* (Oakwood Press, 1948)

Francis, John: *History of the English Railway* (London, 1851)

Gasquoigne, C. P.: *The Story of the Cambrian* (Christopher Davis, 1973 edn)

Gough, John: *The Midland Railway - a Chronology* (RCHS, 1989)

Gray, Adrian: *The London, Chatham & Dover Railway* (Meresborough Books, 1984)
*South Eastern Railway* (Middleton Press, 1990)

Gregory, R. H.: *The South Devon Railway* (Oakwood Press, 1982)

Helps, Sir Arthur: *The Life & Labours of Mr Brassey* (Evelyn, Adams & Mackay, 1872)

Jenkins, S. C., and Quayle, H. I.: *The Oxford, Worcester & Wolverhampton Railway* (Oakwood Press, 1977)

Johnston, Colin, and Hume, John R.: *Glasgow Stations* (David & Charles, 1979)

Joy, David: *The Whitby & Pickering Railway* (Dalesman Books, 1973)

Long, P. J., and Awdry, Rev W. V.: *The Birmingham & Gloucester Railway* (Alan Sutton, 1987)

Maggs, Colin: *The Bath to Weymouth Line* (Oakwood Press, 1982)

Marshall, J.: *Biographical Dictionary of Railway Engineers* (David & Charles, 1978)

Mitchell, Joseph: *Reminiscences of my Life in the Highlands, Vol 2* (Lewis Reprints, 1971)

Mitchell and Smith: *Southern Main Lines; Yeovil to Exeter* (Middleton Press, 1991)
*Country Railway Routes; Bath to Evercreech Jn* (Middleton Press, 1988)
*Country Railway Routes; Yeovil to Dorchester* (Middleton Press, 1990)
*South Coast Railways; Bournemouth to Weymouth* (Middleton Press, 1988)

Mullay, A. J.: *Rails Across the Border* (Patrick Stephens Ltd, 1990)

Popplewell, Lawrence: *Gazetteer of Railway Contractors & Engineers of East Anglia* (Melledgen Press, 1982)

Reed, Brian: *Crewe to Carlisle* (Ian Allan, 1969)

Robertson, C. J. A.: *The Origins of the Scottish Railway System, 1722-1844* (John Donald, 1983)

Rolt, L. T. C.: *The Making of a Railway* (Hugh Evelyn, 1971)
*Red For Danger* (Pan, Rev Edn 1978)

Russell, J. H.: *The Banbury & Cheltenham Railway, 1887-1962* (OPC, 1977)

Smith, D. J.: *Shrewsbury to Swansea* (Town & Country Press, 1971)

Thomas, John: *The North British Railway, Vol 1* (David & Charles, 1969)
*The West Highland Railway* (David & Charles, 1976)

Vallance, H. A.: *The Highland Railway* (David & Charles, 1963 edn)

Webster, N. W.: *Joseph Locke - Railway Revolutionary* (Allen & Unwin, 1970)

Whishaw, Francis: *The Railways of Great Britain & Ireland* (David & Charles reprints, 1969)

Williams, R. A.: *The London & South Western Railway, Vol 1* (David & Charles, 1968)

Various volumes in the David & Charles 'Regional History' and 'Forgotten Railways' series

Public and General Acts of Parliament

Board of Trade, Inspector's Reports

National and local newspapers, *Herepath's Railway Magazine, Railway Times, Railway Magazine, Railway World, British Railway Journal, Railway Observer* (RCTS), *Backtrack.*

# 1
# SOUTH AND WEST

# Hemerdon and Rattery

The South Devon Railway's line to Plymouth opened, amid great rejoicing and a public holiday in the town, on 2 April 1849. It was, the *Plymouth, Devonport & Stonehouse Herald* remarked on 7 April, an event which '. . .cannot fail of being long remembered. . .as of considerable importance to the town and port. . .'

However great the rejoicing on the part of the populace, it was less than a week before the heavy gradient eastwards towards the summit at Wrangerton (sic, but soon renamed Kingsbridge Road) began to take its toll. On Friday 6 April the 6.55 out of Plymouth '. . . met with the detention of an hour and a half by the bursting of a tube of the engine, when nearly at the top of the Hemerdon incline'. It had already been deemed wise to split a very heavy train, and the second portion had almost reached the summit when '. . . a tube bursted, the power of the locomotive was gone, and back ran the carriages beyond Plympton station'.

But how and why was it that gradients such as Hemerdon were constructed? What was the compulsion that required engineers to surmount obstacles which only 20 years before would have been thought wildly impracticable, at least so far as haulage by adhesion locomotives was concerned? Indeed, until but a short time before, inclines a good deal slighter than Hemerdon had been considered impassable

except with cable-assistance and stationary engines.

Well, Hemerdon was not the first of the big inclines, and we will be climbing many of the others in due course, but it was projected in a rather different light from most of them. The Great Western Railway, in conjunction with the Bristol & Exeter Railway, saw Plymouth as a natural extension of their interests, and in 1836 Brunel made a survey of a line from Exeter to Plymouth, following the coast and making use of long viaducts at Teignmouth and Dittisham. A rival scheme proposed an inland but hillier route, some 14 miles shorter at 37 miles. The inhabitants of Exeter were not much in favour of either, being more concerned as to what effect the development of better natural facilities at Plymouth might have on the port in their own city.

But the GWR, the Bristol & Exeter and the Bristol & Gloucester Railways came forward with the money, and Brunel, his coastal scheme abandoned, in due course propounded a notion for an 'atmospheric' system which would surmount the gradients of the inland route with ease. Indeed, he urged, they could well be built even steeper and with greater economy, since extensive earthworks could thus be avoided. As history knows, this experiment turned out to be a costly disaster, but because of it today's railway system is left with the notorious banks at Hemerdon, Rattery and Dainton. Under modern traction they are not now, perhaps, the problem that they were, but they still command respect.

For all Brunel's airy remarks about earthworks, they are still heavy. Some embankments are of considerable height, while between Totnes and Laira there are 30 road overbridges and 32 road underbridges, not to mention seven viaducts and Marley tunnel, 869 yards long. A cutting, albeit a deep one, would actually have sufficed at this point, but a tunnel was insisted upon by Lord Carew, owner of the Marley estate.

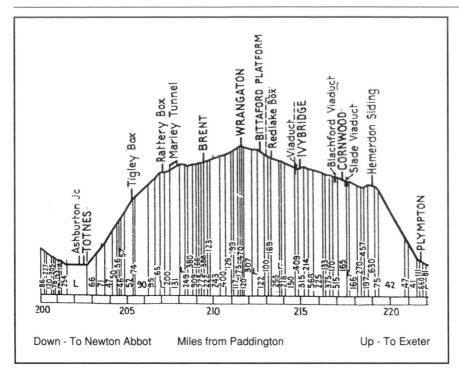

**Gradient profile, Hemerdon and Rattery**

Construction of this section was by Messrs (Joseph) Samuda Bros & Clegg, who found that it presented problems. The work was consequently to take some time, and the engineer's report to the shareholders of 19 February 1845 was noted in the next issue of the *Railway Times*:

'. . .the principal works have been commenced and although some delay has occurred in the progress of the tunnels, and principally at Marley tunnel, by a change of contractors, I expect they will immediately be again in full work.'

'King' Class 4-6-0 No 6013 *King Henry VIII* tops the summit at Wrangaton station with a down express on 16 August 1959. *Peter Hay*

In August 1846 upwards of 1,500 men were working between Newton (Abbot) and Ivybridge. Powers for a deviation had delayed progress beyond Colebrook, and there had also been difficulties over possession of land, but Brunel could report on 29 August 1846 that the job was nearly completed and that he anticipated that the section would be ready for permanent way by the end of the year.

Fights between the navvies employed on the works were not infrequent, though one came to a premature end when one of the protagonists, stripped and ready for action, dropped down dead before a blow had been aimed. The morals of the men and, it must also be said, their living conditions, were causing the SDR directors concern. The navvies lived in barrack-like buildings, in some of which 150-200 men, women and children were crowded, and near Marley tunnel the Reverend John Thompson found others packed into turf or mud lean-to huts 12 feet square, later telling a Committee of Parliamentary Commissioners that he had never seen anything to compare with them. The men went on strike, successfully, for fortnightly instead of monthly pay, Thompson acting as a go-between. They had less success, however, against the shopkeepers of Totnes, who charged them 20 or 30 per cent above the normal rate for second-class provisions.

This, of course, was the principle of the infamous 'truck' system, though in most instances the 'company shop' (sometimes also referred to as the 'tommy shop') was run by the contractor or sub-contractor. This meant, particularly in remote areas, that the contractor got back most of a navvy's pay at considerable profit, and there was absolutely nothing that the latter could do about it - that is, if he wanted to eat. Often payment was made in the form of vouchers exchangeable only at the 'shop', and in this event the navvy had no alternative whatever. It was an abominable situation, which even the most enlightened of contractors admitted was almost impossible to prevent.

What with one thing and

*Above* On the same day Class '45xx' 2-6-2T No 5573 accelerates away from the station with a lightly loaded pick-up goods. *Peter Hay*

another, when Brunel made his report twelve months later, at the end of August 1847, he could say only that the bridges and viaducts were almost finished, that ballast (using a commodity called shillet) was being laid on the completed works, but that between

*Right* Just a year later and steam engines are getting diesel assistance up the bank. Here 'Castle' Class 4-6-0 No 5055 *Earl of Eldon* with an up express is fronted by one of the North British Class '2' locomotives introduced the previous year. *Hugh Davies*

five and six thousand yards of earthworks were still incomplete. The terrain was described as 'mostly slate and shale', but the bridges were solidly built, of rubble-stone, the piers and arches having dressed stone quoins.

The Board of Trade Inspector, Captain Symons, made his examination on 29 April 1848, and in his report remarked upon the good workmanship of the construction. The track was laid in Brunel's broad gauge, of 7 feet $0^1/_4$ inch, and consisted of bridge-rail laid on longitudinal timbers. It was double only up Rattery bank and from the summit section down to Laira, the rest being single. It is perhaps a pity that when this section was doubled, the tunnel mouth of the second bore was faced in red brick, no attempt being made to match the stonework of the original. During the construction of this, in May 1891, a partial collapse in the old tunnel stopped all traffic for five days. When the branch to Kingsbridge from Brent was opened on 19 December 1893, Kingsbridge Road reverted to its original name of Wrangaton.

Any ideas about the use of atmospheric traction over this section had long gone by the time of its opening, but the steep banks from Plymouth and Totnes remained as a legacy. For the traveller from Plymouth the climbing begins beyond Plympton (whose old grammar school has Sir Joshua Reynolds as its most famous former pupil), with about a third of a mile at 1 in 41, a short section at 1 in 47 and then one and a half miles at 1 in 42, whereafter the slope eases to 1 in 75 for a third of a mile, and then still further up to Hemerdon - incidentally referred to as 'Homerton' by Capt Symons in his report. There are still a little under seven miles of steady ascent to the top at Wrangaton, though nothing steeper than a half-mile pitch of 1 in 100/120 just before Bittaford.

The summit is 462 feet above sea level, and 439 feet above the northern base of Rattery bank at Totnes. The profile of the southbound climb is not dissimilar to that of Hemerdon - hard work at first, followed by easier slopes to the top. Totnes station is built on level track, but the engine is working 'against the collar' almost from the start, with a mile at 1 in 66/71 as the line trends westward from its hitherto south-westerly course. Then comes two-thirds of a mile at 1 in 47, and the next mile and a quarter has nothing easier than a short length of 1 in 57 as the valley begins to close in on either side of the line.

The beginning of Tigley cutting heralds the crossing of the 100-foot contour, but the worst is now over. 1 in 90 for three-quarters of a mile eases to 1 in 95, and another three-quarters of a mile at 1 in 90 leads to a right-hand curve and a stretch of 1 in 66. A level section follows, and a pitch of 1 in 200 ends at Marley tunnel mouth, the tunnel itself lying on a slope of 1

in 131. In the remaining three and a half miles between tunnel and summit there is nothing steeper than a third of a mile at 1 in 117.

To those of us familiar with shed facilities at Laira (Plymouth) it comes as something of a surprise to find that the first steam shed there opened as recently as 1901. When diesel traction made its debut on the banks, steam/diesel double-heading could be seen for a while. Laira was made the prototype for the BR Western Region diesel maintenance and servicing depots, and the steam shed closed in June 1965. In 1980-1 it became a servicing point for High Speed Trains (HSTs), and though the timing of these trains between Plymouth and London is now around three hours, the sharp curves mean that they are unable to fulfil their true potential. The only intermediate station remaining open is Totnes, those closed to passengers being, from the Plymouth end, Plympton, Cornwood, Ivybridge, Bittaford Platform and Wrangaton, all on 2 March 1959. Brent survived until 5 October 1964.

# Dainton

The Dainton banks, one in each direction, are shorter and sharper than the two just described, and sharper not just in the steep sense. A series of curves calls for a cautious descent whether heading for Newton Abbot or Totnes, but particularly restricting in the latter case, since to some extent it precludes getting a decent run at Rattery. In the up direction, Aller Junction lies just beyond the foot of the bank, and a mile and a half further on is Newton (not officially known as Newton Abbot until March 1877) itself, where most trains stop anyway.

The bank has a roughly pyramidal outline, with its summit near the small village of Dainton and approximately in the middle of the tunnel that burrows beneath Dainton Common. It owes its steepness to the same cause as Hemerdon and Rattery, and like them it never actually experienced atmospheric traction, though the SDR laid atmospheric pipes for almost the entire eight and three-quarter miles between the towns, built pumping houses at Dainton and Totnes, and installed Boulton & Watt pumping engines in them. Until comparatively recently,

*Right* 'Hall' Class 4-6-0 No 4983 *Albert Hall* assists an unidentified 'Castle' up towards Dainton tunnel. They have charge of the 9.25 Liverpool-Plymouth express, and the date is 8 April 1949, though as yet there is no sign of nationalisation visible on either engine. The signal is Dainton Sidings' distant. *A. F. Cook*

*Below right* The final few yards of Dainton's 1 in 38 on 17 May 1958. The driver of '28xx' Class 2-8-0 No 2843 peers out anxiously as his engine blasts towards the tunnel - it is assisted in the rear by one of Newton Abbot's stud of '51xx' Class 2-6-2Ts, No 5168, kept there for this very duty. *Hugh Ballantyne*

remains of the Totnes pumping house could be seen incorporated into a dairy on the up side of the line north of the station.

Building went well (the contractors were again Samuda & Clegg), and on 28 February 1846 Brunel could tell the South Devon shareholders that 'a considerable portion of the works would be ready to receive permanent way that summer'. The line, laid in broad gauge, and single with bridge-rail on longitudinal baulks, was ready for its first train on 20 July. The train was hauled by a conventional locomotive, and despite great anxiety on Brunel's part that the engine would be unable to cope with the climbs, all was well. One wonders whether, had it not done so, Brunel might not have tried to persist with the atmospheric system. On the other hand, a report in *The Times* of 3 November 1848 says:

'The shareholders in this undertaking have forwarded to the directors a memorial, numerously signed, urging the necessity of a complete revision in the management of the concern, and of the strictest pecuniary economy; and particularly looking at the very great expenditure of capital in the construction of the line beyond that which it was originally estimated [and] at the enormous amount which has been sacrificed in the abortive experiments to effect its working by atmospheric traction. . .'

If the shareholders felt so strongly about it, perhaps Brunel would have failed to sway them in any case.

This short section of railway, apart from the sheer difficulty of the climb, contains few civil engineering features - other than the short tunnel at Dainton (272 yards), the only notable work is the bridge across the River Dart just north of Totnes station. This was built of timber, but the original piers were replaced by masonry in 1864.

The climb is perhaps less arduous from the Totnes side, at least to begin with. After an initial 1 in 254 for a little under half a mile, there is a short length of 1 in 118, another of 1 in 78 and another of 1 in 120. A third of a mile or so on the level preludes the climb proper - a quarter-mile of 1 in 260, another of 1 in 76, another at 1 in 105 and another at 1 in 55. There is now just under a mile to the top, in a succession of short pitches at 1 in 65, 38, 43, 37 and 130, each about ten chains long except the steepest, which is twice that length. Dainton Siding lay immediately south of the simple stone-lined arch of the tunnel mouth.

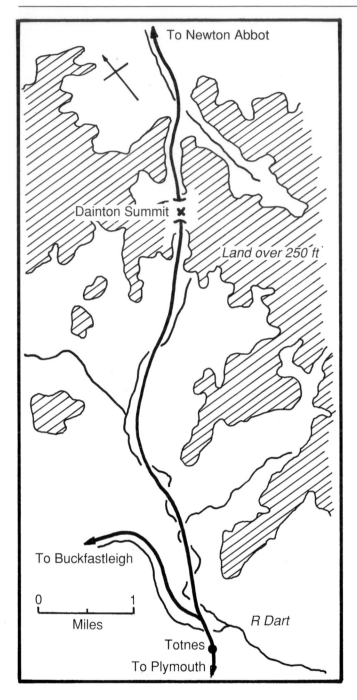

are the steepest used by main-line express trains in the country. In the days when it was common practise to split freight trains on the Devon banks, to recouple a train, as now and then happened, in the darkness of Dainton tunnel must have been something of a feat.

Track was single at first, laid in broad gauge in Brunel's 'baulk road' style. The singleness did not, however, last for long. On 10 December 1853 the *Railway Times* reported:

> 'From Exeter to Newton the line is single, but below that place numerous gangs of men are at present busy in laying down a double line of rails as far as Totness [sic]. In many parts this work is complete, and there will thus be less chance of collisions, there being a deep incline at this part of the line.'

The SDR used its own staff and rolling-stock, but hired locomotives from the GWR until the end of June 1851. For the next 15 years it hired engines from contractors, but this proved expensive, and in 1866 the company bought the forty engines the contractors had been using, and took over the working of the Cornwall and West Cornwall Railways as well. When it became known in 1875 that the Bristol & Exeter had come to an arrangement with the GWR, the South Devon approached that company too. It became GWR-worked under a 999-year Agreement from 1 January 1876, and was formally amalgamated from 1 August 1878. The SDR main line remained broad gauge until the final parts of the GWR system were converted during the weekend of 20-21 May 1892.

# Meldon

North of Brunel's route across Devon ran another line, built by the Okehampton Railway and authorised in 1862 to build a line to that town from Coleford Junction, on the North Devon Railway & Dock Company's line to Barnstaple. An Act of 13 July 1863 gave authority to extend this line to Lidford (now Lydford), where it would join the Launceston & South Devon Railway.

Early railways tended to go over or through obsta-

From the Newton Abbot side the line falls for about half a mile from Aller Junction and then begins climbing in earnest: a quarter-mile at 1 in 98, half a mile of 1 in 57, another quarter at 1 in 71, another of 1 in 46. Stoneycombe Siding, situated here to serve a company quarrying the pink stone of Dainton Hill, is slightly more than a mile from the summit, which is achieved, as on the other side, in short pitches of ten to twelve chains each - 1 in 56, 41, 49, 36, 44, 84 and 190. It is about two and a half miles from bottom to top, which might not sound far, but few engine crews found it easy going! The 1 in 36 and 1 in 37 pitches

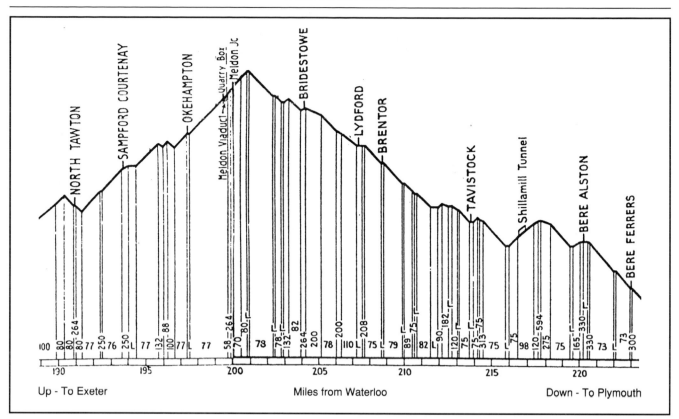

Up - To Exeter          Miles from Waterloo          Down - To Plymouth

**Gradient profile, Meldon**

cles, and there was a very substantial one in the way of this line - Dartmoor. In this instance its builders tried to avoid the obstacle, but even so the line which sets out to cross the watershed between the Rivers Okement and Tamar lets itself in for a good deal of climbing. Indeed, considering the height attained by the line at the summit (950 feet), it is somewhat surprising that it does not seem to have been regarded at a 'major' summit and subjected to the same amount of celluloid and emulsion as, say, Shap, Ais Gill or Masbury.

'The proposed line,' said *The Times* of 9 January 1863, 'is to run from Okehampton to the Launceston and South Devon Railway, near Lidford (sic) and [is] to cost 16,000L.' Fifteen months later shareholders were told that the contract for the construction

of the line had been let to Messrs Robert Sharpe & Sons, who were to build both the initial line to Okehampton from Coleford, and also the extension across the summit at Meldon. 'An application,' pointed out the directors' report in March 1864, 'has been made to Parliament for powers to deviate certain portions of the line in the neighbourhood of Okehampton in order to secure improved gradients - a most important object - seeing that the railway must become a great trunk line.' After the meeting a 'first sod' ceremony was performed by the Countess of

'West Country' Class 'Pacific' No 34023 *Blackmore Vale* (with nameplates removed) has topped the summit at Meldon and is now hurrying downhill towards Exeter past Meldon Halt on 19 July 1958. The gradient can be seen curving right beyond the locomotive, and the summit lies in the cutting above the platform railings. *Hugh Davies*

Portsmouth, the wife of a director, and the event was 'celebrated at a banquet given by the contractors, at which Mr S. C. Hamlyn, the chairman of the company, presided'.

The company's engineer was W. R. Galbraith, but it was to be some years before the line reached Okehampton - it eventually opened on 3 October 1871, accompanied by a ceremonial cream tea. The spring meeting that year had heard that capital had been obtained for the extension to Lydford, and that the contractor had undertaken to complete the line by September 1872. Ten months later about half the works had been completed, and progress was described as satisfactory. This rather complacent view was rudely shattered when, in October 1872, it was stated that the contractor was 'having difficulty obtaining labour'.

Work was reported the following March as being 'pushed forward with the utmost vigour', but later in the year came further delays, and on 30 September 1873 the half-yearly shareholders meeting was told:

'. . .in consequence of the state of the weather, the labour market and the difficulty of obtaining delivery of the ironwork for Meldon viaduct. . . this anticipation [of completion] had not been realised, although the completion of the works within a short period might now be regarded as certain.'

By 1 April 1874 the viaduct and other works were almost complete at last, and Col Hutchinson, of the Board of Trade, made his inspection on 29 September. He was satisfied with what he saw, and shortly afterwards it was announced that the line would, in a few days, be open for traffic, worked by the South Western company, an event which took place on 12 October 1874. The whole project had, in fact, been sponsored by the London & South Western Railway, which was anxious to find a route to Plymouth and the West in competition with the GWR. It had already formally taken over the original Okehampton company, by then called the Devon & Cornwall Railway, in 1872.

A journey over the summit was a slog in either direction, probably harder for trains travelling north-eastwards from Plymouth. Of the three miles between the Tavy viaduct and the approaches to Bere Alston, all but half a mile were taken at 1 in 73, and there was another mile of 1 in 75 before an almost equally steep drop through Shillamill tunnel. Thereafter the ascent began again, with one and a quarter miles at 1 in 75 before an easing through Tavistock. Then climbing became steady except for a brief stretch two miles further on. The next four miles through Brentor

was at 1 in 82, 79, 89, 79, 75, with only three level pitches of less than ten chains apiece. An easing through Lydford was followed by a mile of 1 in 110, and the two miles to Bridestowe including three quarters of a mile at 1 in 78. Then three-quarters of a mile of 1 in 82 earned a brief 'down' before the final 1 in 78 to the summit, two miles broken by one ten-chain 'level'.

In the other direction, the rise from Exeter to Coleford is steady and reasonably gentle. The section thence towards Meldon is, unlike the one just described, still open, though only as a freight branch, and three-quarters of a mile at 1 in 97 and a mile at 1 in 80 give notice of things to come. A minor summit a mile before Bow, and another hump beyond, lead to a mile and a quarter at 1 in 100, half a mile at 1 in 80, and a fall, mostly at 1 in 80, through North Tawton. Then a mile at 1 in 76, an easing through Sampford Courtenay, and a mile at 1 in 77 herald another short switchback section. There is a 1 in 77 for half a mile, and a brief level through Okehampton, its station set high above the town. Another mile and a half at 1 in 77 carries the line to and across Meldon viaduct, after which comes a pitch at 1 in 58, mercifully short. The final 1 in 70 and 1 in 80 which lead to the summit level are each about 30 chains long.

The line was built single at first, but was doubled in 1879. Meldon viaduct, built on a 30-chain radius curve, is of lattice ironwork - it has six girder spans, set on lattice piers, the tallest of which reaches 120 feet. It lies just to the east of Meldon Quarry, still used by BR for the acquisition of granite ballast, and is the only viaduct of its type in the country that is still in use.

The route closed to passengers between Okehampton and Bere Alston on 6 May 1968, while that between Yeoford (Coleford Junction) and Okehampton closed to passengers on 5 June 1972. The line to Barnstaple remains open at the time of writing.

# Mortehoe

**W**e move now to the far north of Devon, where it had been perceived quite early on by railway companies with an interest in Barnstaple that a line

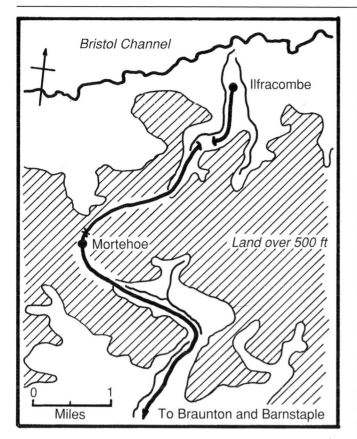

northwards from there to the resort of Ilfracombe would have excellent potential. The problem was firstly persuading others to a similar view, and secondly to get to the other side of the ridge which lay between the towns.

'A meeting,' announced *The Times* of Thursday 19 July 1860, 'was held a few days ago at Ilfracombe for the purpose of promoting the construction of a railway from the North Devon Railway to Ilfracombe. Increased exertions, with a view to carrying out the object of the meeting, were resolved upon.'

Despite these good intentions, it was 1864 before a Bill was placed before Parliament by the Ilfracombe Railway. Notwithstanding its title, the project was promoted by the Devon & Somerset Railway, a pie in which the Bristol & Exeter Railway had a

finger, and broad gauge was therefore proposed. It envisaged a route well to the east of that eventually built, going from Barnstaple via Pilton, Sharwill and Marwood, and ignoring Braunton and Mortehoe. Hard climbing would have been needed to attain a summit on Bittadon Down, possibly 100 feet higher than the eventual one, and a correspondingly steep descent would have been necessary to reach a terminus anywhere near the centre of Ilfracombe.

Narrow and broad gauge factions managed to reach agreement for a mixed gauge line, but the whole scheme then collapsed when the D&S failed to pay its half-share of the expenses. Not unnaturally the LSWR was less than happy about the scheme's failure, but on the other hand cannot have regretted its abandonment when the time allotted by Parliament ran out in 1868. It at once produced a plan of its own, which attained Royal Assent on 4 July 1870.

The contractor appointed was James Taylor, for a contract price of £90,000, and he reported in February 1871 that the route was being marked out. The first sod, however, was not cut until 27 September, and by December the local press was anticipating an imminent arrival of navvies to build the line. When work began there was the usual crop of accidents among the men, though only two fatalities seem to have been recorded, one occurring when a bank which a navvy was undercutting, somewhat predictably, fell on him.

The summit cutting, the first section to be started, was the last to be finished - in August 1872 it was less than half-done. By 24 January 1874 the tunnel at Slade was half-finished, and completion was expected by March: a clear run of railway was now ready between Barnstaple and Mortehoe. On 16 June 1874 the first train crossed the iron bridge over the River Taw into the town. The summit cutting was finished

**An old, undated print looking south from Ilfracombe station. Beyond the platform and the goods shed the line can be seen climbing steeply away past the signal box. The gentleman with the broom has no doubt been instructed to do what he can to remove the light fall of snow which has arrived during the night.** *Lens of Sutton*

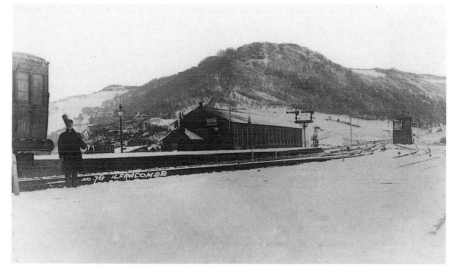

on 27 June, and a trial run along the whole line took place on the 30th; the first public train ran, filled to capacity, on 20 July. It would seem that Taylor lost money on this contract, for the end cost of the line was £130,000, or around £8,600 per mile.

The first miles, along the estuary of the Taw, were easy going, and climbing in earnest did not begin until departure from Braunton, a little under five and a half miles from Barnstaple Town. A 30-chain pitch of 1 in 75 was followed by a slightly shorter one of 1 in 100, and then half a mile at 1 in 88. A quarter mile of 1 in 120 led to three quarters of a mile at 1 in 80, but this was by no means the toughest stretch. An easing to 1 in 300 merely flattered to deceive, for the engine driver was now faced with a little over a mile and half at 1 in 40. A ten-chain level then gave a short breather, but there followed a further two miles, again at 1 in 40, before an easing to 1 in 330 led past Mortehoe (Morthoe until May 1902, and Mortehoe and Woolacombe from 5 June 1950) to the summit, 633 feet above sea level. Trains achieving this peak had made a vertical rise of 593 feet in just over six miles from Braunton.

From the opposite direction things were little easier. Ilfracombe's platform stood 257 feet above sea level and on a gradient of 1 in 300. Crews knew that they must climb 376 feet in less than three and a quarter miles, and they could waste no time about it. At the platform end the gradient became 1 in 55, and 15 chains from the buffer-stops turned into a slog at 1 in 36. Slade tunnel was passed in a little more than half a mile - it was mercifully short in the engine-crews' view, though not short enough for some. Lurid tales are told of engines slipping in the tunnel and emerging with a blackened and shaken crew at the southern end. Certainly the crews had no respite for two and a quarter miles, at which point the gradient eased briefly to 1 in 75, then levelled for just under a quarter of a mile. Even then there were still a further 30 chains or so at 1 in 77 before the hard-worked engine at last reached the top.

The line was built as a light railway, with flat-bottomed rail fastened direct to the sleepers with fang bolts and spikes. The 60 lb per yard rail of the lower part of the line gave way to 75 lb rail on the steep gradients, and the ballast was broken stone and shale. There was only single track to begin with, but it was doubled between Braunton and Mortehoe in 1889, from Pottington to Braunton in 1890 and through to Ilfracombe in 1891. At this time it acquired standard LSWR permanent way.

Single-engine working normally sufficed because lengthy local trains were not required, but double-heading was often resorted to on busy summer Saturdays. Services on the branch reached a peak dur-

ing the summer of 1909, when there were seventeen trains in each direction. During and after the Great War the line declined in importance, but revived as part of the Southern Railway in the 1930s to peak again in 1939 with a weekday quota of eighteen down and sixteen up trains, and twenty-four each way on Saturdays. The final day of steam working was 5 September 1964, and two years later the weekday service was nine trains each way. As road transport increased, the branch began making a loss - the last train ran on 3 October 1970, with 500 people on board, and the track was lifted five years later, after a scheme to take it over privately had failed.

# Whiteball

**W**hiteball, sometimes known as Wellington, bank has two claims to fame: the lesser is that for a short time a point near Beam Bridge, a mile and a quarter below the summit (roughly where the gradient changes from 1 in 86 to 1 in 80), was the terminus of the Bristol & Exeter Railway. This is no place in which to discuss the pros and cons of the other feat - *City of Truro* can scarcely speak for itself concerning its claimed 100 mph-plus exploit in 1903, but abler pens than mine have already done it that service, and no doubt will again.

The Bristol & Exeter was conceived as a logical extension of the Great Western from Bristol, though it was a much less well-off concern and the work went slowly, more slowly than many shareholders would have wished. Brunel was its Engineer, a survey was made by one of his assistants, William Gravatt, during November 1835, and the first section of the line opened to the public between Bristol and Bridgwater on 14 June 1841. The continuation to Taunton opened slightly over a year later.

The next stage was to Exeter, but the Blackdown Hills lay across its path, forming a major impediment between the valleys of the Tone and Culm. Work began between Taunton and Wellington in 1842, but the eight and a half mile section did not open until 1 May the next year, largely because the Great Western Canal Company delayed the work by insisting that the B&E must stick strictly to the letter of the Act in regard to a bridge across its canal. Work on the line

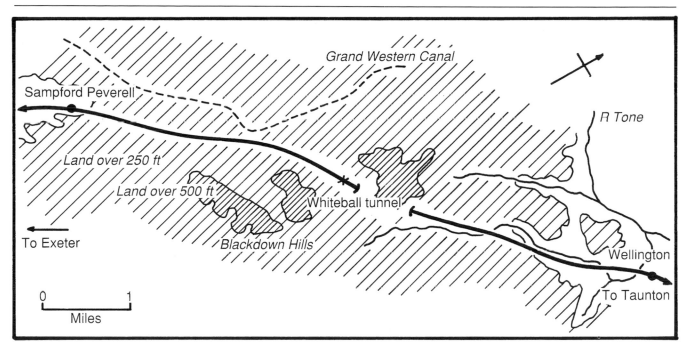

No 5051 *Drysllwyn Castle* and No 4930 *Hagley Hall* pound up towards Whiteball tunnel with the up 'Great Western Limited' from Newton Abbot to Bristol on 14 July 1985. In the foreground is the end of Whiteball's down goods loop; there were also up and down sidings for refuging slower-moving traffic at the summit. *Hugh Ballantyne*

beyond Beam Bridge also began in 1842, and in August Brunel reported that the '. . .heavy cuttings in the neighbourhood of White Ball Tunnel have been carried on vigorously, and are in a very forward state'.

The tunnel itself was let in four contracts, and by January 1843 nine shafts had been sunk to rail level, with a good deal of the heading cut too. There was a delay when one of the contractors failed, but the tunnel, 1,092 yards long, was complete apart from track and ballast by February 1844. A total of 14 shafts had been dug and refilled by the time the job was done. It was not good material to work with, consisting of marl, sand, quicksand, sandstone, gravel and a hard conglomerate, and the tunnel required a brick lining two feet thick throughout.

There was, it is said, a great deal of disruption in the surrounding villages while the gang of more than 1,000 navvies employed on the tunnel and its approaches were in the area. There were a number of fatalities among the workmen too, many due to their own foolhardiness - in *The Railway Navvies* Terry Coleman tells of a worker in Whiteball cutting who was twice taken to task by his ganger for undercutting too far. The navvy took no notice - after all, the work went more quickly the way he was doing it. But a quarter of an hour later the overhang collapsed, with the inevitably fatal result.

The bank itself runs south-westward up to the tunnel, and really begins well before Beam Bridge. Gentle gradients out of Taunton lead to milepost 145 (from Paddington), and a mile of 1 in 369 leads to another of 1 in 203. That is the steepest section for a mile or so, after which there is a mile at 1 in 174. A slight easing beyond Poole Siding brings a steepening to 1 in 170 for half a mile and a brief stretch of level track through Wellington.

Now the going gets harder. It is three and half miles to the summit from here, which are covered in four pitches more or less equal in length at just under a mile each - first 1 in 90, steepening to 1 in 86 and then to 1 in 80. The fourth takes the line through the tunnel at 1 in 127, and across the Somerset/Devonshire border, easing to 1 in 203 for the final stretch to the top at Whiteball Siding.

This line was always double, laid with bridge-rail on longitudinal timbers. Not being a particularly rich concern, the B&E had leased itself to the GWR at a guaranteed rent charge of 5 per cent for three years from January 1846, and 6 per cent in perpetuity thereafter. By 1848, however, the company's finances were healthier, and to the chagrin of the GWR the 'Exeter' decided to run its own line after the first part of the lease ran out in January 1849.

A successful job it made of it too, building its own locomotives (one of which was recorded at 80.6 mph

during a descent of Whiteball bank) and stock at Bristol. It was only when the threat of an expensive conversion from broad to narrow gauge became inevitable that the company once more sought shelter beneath the Great Western wing, to be re-leased from 1 January 1876 and absorbed from 1 August. It was another sixteen years before the GWR got around to converting the main line, during the weekend of 20-21 May 1892.

# Semley, Milborne Port, Hewish and Honiton

It is said that when the first sod of the Salisbury & Yeovil Railway was cut, at Gillingham (Dorset) on 3 April 1856, the company had a mere £4 2s 4d in the bank. Thanks to generous terms which it managed to get from the LSWR for working the line, its first dividend was paid in 1861. The shareholders thereafter benefitted phenomenally, and by 1877 were receiving 12.5 per cent on their holdings. It did not last, of course, but in any event another good offer by the LSWR persuaded the shareholders to vest their company in it from January 1878.

A line running westward from Salisbury would have Exeter as its obvious destination, though a route thence via Dorchester was being canvassed at the time. A special meeting on 16 January 1856 agreed to the route proposed by the Salisbury & Yeovil Railway: it had London & South Western prompting, and the possibility of extension to Exeter very much in mind. At this time both the LSWR and the GWR were competing for the West of England traffic, and no love was being lost between the neighbours.

The line had Yeovil as its immediate destination, however, and because it ran, as it were, 'across the grain' of the hills instead of parallel with them, the first section turned out to be something of a switchback, with summits at Semley and Milborne Port. Contractors were Brassey & Ogilvie and Leslie & Davidson, who, according to *The Times* of 5 February 1859, were 'proceeding rapidly with the works'. Delay was experienced in completing the station at

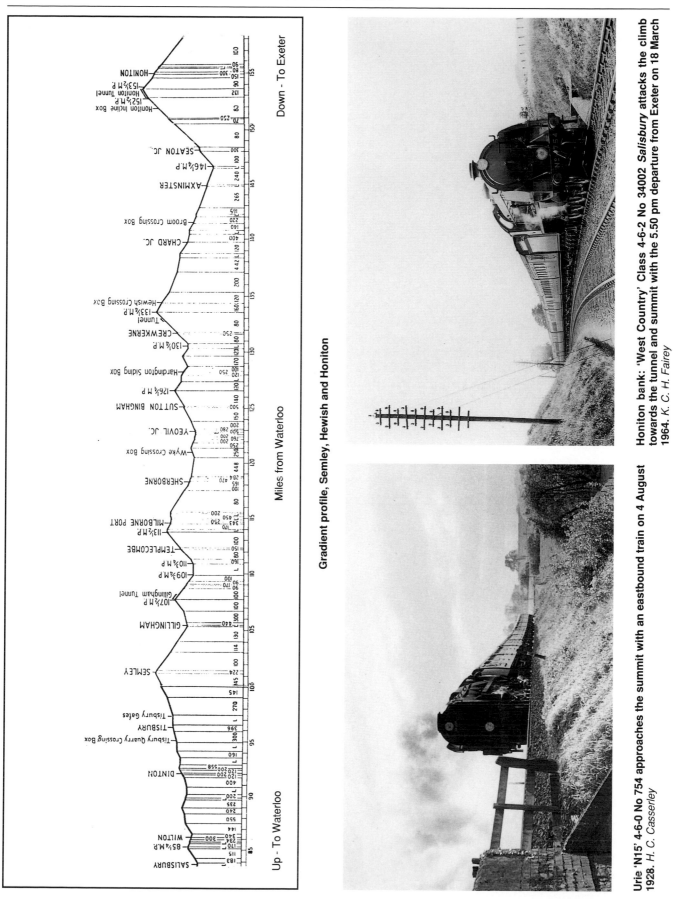

**Gradient profile, Semley, Hewish and Honiton**

**Honiton bank: 'West Country' Class 4-6-2 No 34002** *Salisbury* **attacks the climb towards the tunnel and summit with the 5.50 pm departure from Exeter on 18 March 1964.** *K. C. H. Fairey*

**Urie 'N15' 4-6-0 No 754 approaches the summit with an eastbound train on 4 August 1928.** *H. C. Casserley*

On the same day 4-6-0 No 827 bursts from the west portal of Honiton tunnel with only a few yards to go to the summit. *H. C. Casserley*

Salisbury, but there seemed to be no doubt that the first section, to Gillingham, would be ready for an early spring opening. The estimate was not so far out, the line opening to Gillingham on 2 May 1859, to Sherborne on 1 June 1860, and to Exeter officially on 18 July 1860, to the public a day later, worked, naturally enough, by the LSWR.

Between Gillingham and Sherborne lay Buckhorn Weston tunnel, which pointed up one of the hazards faced by contractors tendering for this sort of work. Excavation at one end cost a mere £12 per yard, but at the other, only 742 yards away, the stratum was so altered that the cost was ten times as much. An incautious contractor could easily bankrupt himself with a cursory survey, but this was the sort of mistake that Brassey did not make.

In the down direction the line follows the valley of the River Nadder for about two miles beyond Tisbury, to a point where it bears to the right, forsaking the Nadder for the rather smaller Sem. It then begins to rise, climbing for some four miles at 1 in 250 and 1 in 145 to a summit of around 400 feet at Semley Hill. Semley station was sited about half a mile beyond the summit, and three times that distance from its village. The climb in the other direction (ie towards Salisbury) is even steeper, involving almost four miles of gradients at 1 in 130, 114 and 100.

Down trains, after descending this slope, are then faced by a three-mile climb through Templecombe to milepost $113\frac{1}{2}$ (near Milborne Port) at 1 in 160, 80 and 150, with a final one and a half miles of 1 in 100.

The Exeter extension had been authorised to the LSWR on 21 July 1856, well before this opening; it proved to be no easier, from the working point of view, than the previous section. Three million cubic yards of earthworks were required, and the contractor, John Taylor, used 3,000 men, 600 horses and two locomotives in its construction. The section that gave the most trouble was that including Honiton tunnel, at the top of the climb, which pierces the ridge between the Rivers Axe and Otter. A layer of sand overlies the marl through which the tunnel is cut, and water percolating through this slowed the work down. At 1,345 yards it was to be the longest tunnel on the LSWR.

The main engineer was John Edward Errington, who had been born in Hull on 29 December 1806, and had his training in Ireland and working on railway surveys in England. He was assigned to do preparatory work on the Grand Junction line, where he met Joseph Locke, and the two were subsequently associated in many projects. Errington began work on the Salisbury-Exeter line in 1856; it was finished just before his death, at the early age of 55, in 1862. Coincidentally, the last work that Locke did was also

On 2 August 1928 4-6-0 No 456 speeds past Hewish Gates signal box with an up express. Note the long-armed LSWR signal, other samples of which can be seen in the Ilfracombe picture on page 17. *H. C. Casserley*

on this line, on the Salisbury-Yeovil section.

Errington's assistant here was William Robert Galbraith, a Stirling man some 13 years younger. From 1855 he had been employed mainly on LSWR projects, and after Errington's death he was appointed Engineer for all new works on the railway. He was to build many lines in southern England during the next 40 years, and also worked in Scotland.

Between Yeovil and Honiton a second ridge had to be crossed, its summit coming near Hewish, two miles beyond Crewkerne. Just beyond milepost 130¼, which is on one of the few level sections on the line, there is a mile of 1 in 80. An easing to 1 in 250 takes the line through Crewkerne station, and then there is a return to 1 in 80 for one and three-quarter miles to the top, passing through Crewkerne tunnel (206 yards) on the way. A long, easier descent of 13 miles brings the line down through Chard Junction and Axminster to milepost 146¼.

This point (the distance is measured from London) is the lowest since Salisbury, and lies midway between Axminster and Seaton Junction. It is here that the climb of almost seven miles to Honiton summit begins. A mile and a quarter of 1 in 100 leads to an easing through Seaton Junction, but beyond here the line curves away from the river to use the north-eastern flank of a natural valley in which flows the Umborne Brook. Almost at once the train is climbing at 1 in 80, a gradient maintained for the next two miles, after which half a mile at 1 in 70 leads to a brief easing to 1 in 250 followed by 1 in 80 again for all but two miles. As the tunnel is entered the slope eases to 1 in 132, and the summit of the climb, 500 feet above sea level, is reached at the western portal of the tunnel, shortly before milepost 153½. Travellers in the opposite direction have a climb of four and a half miles through Honiton at mostly 1 in 90/100.

The opening day was much affected by rain, which seems not to have dampened proceedings for the train carrying the company's Directors stopped at each station *en route* between Yeovil Junction (then called Stoford) and Exeter to be given Addresses from local dignitaries. Their welcome at the destination was notably quiet, however - after all, the broad gauge Bristol & Exeter had reached the city sixteen years before, so railways were nothing new. Most of the line was built single at first, and doubled in stages, though the stretch between Axminster and Honiton was ready on opening day, and may have been used from the start, despite the fact that authority to do so was given only in a letter dated 31 July.

It has not been an easy route to work. On a test run in 1947 one of Bulleid's new-fangled 'Pacifics' of the 'Merchant Navy' Class, *Blue Funnel* (later No 35013)

is recorded as having entered Honiton tunnel at 62 mph hauling 345 tons from a standing start at Sidmouth Junction. But this was by no means a usual achievement, although the fastest timing between Waterloo and Exeter was three hours for the 171¾ miles, which was no mean feat. The line is now singled between Wilton Junction and Pinhoe, Exeter, except for the section from Templecombe to Yeovil, with passing places at Tisbury, Gillingham, Chard Junction and Honiton; as a result, today's journey takes around three and a half hours. Semley was closed to passengers on 7 March 1966, as were also Chard and Seaton Junctions. Sidmouth Junction was re-christened Feniton on 3 May 1971.

# Evershot and Bincombe

The efficacy of sea-bathing at a place that became Melcombe Regis had been advocated as early as 1763, and visits by King George III between 1789 and 1811 ensured the popularity of the watering place. Weymouth, situated south of the Backwater, had a fishing trade unserved by rail, and though it did not appear in early GWR projects in the direction of Dorchester, the Bristol & Exeter had plans for a line to the town.

Though an impecunious concern, the Wilts, Somerset & Weymouth Railway (originally the Wiltshire & Somerset) was backed by the GWR, which took it over only six years after its incorporation on 30 June 1845. At the time of the absorption it had opened (on 5 September 1848) just under 14 miles of broad gauge line from Thingley Junction to Westbury, and was clearly in no position to go anywhere else unaided.

This is not to say, however, that no work had been done on the southern section during this time - the reports of company meetings show quite the contrary. There were two summits for Brunel and the resident engineer, a man named Peniston, to surmount, and the first of these, at Evershot, presented difficult geological problems. Having traversed the deep gorge cut through Yeovil sands by the River Yeo, the line then had to climb across faulted deposits to reach the chalk uplands by which it descended into the valley of the

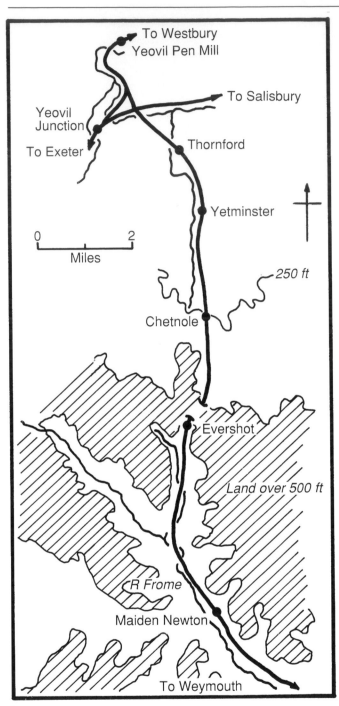

1846. At Evershot shafts had already been sunk to the crown of the tunnel, and works near the summit were in full swing by that August when George Wythes, of Brighton, was awarded a £95,500 contract for the Maiden Newton-Dorchester section, south of the summit. Contractor for the Yeovil to Maiden Newton stretch was A. W. Ritson, whom we shall meet again at Whitrope, and who, among many other contracts, also built part of the Midland's London Extension. Money began to run out, however, and work was concentrated on the section between Thingley and Westbury. In his report to the WS&W Board on 28 August 1848, Brunel stated:

'Between Yeovil and Dorchester not much progress has been made since my last half-yearly report. At Holywell tunnel [now known as Evershot] we have proceeded slowly, but so as to

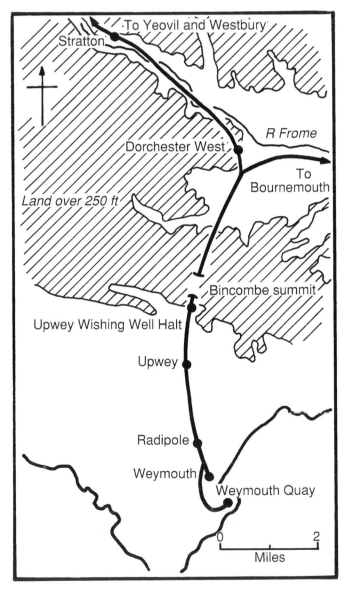

River Frome. Because of the substantial climb involved in the first section of the route, Brunel had suggested in 1844 that the atmospheric system should be used, and W. S. Moorsom, Engineer of the Southampton & Dorchester Railway which was aiming at Dorchester from the east, thought it might also help him over Bincombe. As things turned out, perhaps it was as well that the idea was rejected.

A difficulty in getting surveyors and draughtsmen, in great demand for other projects, delayed a start on the southern section, but work began in February

Upwey Wishing Well Halte in the early days of the century. The station stood on Bincombe bank, just below the tunnels, and in this picture an auto-train is waiting to leave for Dorchester. Presumably it has time in hand, for the gangers working beyond the short tunnel seem in no hurry to get out of the way! *Lens of Sutton*

secure the completion of this work in time for the rest of the line, should these works be proceeded with more rapidly.'

It sounds as if he was hedging his bets a little!

Meanwhile, of course, work was also proceeding south of Dorchester. The inhabitants of Weymouth complained as early as November 1845 that they wanted some action, but Parliamentary authority was needed for a deviation at Bincombe, so they perforce had to wait. Brunel arranged a contract with Messrs Dodson & Munday of Weymouth to complete the Dorchester-Weymouth section of the line for £112,000 in 22 months.

On 28 August 1848 Brunel told the Board:

'In the neighbourhood of Dorchester, and thence to Weymouth, where the works are heavy, they have been progressing steadily; and the Bincombe tunnel, which is the principal work, is nearly completed. About 130 [of 814] yards remain still to be executed.'

Bincombe bank was no easy matter, particularly as here, when, on 5 September 1965, 'Battle of Britain' Class 4-6-2 No 34066 *Spitfire* has a twelve-coach Channel Islands Boat Express to struggle with. Banking assistance is being given in the rear by BR Standard Class '4' 2-6-0 No 76014, which will drop off beyond Bincombe tunnel. *Hugh Ballantyne*

A year later, the directors' report to the shareholders, as quoted in the *Railway Times* of 1 September 1849, told them that the most important parts of the line had been '. . .brought nearly to a state of completion. The tunnel is. . .all but finished; and a few works will suffice for its entire completion.'

At this point the money really did run out. All work was stopped, except north of Westbury, and Wythes, who had all but completed his contract, claimed compensation for the delay; his contract was later completed by G. Hennett. The directors decided to sell the Company to the GWR, a step which became reality as from 14 March 1850, though Parliament did not ratify it until 3 July 1851.

Meanwhile, in 1847, the Southampton & Dorchester Railway (to become part of the LSWR the next year) had reached Dorchester. Somewhat optimistically the inhabitants of Weymouth prepared for the arrival of the railway by changing to Railway Time on 1 January 1852. They had to wait another five years before the line arrived!

Application was made to Parliament for an extension of time in 1856, when it was estimated that a mere three or four months' work would finish the job - however, it was another year before Colonel Yolland inspected the entire line from Yeovil to Weymouth, on 15 January 1857, and it was opened five days later, the first train leaving Weymouth at 6.15 am.

The WS&W appears to have treated its workers very much better than many other concerns of that time - or, indeed, later. A church and free school was set up in Weymouth, the railway company contributing, and it also made grants to chaplains. Brunel, on discovering that the truck system was operating on the Radstock branch, ordered it to be discontinued. Not that this completely avoided trouble, and there was an attack on a public house in Maiden Newton following the death of a navvy in April 1846.

And what of the inclines themselves? Though Bincombe seems to grab most of the limelight, Evershot is actually considerably steeper. A train southbound from Yeovil rises very gently at first, until Yetminster is reached. The station stands on a slope of 1 in 256, but this soon increases sharply to 1 in 151, and, after a very brief level pitch, to 1 in 75. This is for about a quarter of a mile, and is followed by successive lengths at 1 in 65 and 1 in 53, with Chetnole station dividing them, and each rather more than half a mile long. The final one and a half mile drag to the top is at 1 in 51, and takes the line through the 308-yard tunnel to the summit, about 500 feet above sea level, immediately to the south. A rather easier descent into the Frome valley follows, with short banks of 1 in 95, 69, 118, 79, 150 and 114, before levelling out towards Maiden Newton after two and a half miles. There is another fall beyond, beginning near Frampton tunnel, and the line rises again to Dorchester.

Bincombe summit is attained more steeply from the southward side, the approach from Dorchester being a straightforward one and a half mile pitch of 1 in 91, the summit level beginning about ten chains north of the tunnel mouth. From Weymouth, drivers had a much harder job of it. There is quite easy going to Radipole, just over a mile from the terminus and situated on a slope of 1 in 187, but the line angles steeply upward soon afterwards, hitting a mile and a third of 1 in 74. This ends shortly beyond Upwey, where it becomes even steeper at 1 in 50, maintained for a mile. Three quarters of a mile of 1 in 52, beginning at the site of Wishing Well Halt, takes the line through the tunnel, levelling at the north portal for about ten chains before running down to Dorchester.

The line over Evershot was originally single, but was doubled between Yeovil and Evershot in 1858. Further doubling, to Maiden Newton, had to wait until 1882, to Grimstone & Frampton until 1884 and Dorchester until 1885. This was laid in broad gauge, of course. South to Weymouth was double track, in mixed gauge. The broad gauge rails were removed, or the track converted, between 18 and 22 June 1874. The whole line north of Dorchester West has now reverted to single track - Yeovil-Maiden Newton on 26 May 1968 and from Maiden Newton to Dorchester on 9 June; there are crossing places at Yeovil and Maiden Newton. In steam days banking engines were kept at Yetminster: trains needing assistance had to come to a halt there, and, if stopping at either Chetnole or Evershot, had the banker coupled. At Evershot it was either uncoupled, or dropped off. Evershot station, which had watercranes, closed completely on 3 October 1966, as did Grimstone & Frampton.

South of Dorchester, Monkton & Came Halt opened as Came Bridge Halt on 1 July 1905, retaining its original name for three months. It closed on 7 January 1957, as did the other halt on the section, Upwey Wishing Well Halt. This had opened a few weeks before its counterpart, on 28 May 1905. Upwey station was opened in 1871, and closed 15 years later when Upwey Junction (for the Abbotsbury Railway) was opened, 35 chains to the south, on 19 April 1886. Radipole Halt opened on 1 July 1905 and closed on 31 December 1982.

Banking was necessary from Weymouth, of course. Trains in excess of seven coaches were usually assisted, the banker joining the train outside Weymouth station and being detached at Bincombe Tunnel signal box. Trains requiring help beyond there had their assisting engine attached in front, as it always had to be, in any case, in fog or falling snow.

# Micheldever

To reach Southampton from London, the London & Southampton Railway needed to cross the chalk ridge that lay across its path. Following the lead given by the first prospectus, of 21 October 1830, which said 'The district. . .in no part presents difficulties which cannot easily be surmounted. . .', this has generally been regarded as one of the lesser problems facing railway engineers, but there were two changes of plan and a change of engineer before it was completed.

The route authorised by Parliament on 25 July 1834 was to curve south beyond Basingstoke to a summit beneath the 593-foot high Popham Beacons, where it would be in a tunnel a mile long. It would then fall more gently towards Winchester. From milepost 44$^1$/$_2$ a slope of 1 in 300 for six miles would bring the line to 378 feet high and a level summit section of two and a half miles, followed by a 1 in 300 fall between mileposts 53 and 64 and at 1 in 194 for four and a half miles thereafter.

At the first meeting, on 23 October 1834, Francis Giles, the Engineer, reported that work had begun on other parts of the line. All was not well though, for the work went slowly, costs rose, Giles's estimates became wildly optimistic, and the whole concern became something of a laughing-stock. Plans for a deviation at Popham were announced in August 1836, but confidence in Giles's ability had gone, and on 13 January 1837 he was replaced by Joseph Locke.

Locke was born in 1805, and learned his business under Stephenson on the Liverpool & Manchester Railway. Still young, he engineered the Grand Junction Railway, and shortly after his appointment to the L&S was supported by Brunel and other notable engineers of the day to election as an FRS, on 22 February 1838, at the unusually early age of 32. Locke brought with him, as R. A. Williams has put it, 'a fresh and invigorating air to the undertaking'. Giles's contractors were small, and Locke's biographer, N. W. Webster, has remarked that '. . .there was no coherency about the work. He was, in fact repeating the errors of George Stephenson.' Locke's takeover effected a transformation. He removed at once all the small, inefficient contractors, appointing Thomas Brassey (of whom more in due course) in their place,

and awarding him the Basingstoke-Winchester contract. Agents were P. Ogilvie and others.

The deviation at Popham, authorised on 30 June 1837, was eight miles long, leaving the original route at East Oakley to go, via Ash, Overton and Micheldever, to Weston Colley. It would be longer than the original route, but it replaced the mile-long tunnel with three short ones totalling about 30 chains: Litchfield (196 yards), and two at Popham, of

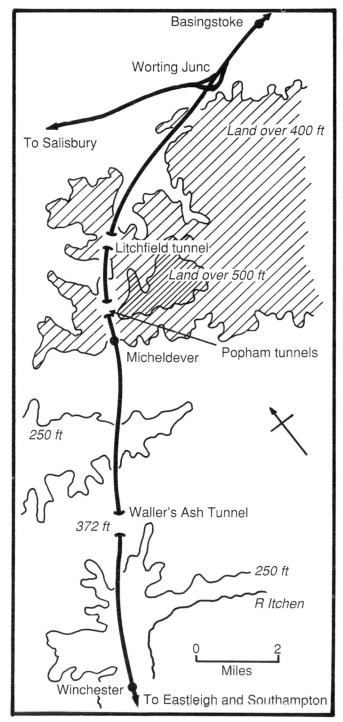

470 yards all told, with a 130-yard break between them. Waller's Ash tunnel (490 yards), between Micheldever and Winchester, was not affected by the deviation. Gradients were easier - now, from Basingstoke, a rise of 1 in 249 for three and three-quarter miles leads to a brief respite and a final two miles to the summit in Litchfield tunnel, just short of milepost 56. Thereafter the line falls at a steady 1 in 252 through Micheldever and Waller's Ash, and on at 1 in 349, 249 and 404 to Winchester, a distance of ten and three-quarter miles from the summit. There is a further fall for five and a half miles at 1 in 252 through Shawford. The average gradient for the 15.5 miles towards Southampton from the summit is now 1 in 253.3, against the 1 in 269 of the original.

Though there was some opposition to the new line, not all were against it. Sir Thomas Baring, a local landowner, became concerned at the dangerous conditions under which the navvies worked, and subscribed to Hampshire County Hospital in Winchester, where many of the casualties were treated. This encouraged other contributions, and even the LSWR Directors were moved to give £100, among the first instances of an employer contributing to the health care of its employees.

The half-yearly meeting on 27 February 1839 was told:

'The work is proceeding most satisfactorily, although the section still presents a large quantity of unfinished earthwork; but the energy which is evinced. . .affords the directors entire confidence of Mr Brassey's contract at the stipulated time, viz the 1st of May 1840. . . Of the 3,200,000 cubic yards of cuttings and embankments required to be removed for the formation of the road in this district, 1,800,000 yards are already executed, leaving 1,400,000 yards to be removed.' (Herepath's *Railway Magazine*, April 1839)

It was also noted that the weight of the rails had been changed from 63 lb per yard to 75 lb.

Brassey did not disappoint the Directors, despite a shortage of workers and an appallingly bad winter in 1839-40, when more rain fell than in any other in living memory. It caused many earthslips on both cuttings and embankments, and Brassey had to draft in yet more hard-found men to make the repairs; but even so, the line was opened, as planned, on 11 May 1840. The Directors and 'bands of music' left Nine Elms at 8.00 am and arrived at Southampton amid a 21-gun salute at 11.00 am. After spending two hours at Southampton (Terminus) - now closed, though extant as a listed building - the guests retired to Brassey's camp at Warren Farm, near Andover Road station (now Micheldever), for 'delicate viands and rare wines' provided by the contractor. The festal air of the train crews apparently aroused some apprehension among the passengers, but the only casualty was a dog decapitated by the train, while Northam crossing gates were run through in 'an excess of joie de vivre'.

Francis Whishaw, in his fascinating contemporary descriptions of the early railways, tells us that the L&S used rails of 63/73 lb per yard laid in chairs spiked to kyanised sleepers. Five tanks for the treatment of these were prepared at Warren's Farm, the sleepers being left in solution of mercuric chloride for six to seven days. Ballast was chiefly gravel, and the space between the tracks was set at 6 feet 5 inches, with the freeway outside at 4 feet 7 inches. Popham tunnels are cut through chalk, and are 25 feet wide by 22 feet high - each was worked from a single vertical shaft about 94 feet deep by 6 feet in diameter. Waller's Ash has the same cross section as Popham, but is cut through flinty chalk - two shafts were needed here, of 9 foot diameter. Lichfield (sic) is through chalk and flints with small veins of clay, again with the same cross-section as the others; a single shaft, 9 feet in diameter, was used in its con-

**Micheldever station was for many years the best-preserved of the original stations - even now the building stands, though the surrounding canopy has disappeared since this *circa* 1920 picture was taken. Beyond the station the line curves towards the tunnel mouth and Basingstoke, while on the right lie the sidings serving the quarry which provided so much spoil for the embankment that extends southward behind the camera.** *Lens of Sutton*

struction. The west portal lies 58 feet deep, the east 65 feet. All the tunnels are lined with brickwork varying between 9 and 14 inches in thickness. The produce of the tunnels was deposited in spoilbanks.

The present-day official lengths of the tunnels vary slightly from those noted above, Litchfield being 198 yards, Popham No 2 199 yards and No 1 265 yards. Waller's Ash, midway between Micheldever and Winchester, is 501 yards long. It appears to have given no trouble at first, but in March 1842 a fall was reported to have caused damage, and bricks in the arch were slipping. A vein of clay in the chalk was to blame, and this had given way beneath the pressure of the chalk on the roof-lining of the tunnel. Repairs were in hand when, on 1 April, 23 feet of arch collapsed, killing four workmen. The line was back in use two days later, but a further fall later put the line out of action for another 24 hours.

Micheldever remains now, as it was then, the only intermediate station on the summit section. Two roads through the station were converted to four in 1904, and a new down platform was built. The original building still stands, albeit without the all-round shelter it once had. The embankment lower down the gradient was widened in 1902 with spoil from the station area to make room for two goods loops, whose usefulness was proved when the line was electrified in 1966.

As a tailpiece, it may be of interest to note that though some doubt was expressed at the wisdom of building a line between London and Southampton, John Francis was able to write in A History of the English Railway:

'So close and cautious had been Mr Chaplin's [Chairman of the L&S] estimate of traffic, that within three months receipts amounted to the sum proposed.'

Francis also noted that the cost of the line had been £5,550 per mile, compared with the London & Birmingham (£8,450), the Great Western (£9,800) and the London & Brighton (£12,800). This must stand a tribute to the abilities of Locke, who was later to gain a reputation for quality allied with economy.

# Sole Street

Like the Wilts, Somerset & Weymouth, the London, Chatham & Dover Railway was an impecunious undertaking. It spent periods in receivership, yet somehow always seemed to be able to bounce back - perhaps its position, near and in London, allowed it to do this. However it was, the company seemed always to be seeking ways to expand its influence, and when it saw an area of country unserved by railways between its own lines at Rochester and Bickley, it, as we would say today, went for it.

Its Act, passed on 23 July 1858 in the face of stiff and wholly expected opposition from the South Eastern Railway, aimed to provide '. . .a direct and independent Communication by Railway between Dover, Canterbury, and the district of East Kent, and the Ports and Places of the Coast thereof, and the Western and Southern Parts of the Metropolis. . .' The major problem, at least in train operating terms, was one of levels. A substantial ridge of chalk, skirted to the north by the South Eastern's line to Gravesend, lay across the proposed route.

Engineer for the line was Joseph Cubitt, son of Sir William Cubitt, born in Horning, Norfolk, on 24 November 1811. He had been apprenticed to Fenton, Murray and Jackson (for whom his uncle, Benjamin, was Engineer) and he helped his father on the SER until 1846, when he moved to the GNR, again under his father. On his father's retirement in 1855 he became a consultant engineer, and built several lines in England and Wales, of which this was one. The contractors were Peto, Betts & Crampton, who, according to The Times of 26 August 1858, undertook to complete the western extension by 1 October 1860.

For once the work appears to have gone to plan. The directors' report of February 1859 said that '. . . the company are in possession of nearly the whole of the land, and the contractors. . .are pushing on the works with vigour at all the heaviest points'. On 31 October 1860 the Directors made their first trip over the new line - they were given lunch near Cuxton, looking across the Medway valley, and dined, in state no doubt, at the Crystal Palace. The line's official opening was on Monday 3 December 1860, but the train unfortunately broke down, leaving its passengers stranded between Farningham Road and Meopham.

The ridge rises steeply almost immediately west of Rochester Bridge, the old Roman road, now the A2, going straight up it. This was clearly impractical for the railway, so, having crossed the Medway, it veers sharply to the left, which enables up trains to take a diagonal course up the slope. There are short pitches of 1 in 106 and 132, interspersed with equally short

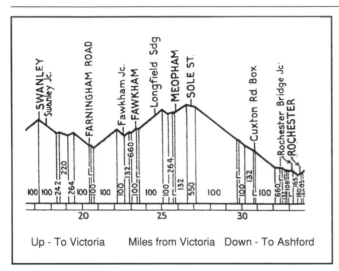

**Gradient profile, Sole Street**

levels, and then a third of a mile at 1 in 660 for about 30 chains. Then the work begins, about a mile and a half from Rochester station, where there will, almost invariably, have been a stop. A mile and a quarter of 1 in 100 begins it, after a brief level stretch at Cuxton Road signal box; something over half a mile of 1 in 132 serves only to lead to another length of 1 in 100. This is comparatively short, about half a mile, but the level beyond is even briefer, and then the train is into the long pull towards the summit, 1 in 100 throughout for two and a half miles. Even when this eases, the climb is not over, for half a mile of 1 in 550 still separates the train from the summit.

Halfway along this length stands Sole Street station, which in steam days must have been a godsend for drivers whose breathless engines needed a 'blow-up'. Beyond the summit, which lies perhaps 200 yards on, the line drops at 1 in 132, through Meopham, and apart from some short upward slopes, again at 1 in 100, it is mostly downhill to Farningham Road. The real switchback begins now, the 1 in 100s alternating frequently until Bickley is reached.

St Mary Cray had a population of 1,464 in 1861 and was the most important intermediate station. It was in a soft-fruit-growing district, so that there was not only manure as inwards traffic, but also a heavy outward flow of fruit during the season. The station was rebuilt in 1958-9 when the line was quadrupled in connection with the Kent Coast electrification scheme. When the line opened the LC&D could offer a time between Canterbury and London of 2 hours 10 minutes. BR today provides a 1 hour 25 minute service.

*Above left* The 5.20 pm up Ramsgate-Victoria train heads up Sole Street bank on 1 September 1958, headed by 'King Arthur' Class 4-6-0 No 30796 *Sir Dodinas le Savage*. *Peter Hay*

*Left* Sole Street station, built on a gradient of 1 in 550, is a quarter of a mile from the summit of the climb. Beyond the overbridge the line can just be seen falling away at the top of the 1 in 100. *Allan Mott*

# Guston

The South Eastern and the LC&D had been at loggerheads for years, and to say that their dispute was bitter is to put it mildly, so the Dover & Deal Joint Railway was something of an achievement in itself, never mind the engineering problems. The result was one of the more spectacular lines in southern England.

Authority to build the line between the two towns was given on 30 June 1874, when the line was vested jointly in the two promoting companies. It was short, a mere eight and a half miles, and was to run from Buckland Junction, about a mile north of Dover (Priory) to an end-on junction with the SE branch from Minster at Deal. The first sod was cut by Lord Granville on 29 June 1878, so it will be noted that by then four years had already passed since the Act had become law; a second, dated 14 August 1877, and a third in 1879 had been necessary to allow work to continue.

The harvest delayed the initial marking out. The contract for construction was won by T. A. Walker, who undertook the work for £147,644 2s 8d. This is a large sum for a mere 8.5 miles, but houses had to be demolished at Dover, land costs were high, and a 1,412-yard tunnel had to be cut at Guston.

The line finally opened, officially, on 14 June 1881, three years after works had begun, with a public opening next day, the first train hauled by an engine from each company. Another Act of Parliament that year allowed a junction facing north to be laid in at the Dover end of the line, so that the L&CD had direct access to Deal. This was opened on 1 July 1882.

The profile of the line is a substantial gable, and it is difficult to know which side to approach from first! But since the name of the company put Dover first, let us start there. The line branches sharply to the right from the Dover-Canterbury route at Buckland Junction, and at once is on a gradient of 1 in 105 and a severe horseshoe curve. Within ten chains the slope has steepened to 1 in 80 and within another ten chains is steeper still at 1 in 60. This pitch is slightly longer, at 15-20 chains, and is followed by two-thirds of a mile at 1 in 69. The next mile lies in three separate pitches, the centre one slightly shorter than the other two, of 1 in 71, 74 and 68 respectively. Already

the line has risen substantially, yet is still a mere one and three-quarter miles from Buckland Junction. As it approaches the tunnel the gradient eases slightly to 1 in 71, and this is maintained through the bore, easing further to 1 in 75 for a quarter mile at the far end. Now, suddenly, the line has reached its summit on the plateau of the Kentish Downs, some 400 feet above sea level, in a deep cutting spanned by two overbridges. The vertical rise from Buckland Junction has been 270 feet in a shade under 2.5 miles. In an article in *The Railway Magazine* of July 1953, the Rev A. Mace relates how, during the Second World War,

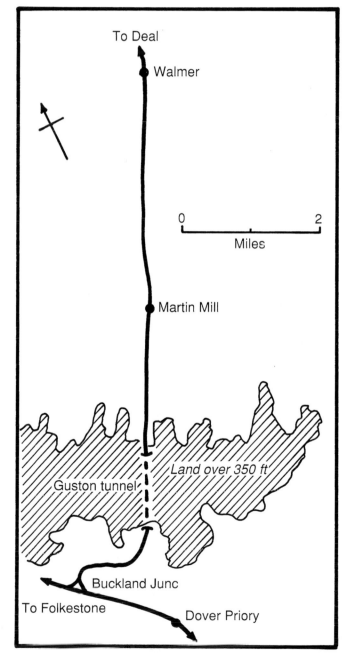

siege guns were kept here to reply to the heavy German shelling from France, being then quickly moved out of danger into the tunnel.

From the other side, the line has to climb further, but has six miles in which to gain the height required. It begins almost at sea level; a stiff pull of 1 in 88 on a right-hand curve for a quarter of a mile leads out of Deal, but an easier mile at 1 in 260, 140, level and 120 follows. There is three quarters of a mile at 1 in 70, through a cutting spanned by an overbridge, and an easing (1 in 1600) into the station at Walmer. In 1953 Mace observed that original D&DR chairs survived in the goods yard here at that time. A long, hard stretch follows, with successive pitches of 1 in 120, 67 and 72 for the next mile. Then comes a quarter-mile at 1 in 64 and half a mile at 1 in 71. Another half-mile at 1 in 69 is followed by a short level of about 15 chains and a brief pitch of 1 in 200. Half a mile of 1 in 120 leads through Martin Mill which then eases to 1 in 280 and 1 in 400 for successive quarter miles. At last, just as train crews must have begun to wonder where the top had gone to, a three-quarter-mile pitch at 1 in 210 leads there.

There were six daily trains each weekday at first, run by the LC&D, with four SE trains extended from Deal, and for many years this was the general pattern. By 1953 there were 25 up (towards Dover) and 24 down trains daily. The current service is roughly hourly, augmented at times when people are travelling to and from work.

# 2
# LONDON, MIDLANDS AND EAST

**F**ive of the London main-line termini have substantial gradients beyond their platform ends. None is long in comparison with the majority of those we have seen so far, but a brief mention at least must be made of them. In addition, several lead to substantial summits further from the City, so it seems proper to deal with these in sequence rather than dart from one to another. And, lest it be suggested that the order in which they are taken indicates a bias of any sort, let us take the only one belonging to the 'Southern' companies first, and then progress from east to west.

**Grosvenor bank on Derby Day, 7 June 1957. 'Schools' Class 4-4-0 No 30939 *Leatherhead* heads up the 1 in 52 out of Victoria with a Royal Train to Tattenham Corner. The lines leading to the carriage sidings can be seen in the foreground.** *Peter Hay*

# Victoria (Grosvenor Bridge)

**T**he climb from Victoria station is short, steep and curved. It owes these properties, in part at least, to the fact that it is built on the site of the basin of the Grosvenor Canal, facing west, and the line must

needs cross above the River Thames, facing south.

It was realised by the companies approaching London from the south that if the river could be crossed, a station near the West End would be highly desirable. The London, Brighton & South Coast Railway in particular hankered after a West End terminus, even more so after the Crystal Palace was moved to Sydenham when the Great Exhibition closed. A station at 'Pimlico' - which was only nominally in that district, for it lay immediately south of the river and slightly to the west of the present line - was opened to the public by the West End of London & Crystal Palace Railway on 29 March 1858. The line was worked by the 'Brighton', which absorbed the smaller company under an Act dated 23 July 1860. Possibly with just such a scenario in mind, the 'Brighton' itself had promoted the Victoria Station & Pimlico Railway, incorporated on 23 July 1858, to build 73 chains of line from Stewart's Lane across the river to a new station.

Victoria was built by John Kelk, and the 'Brighton' side of it was designed by that company's resident engineer, Robert Jacomb Hood. The LB&SC provided half the cost, and was thus entitled to half the station - the remainder was leased to the LC&D and the GWR, which ran a broad gauge service into platforms on the north side until about 1866, and a standard gauge service until 1915, remaining a lessee until 1933. The 'Brighton' opened its half of the station on 1 October 1860, and the rest was opened on 25 August 1862.

Grosvenor Bridge was designed by John Fowler, the engineer of the VS&PR, assisted by Benjamin Baker and W. Wilson. It was 930 feet long, and 30 feet 9 inches wide between the parapets. When completed it had cost £746,936, which looks an even larger sum if it is set beside the estimated cost of the entire railway - £450,000 - as authorised in its Act. Construction began on 9 June 1859, and although work was slowed by a strike that autumn, the first train rumbled over precisely one year later; it was the first to have crossed the Thames by rail in the London area.

That first train left Victoria station at 5.45am, and by the end of the day no fewer than 94 trains had used the bridge. It originally carried two tracks only, of mixed gauge, but in 1864 Sir Charles Fox began a widening operation by building a second bridge, which allowed an extra five tracks, all of standard gauge. Later two more were added by the 'Brighton' under an Act of 1898-9. In 1967 steelwork for a widened bridge was provided by Redpath, Dorman Long, to carry twice the load and one extra track, but the space thus created remains unused.

A station at Grosvenor Road, on the end of the bridge, was opened in January 1867, at first as a ticket platform, but on 1 November that year as a full station by the LC&D, and on 1 November 1870 by the LB&SC. The track up to Grosvenor Bridge was roofed over at first, to minimise inconvenience to the residents - one suspects it also aided adhesion in bad weather. Thankfully no accidents having the gradient as either cause or abetter have occurred at Victoria.

The gradient begins with 400 yards of 1 in 290 from the platform ends, but as the curve takes effect, so does the slope, with another 400 yards of 1 in 62, which lifts the line above the Grosvenor Road carriage sidings - now an EMU depot - and ends only as the line runs on to Grosvenor Bridge itself, which is, of course, level. On the south side of it there were also, to begin with, sharp slopes down at 1 in 50 to the VS&PR's junction with the WEL&CPR and 1 in 53 up beyond the bridge which took the LSWR line to Nine Elms. Powers for an overbridge to remove this nuisance were obtained in 1862, and it opened on 1 December 1867.

# Liverpool Street (Bethnal Green)

The Great Eastern Railway at first used the old Eastern Counties Railway terminus at Bishopsgate. First moves for building a new, bigger terminus nearer the City began soon after the formation of the GER in 1862, and building was authorised on 29 July 1864, after which some preliminary work began. But in 1867 a Receiver was appointed to look after GER affairs, and such matters as new stations were shelved.

It was two years before the Receiver could be disposed of, and in 1869 work on the planned station began again. A choice between a high or low level approach was offered; the latter was preferred because a connection with the Metropolitan Railway was considered important. The line therefore had to be carried down from the viaduct by which it had reached Bethnal Green, on a gradient of 1 in 70 for 30 chains, in order that it could cross under Brick Lane. It then curved to the left to bring it to platforms beside, but lower than, the North London Railway's station at

*Right* Gradient profile, Bethnal Green and Brentwood

*Below right* Hauling the 5.54 pm Liverpool Street-Norwich express, 'Britannia' 'Pacific' No 70007 *Coeur-de-Lion* climbs Bethnal Green bank on 4 June 1958, and passes an 'N7' 0-6-2T labouring up the incline with a stopping train for Enfield Town. *Brian Morrison*

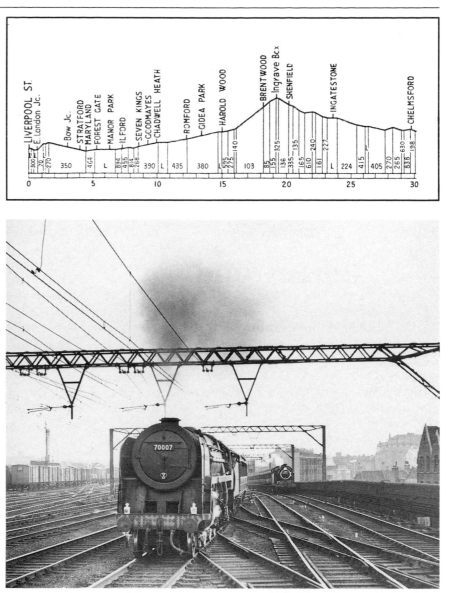

Broad Street. Extensive tests in 1869 showed that this gradient could be feasibly worked by the company's current stock.

Planning and building were in the charge of the General Manager, Samuel Swarbrick, who would brook no interference from the Board. A later GER Chairman, Lord Claud Hamilton, complained bitterly in 1923 that the result of this somewhat high-handed action was greatly inconvenient to the travelling public and that every 'heavily-laden train has to commence its journey at the bottom of an incline'.

The line down to the new station was to be in cutting, with retaining wall on either side, not to mention a sort of semi-tunnel beneath the old Bishopsgate station. It was a major operation, and with the new station occupied the early 1870s. A temporary structure opened for suburban traffic in February 1874, and the station opened fully on 1 November 1875, when Bishopsgate was turned over entirely to goods. The Metropolitan Railway used platforms 1 and 2 for five months, until its own station was finished, but the suggested through workings subsided in a morass of arguments about charges. The connection was used only for special workings, which ended in 1904, and the junction was removed three years later, but traces of the tunnel can still be seen at the east end of Liverpool Street LUL station.

Before the new station was ready, a small station for the suburban traffic was built on the new line, directly beneath Bishopsgate, and called Bishopsgate Low Level. It opened on 4 November 1872 but was closed on 22 May 1916 as a wartime economy. It never re-opened, but a forlorn-looking platform can still be seen on the up side of the cutting.

By the 1880s the suburban traffic down the hill to Liverpool Street was increasing rapidly, and the sta-tion was extended on the east side, a third pair of tracks being provided between Bethnal Green and the terminus; they came into use in 1891. Since then the 1 in 70 has seen the passage of the Great Eastern's famous 'Jazz' service - introduced in 1919 and so called because of the coloured strip painted above the door, which denoted the class of the compartment. It was possibly the most intensive suburban service ever run, when, hundreds of times daily, grimy tank engines plied their articulated stock up the bank to Enfield, Walthamstow, Chingford et al and back again.

During the Second World War Liverpool Street gained an unenviable reputation for dirt and murk, but nothing of very great note happened during the time the LNER was in charge. Electrification of the Shenfield route began in 1937, but was suspended during the war. A part-service began in September 1949, and the full service on 11 November.

Electrification was extended to Chelmsford and Southend in 1956, and the service up Bethnal Green bank is now completely electric. As for the station itself, all memories of the gloom of former years have gone following the magnificent rebuilding carried out in recent years.

# Brentwood

The Eastern Counties Railway became, perhaps, the best-hated line in the country, its inefficient service a byword. It had set out to build a railway from London to Yarmouth, but gave up when it had completed 51 miles to Colchester, only reaching its originally intended destination by absorption of other concerns. However, it is on the line to Colchester that the section now concerning us occurs - that which crosses Brentwood Hill. It gave great trouble and cost a lot of money to conquer, which no doubt contributed to the fatal lack of that commodity felt by the company on arrival at Colchester.

To build a line into East Anglia was a very laudable ambition, since the area, though primarily agricultural, had other industries ill-served by a poor road system. The line's engineer was John Braithwaite, who, with Ericcson, had been an unsuccessful competitor in the Rainhill Trials of 1829. Authority to build the line was obtained on 4 July 1836, and the first trains ran from a temporary terminus at Mile End to Romford on 20 June 1839. Extensions at each end, to Brentwood and Shoreditch, followed on 1 July 1840, and there things came to a stop for the time being because the shareholders thought the whole affair was costing a good deal more than they had anticipated. Robert Stephenson was called in, and confirmed Braithwaite's estimate of £520,000 required for completion to Colchester. In 1840 Parliament approved extra share capital of £350,000.

Francis Whishaw paid a visit to the incomplete ECR, and in his subsequent book mentions the cutting at Brentwood as being unfinished. He observed also that:

'. . .the gradients are entirely of the first class, except the Brentwood Incline, which rises to the summit level with a gradient of 52.80 feet [1 in 100] for a length of nearly three miles. This incline would have been less objectionable had there been a short level plane in the middle, to check the engines' velocity while making the descent.'

But work was continuing on Brentwood Hill, and the *Norfolk Chronicle* of 2 February 1839 reported that the company was about to let 'the whole ground from Brentwood to Colchester'. One John Burge won the contract, but came to regret it, for Braithwaite's report to the Directors in August 1839 referred to the extreme difficulties in cutting through Brentwood Hill, and remarked that the contractor

'. . .had some trouble keeping the roads in order, owing principally to the late unfavourable weather and having run through two veins of black sand, yielding a little water, which by the constant traffic of the horses, was trodden into the appearance of a quicksand; this obstruction no longer exists, having got into a different stratum, and leaving only 30,000 cubic yards remaining to be excavated from Brentwood Hill.'

Alas, he was too optimistic, and his figure of 30,000 cubic yards a gross underestimate. Throughout the next year progress was slow due to shortage of funds, and many works had been suspended. By February 1841 more contracts were being let towards Colchester, and the works east of Brentwood Hill were proceeding to Braithwaite's satisfaction. On 13 August 1841 the *Chelmsford Chronicle* reported:

'Contract 22 - Brentwood Hill West: Since the commencement of this work the contractors have prosecuted the cutting with vigour; 140,000 cubic yards [so much for 30,000!] have been run to spoil, being nearly one third of the amount of cutting required to complete this, the heaviest work, which leaves no doubt that the upper portion, to within 30 feet of the formation, will be finished, trimmed and drained before the winter months set in.

'Contract 12 - Brentwood and Shenfield: the excavators are proceeding at the west end of Shenfield Common, where about 40,000 cubic yards have been carried to spoil, and on the western side of Mountnessing Hill, where about 8,000 yards have been carried into embankment.'

Contract 22 was completed by a local concern, James & Thomas Hill of Brentwood, who were awarded it

**Above** Not long in traffic after trials, BR 'Britannia' 'Pacific' No 70001 *Lord Hurcomb* heads up Brentwood bank at 30 mph with the down 'Norfolkman' on 24 March 1951. Two of the first four coaches - Thompson stock - have already acquired carmine and cream livery, while the Gresley brake composite retains its teak. *E. D. Bruton*

**Right** On the same day but travelling in the opposite direction, Class 'B12/3' No 61557, having probably stopped at Shenfield to set down, is now accelerating hard down Brentwood bank just below Ingrave summit. There was no trace of this train in the timetable, and neither was it labelled, but it did convey a buffet car. Possibly it was a relief service. *E. D. Bruton*

on 12 February 1841 after several other contractors had failed. Sand was the main problem, but the Hills either overcame this themselves or took over after the problem had been solved - the date, and the fact that they were local, rather implies the former. The contract length was a mere 26 chains long, but it included the removal of 470,000 cubic yards of spoil and cost the company £23,846. In contrast, W. S. Simpson, who was given Contract 12 in Shenfield Parish on 27 April 1841, had 100 chains for which he charged £35,000. The Hills, incidentally, disposed of much spoil at the top of the cutting, and to this day the 'Tips' are the scene of much juvenile activity and enjoyment.

The usual contretemps between locals and navvies occurred, and in September 1841 a complaint was made about a shortage of constables in the Mountnessing area. A summons was issued against one of a group of labourers 'who had misconducted himself in the Ipswich Arms, Ingatestone'. In 1839 the *Essex Standard* noted the case of John Edwards, an ECR gangman, who had been committed for non-payment of 4s 6d to Ephraim Weaver, a labourer. Edwards claimed he had withheld the money because Weaver had been fighting, and the case was dismissed. Less successful was a brickmaker named Brignell, who was summoned by William Gover for refusing to pay him £2 14s 3d - Gover got his money.

Luggage trains ran for three weeks before the line's opening was announced in the *Essex Standard* of 24 March 1843 for five days later, and in due course Braithwaite drove the inaugural passenger train. 'At the various stations and bridges throughout the line,' reported the same journal on 31 March, 'crowds of the inhabitants of the adjacent villages had assembled, by whom the passing train was cheered in the most enthusiastic manner.' The *Chelmsford Chronicle* reported the opening too, of course, noting that the train was 'well filled and decorated with tasteful flags.'

From Bethnal Green the line falls to Maryland, only recovering the height achieved in one mile between Liverpool Street and Bethnal Green summit at Chadwell Heath, some five and a half miles on. From here a mile on the level is succeeded by a mile and a half at 1 in 435, which brings the line to Romford. A long 1 in 380 leads past Gidea Park, and a short level ends at Harold Wood. As a preliminary to the main climb, half a mile of 1 in 595 begins here, followed by another half-mile of 1 in 275 and about ten chains of 1 in 140. Two miles at 1 in 103 take the line to Brentwood station. Half a mile at the stiffest gradient (1 in 85) comes next, but despite an easing to 1 in 155 there is little respite, for it is still half a mile to the top, which comes at Ingrave.

From Chelmsford the climb is less severe, beginning with an undulating section for about two miles. Then comes a one and a half-mile pitch of 1 in 405, a short level and three quarters of a mile at 1 in 415. A mile and a half of 1 in 224 lifts the line to a longish level through Ingatestone, followed by pitches of 1 in 227, 161 and 240. After half a mile down at 1 in 610, it is all climbing to the top. Successive half-miles of 1 in 165 and 135 ease to 1 in 335 to Shenfield, but then comes three-quarters of a mile of 1 in 136 before a final quarter mile of 1 in 325 reaches Ingrave.

The ECR originally laid its track to a gauge of 5 feet, but this was soon perceived as inconvenient. Between 5 September and 7 October 1844 conversion was carried out in sections, on each running line in turn to avoid disrupting the traffic, at a cost of £1,000 per mile. Brentwood station was described in 1848 as 'one of the handsomer smaller stations on the Eastern Counties Railway'. It was demolished to make way for track widening, completed between Romford and Shenfield on 1 July 1934. Electrification was delayed by the Second World War, but was completed by November 1949.

# Elsenham

The Northern & Eastern Railway, incorporated on the same day as the ECR (4 July 1836) had as its main ambition a line for 53 miles between Islington and Cambridge 'with a view to its being extended hereafter to the Northern and Eastern Counties of England'. In the event it failed to reach, at any rate by its own volition, either of the places it was nominated to serve.

By 1842 it was running to Bishop's Stortford from the ECR terminus at Shoreditch, but there was no money left, and in 1840 the company had abandoned its powers to build further. In 1843, after finances improved, authorisation to extend to Newport (Essex) was granted, and the following year the ECR, having acquired sanction to build to Cambridge and beyond, took the line over on a 999-year lease. Like the ECR, the N&E had been laid to a gauge of 5 feet, which the ECR converted at the same time as it dealt with its own line. It is this section of the line to Cambridge that contains the banks on either side of Elsenham.

The route has been rising steadily ever since leaving London, reaching Bishop's Stortford without anything horrendous in the way of gradients. Now, however, it was confronted with the escarpment of a chalk ridge that sweeps south-west from Norfolk and turns south near Marlborough. Clearly it was too steep for a direct assault, so the engineer chose what mountaineers would call a traverse, gaining height by a diagonal route towards a gap at the village of Elsenham. From there it is mostly downhill to Cambridge, though, as with most generalities, there is an exception at Audley End.

Work began fairly promptly - Robert Stephenson was chief Engineer, with a man named Borthwick as his resident. The *Railway Times* of 10 August 1844 reported that shareholders were told at their half-yearly meeting that works were already in active progress. In January the following year, the Directors

'. . .have much pleasure in announcing. . .that they have concluded an arrangement by which the contractors [Messrs Grissell & Peto (the same Peto as we have already met, but with a earlier partner)] are pledged to complete and deliver to the company, on the 1st of July next, the whole of the extension lines between Cambridge, Newport, Ely and Brandon. . . [They] are not bound to deliver the portion of line. . .between Newport and Cambridge until the end of July 1846, but having. . .been unceasing in their efforts to carry on the works rapidly. . . these extension lines will be finished and earning income 13 months earlier than the date for completion fixed by their contracts.'

This, even today, would be a notable achievement, and the line was open to Cambridge on 29 July 1845 and opened throughout the next day. The work on

the 10.25-mile Bishop's Stortford-Newport section was split into two parts executed by a Mr Earle under three contracts:

No 1 Hockerill: Bishop's Stortford to Elsenham
£42,962

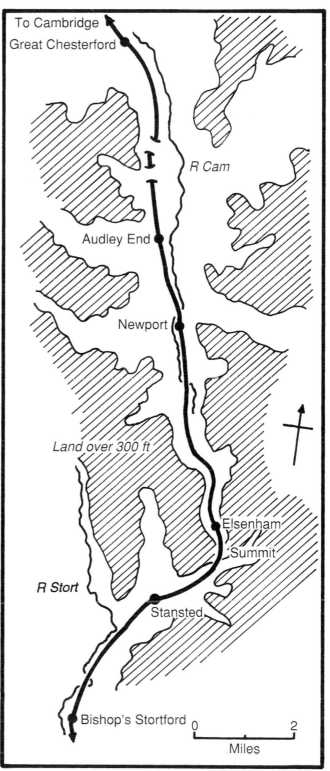

**Elsenham early in the 1950s. Class 'B1' 4-6-0 No 61286 has just topped the summit south of the station, and is now leading its train over the level crossing and into the northbound platform.** *D. Hufford*

No 2 Newport: Elsenham to Newport £35,981
No 3 Subsidiary: double track, buildings, etc £15,831

Total £94,774

This has interest in that the average cost for this section, one of the heaviest so far as earthworks are concerned, was only about £9,250 per mile, against £12,013.50 per mile over the whole line - no doubt the cost of the Audley End tunnels enhanced the overall figure.

For two miles after leaving Bishop's Stortford the terrain is straightforward, but at this point a pitch of 1 in 232 leads up to Stansted station. There is a level section of a third of a mile, succeeded by half a mile of 1 in 124, while the final length to the summit, about three quarters of a mile long, is at 1 in 107. Elsenham station, situated a few yards after the gradient levels out, was built by Thomas and William Piper for £1,867. The summit level is half a mile long, and is followed by descents to a point half a mile beyond Newport. It had been intended to follow the valley of the River Cam gently down to Cambridge from here, but the owner of Audley End objected, insisting on tunnels through Littlebury Hill. Thus, in order to lessen the amount of tunnelling as much as possible, the line must needs climb once more, which it does first at 1 in 300 for half a mile. There is then a third of a mile which is level, followed by two-thirds going up at 1 in 130. This summit is reached at Audley End, after which one goes downhill all the way to Cambridge.

The climb is actually longer from the Cambridge side. Beginning in earnest at 1 in 265 near milepost 50 (from London), further short pitches of 1 in 747 and 257 lead to a half-mile level through Whittlesford station. Half a mile at 1 in 267 lifts the line to another short level, and two miles at 1 in 320 bring it to Great Chesterford. There are then successive three-quarter miles at 1 in 163, 135 and 153, and a quarter-mile at 1 in 381 before the gradient eases to 1 in 741 to cover the remaining mile to the Audley End level. A brief downslope follows, as already described in the opposite direction, and climbing begins again with a short 1 in 330 and level through Newport. Each of these pitches is about 300 yards long, and half a mile at 1 in 182 begins immediately south of Newport station. This eases to 1 in 254 for a shade over a mile, increasing again for a further one and a half miles to 1 in 176. A final mile at 1 in 322 takes the line to the level through Elsenham station.

The line has been well-used, though the route difficulties just described have kept journey times longer than some would have preferred. Some rationalisation of stations has occurred, but with the exception of

Cambridge it is generally the ones at the London end that have received facelifts. So far as the section under discussion is concerned no stations have closed to passengers, though the branch to Saffron Walden and Bartlow from Audley End, and the Thaxted line from Elsenham, closed on 7 September 1964 and 15 September 1952 respectively. Electric services to Cambridge began on 19 January 1987, and that, combined with new traffic to Stansted Airport along a new branch opened to the public on 19 March 1991, means that the line is probably busier now than it has ever been before.

# King's Cross (Holloway)

Not far from Euston (see page 53), but later, the Great Northern Railway opened a temporary terminus at Maiden Lane (now York Way) on 7 August 1850. Like Camden Town, this too was on the north bank of the Regent's Canal, and, also like the L&B, the GN had decided that the line to its intended terminus would pass underneath it (although, as we shall see, the L&B ultimately decided on a crossing).

No doubt the Great Northern was relieved that Maiden Lane was only temporary, because the situation, in facilities which quickly proved woefully inadequate, soon became chaotic. What must have been a very welcome extension through Maiden Lane (or Gasworks) tunnel to the present station at King's Cross was opened on 14 October 1852. There had been a bank of 1 in 107 down to Maiden Lane anyway, and since the temporary station was on a level with the canal it meant that the gradient was doubled in length, though the pitch of the slope did not alter.

Much has been made of the difficult start from the platform end at King's Cross, and the official gradient profile shows a level to the southern tunnel mouth and up at 1 in 107 thereafter for about a mile and a quarter. In fact, there is a dip down to the tunnel mouth, continuing into the tunnel, and only after a few yards therein does the line begin to rise. If you doubt it, go and see for yourself; the row of lights attached to the wall inside the tunnel makes it plain enough.

Ex-GCR 'Director' 4-4-0 No 5507 *Gerard Powys Dewhurst* lays a smokescreen across Belle Isle as it blasts away from Gasworks tunnel under the North London Railway bridge. It is clearly an important Pullman train, but the effect is rather spoiled by a distinctly grubby Gresley full brake behind the tender. The engine's clag won't make it any cleaner! *H. C. Casserley*

Not that beginning the climb in tunnel made things any easier in steam days. It was not unusual for trains to have difficulty here, and it is fairly well known that the lights were installed in the tunnel after an occasion when a train had slipped backwards; at least crews in the dark would then know which way they were moving! The section never used cable-haulage, but banking assistance, generally at the rear, was given whenever required and available. There was, at first, only a single tunnel under the canal, but a second was opened on 4 March 1878 and a third, on the west side, in June 1892. Further up the bank, a second Copenhagen tunnel, so that freight trains could move straight to the yard, had been added in August 1877, and a third bore joined the others on 20 June 1886.

The gradient has provided its share of accidents, but only one, mercifully, has had fatal consequences, when in 1945 a Leeds express stalled in the tunnel, and slipped back. A signalman tried to divert the train, but was just too late - the bogies of the last carriage had crossed the pointblades before they moved, and two passengers were killed in the resulting derailment.

To the west of King's Cross station lay the notorious 'Hotel Curve', a link with the nearby Metropolitan Railway. The 'Suburban' platform was opened on 1 February 1878, and was approached by a gradient which included pitches of 1 in 35 and 48 - it was on a 7-chain radius curve too, which was no help - and it was undoubtedly one of the drivers' least favourite stretches of line. It was the soul-destroying duty of a GN employee to spend his time applying fresh sand to the rails after each train had passed. Starting a packed commuter train on the 1 in 60 that the slope eased to at the platform was something of a nightmare as well as a lottery.

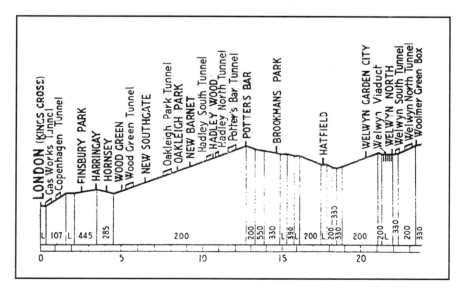

Gradient profile, Holloway, Potters Bar and Woolmer Green

Double-heading on Holloway bank in April 1952: Class 'B1' 4-6-0 No 61392 and 'B17' 4-6-0 No 61671 *Royal Sovereign* lift a King's Cross-Peterborough train out of Gasworks tunnel and past Belle Isle. *Peter Hay*

# The 'Northern Heights' (1): Potters Bar and Woolmer Green

**W**hile the London & Birmingham was far enough west to be able to skirt the 'Northern Heights', the Great Northern and the Midland Railways were not so lucky. The GNR was first, having opened from Maiden Lane to Peterborough in 1852, and for a number of years the Midland used its line to reach London. By 1863, however, congestion was becoming acute, so the Midland promoted its own line into London by extending south from Bedford.

Both had to pierce the wide bed of London Clay which rises to a height of some 478 feet near Elstree. The GN, being first in the field, was able to choose a slightly lower route by way of Potters Bar, but this still involved a none too easy climb, particularly in view of the sharp rise up Holloway bank. There were two ways of doing it - use a steady gradient and resort to tunnelling, or take a steeper, switchback approach.

The Great Northern took the former option, and, as a boy, this author at least found the succession of nine tunnels (though he could never remember them in the right order!) and a viaduct between Woolmer Green and the terminus by far the most exciting route to the capital. Heavily laden trains leaving London no doubt found it exciting too, but for rather different reasons.

The permanent survey of the route was done by William Cubitt, who had been appointed Engineer-in-chief on 23 September 1844, when Locke withdrew. Cubitt's son Joseph acted as superintending Engineer under his father. In November 1846 Thomas Brassey undertook to construct the railway between Maiden Lane and Peterborough, the 59 miles to Huntingdon by 1 July 1849 and the remaining 17 to Peterborough by the 1 November following, with a penalty clause of £5,000 per month for non-completion. It sounds a horrendous bargain, since the work included no fewer than eight tunnels, two viaducts, a bog to cross and the removal of some 9.75 million cubic yards of spoil. The contractor's three agents for the section were Messrs Bartlett, J. Milroy and Stephen Ballard, all trusted and often-used men.

Work went more slowly than expected, but in July 1848 Joseph Cubitt was able to report quicker progress. Tunnels had been left in abeyance and the section north of Hitchin was as yet untouched, but more funds were allocated to both items (£50,000 a month was to be spent on construction) and by the following February things had improved greatly. Clearly Brassey knew what he was doing, though, for the 5,000 to 6,000 men he employed between London and Peterborough finished on time, even drawing a

*Right* An up express emerges from Hadley Wood North tunnel heading south through Hadley Wood station on 1 June 1958. Work has begun on the widening and the cutting of the new tunnel, and various items of the contractors' impedimenta can be seen in the background. *A. E. Bennett*

*Below right* Ex-LNER Class 'K3/2' 2-6-0 No 61868 emerges from the other end of the tunnel on 14 April 1951 with a down fish van train, travelling up the 1 in 200 at about 30 mph. *E. D. Bruton*

somewhat grudging approval from John Herepath, who wrote in his April 1850 *Railway Magazine* that:

'. . . the North Mimms tunnel [Potters Bar]. . .is bricked through from end to end and partly ballasted. All the other tunnels on Mr Brassey's contract (except the Tottenham [Wood Green] tunnel which yet requires about 50 yards to complete it) are not far from completion.'

Herepath also comments on the fact that land bought for quadruple track has had only double track laid, but observes pointedly that even this is preferable to 'spending millions and having nothing to show for it'.

The *Stamford Mercury* of 2 August 1850 announced a successful inspection 'on Tuesday last', but in fact the Inspector, accompanied by about 400 Directors and guests, did his duty on Monday 5 August, and the line opened on Wednesday the 7th.

Having successfully, one hopes, surmounted Holloway bank, there is a half-mile level which leads to a mile and a quarter of 1 in 445 through Finsbury Park, which ends at Harringay. Then, the line having fallen at 1 in 265 for a mile through Hornsey, a long pitch of 1 in 200 begins about halfway between there and Wood Green. It continues unbroken for the next eight miles, through the tunnels at Wood Green, Barnet (previously Oakleigh Park), Hadley Wood South and North (384 and 232 yards respectively) and Potters Bar, at 1,214 yards the longest in the sequence. The climb ends at Potters Bar station, half a mile beyond the north por-

tal of the eponymous tunnel.

One says that the climb ends, but in fact it doesn't really, because there is more still to do to take the line over the same chalk ridge we have just climbed at Elsenham. But for the moment the line goes easily enough downhill for the next six miles, about a third of which is at 1 in 200 and the rest rather easier. A mile or so beyond Hatfield comes the trough, the climb from which begins with about 30 chains of 1 in 330 and continues with a shade over two miles at 1 in 200. Half a mile beyond Welwyn Garden City station a quarter-mile dip at the same gradient leads on to the

**Blue-liveried Class 'A4' 'Pacific'** *Dominion of Canada*, **complete with presentation bell, accelerates from a signal check at the top of the climb, and begins to take water at Langley troughs. The train is the 9.30 am King's Cross-Newcastle express on a chilly morning, 12 May 1951.** *E. D. Bruton*

40-arch Welwyn (or Digswell) viaduct, a magnificent feat of engineering in blue brick, which is 519 yards long and at its highest point stands 97 feet above the little River Mimram. Welwyn North station is at the north end of the viaduct, as the line begins to climb again at 1 in 330. It steepens to 1 in 200 halfway through Welwyn South tunnel (446 yards), this slope continuing for a mile during which it passes through Welwyn North tunnel, longer at 1,046 yards. Woolmer Green signal box once marked the point at which the gradient eased to a final 1 in 330 to the summit, just a few feet higher than the one already topped at Potters Bar.

The first stations on the line were at Hornsey, Colney Hatch (after many changes of name, New Southgate since 1971), Barnet (renamed New Barnet in 1884), Potters Bar and Hatfield. A station was opened at Seven Sisters Road in 1861, near the Hornsey Wood tea gardens, but after Hornsey Wood was renamed Finsbury Park in 1869 that became the name of the station also. Wood Green was added in 1859, Oakleigh Park in 1873, with Harringay and Hadley Wood both in 1885. As London expanded a platform on the main line at Welwyn Garden City was opened in 1920, and a fully-fledged station there on 20 September 1926. A new station at Brookman's Park was also opened that year. The latest addition is Welham Green, between Brookman's Park and Hatfield, which was opened in 1986.

With the increase in commuter traffic came also an increasing bottleneck as more and more trains competed for the double track section south of Potters Bar. Finally, in 1959, a section of widening was completed between New Barnet (four-tracked since 1892) and Potters Bar, including the bores of three new tunnels parallel to the originals. The short section including the viaduct and Welwyn tunnels remains double-tracked to this day.

Government grants enabled electrification, after many years of stagnation, to became a reality on suburban services out of 'The Cross' in November 1976, to be joined ten years later by the outer suburban service to Peterborough. Now electric expresses reach Edinburgh in three and a half hours, making light of Holloway and the rest.

# Stoke

For as long as people remember steam engines, Stoke bank will have a place in railway history. It has to be said, however, that, speed records apart, there is very little that is sensational about it. It is no longer than many and considerably less steep than most, but it is straightish, and there are no impediments such as major stations at the bottom. It was built by the Great Northern Railway, which, other than Brunel on the Great Western, had speed in mind more than most.

When the Great Northern Railway Act was given the Royal Assent in 1846, it was hitherto the longest (285.5 miles) and most expensive (£5.6 million) line to be authorised by a single Act. It opened between London and Peterborough on 7 August 1850, a loop line from Peterborough to Doncaster via Boston having already opened during the previous two years. The cut-off to Doncaster via Grantham and Newark, nicknamed the 'Towns' line, was slower to materialise.

Work, of course, had begun before the line to Peterborough opened, a Directors' report on 11 August 1849 stating that the survey and working plans were complete, and that they were 'about to let the work from Corby by Grantham [Corby Glen] to Hougham, a distance of fifteen miles, on which the works are heavy. . .' The contract for this length was taken on the 6th of that month by Thomas Jackson of London, at a price of £229,883. He broke ground at the end of January 1850, and by 26 April the *Stamford Mercury* could report that work was '. . .rapidly advancing in the neighbourhood of Grantham. . . shafts are sinking for all the tunnels, and cuttings are commenced in many places'.

A fine winter in 1850-1 'enabled the contractors to urge on their works with greater speed than usual. . .' (*Stamford Mercury*, 18 April 1851), that journal at the same time remarking that the very heavy works 'are said to be of a strong and substantial character, and reflect great credit on the contractors'. That August the contractor gave each of his clerks, engineers and heads of department £5 and eight days leave to visit the Great Exhibition and London.

The work was not without its tragedies. John Jones, a 48-year-old navvy, died when he burst a blood vessel in stooping to do up his child's shoe, and in 1851 a young man named Booth 'lost an arm when he fell on

a cutting at Little Ponton, and a wagon crushed it'. Another young man was killed in the same spot a week later. That July the *Stamford Mercury* observed that accidents were becoming numerous and recommended that overseers should take more care. 'Evidently the navvies are too careless,' it said virtuously. But perhaps the most remarkable accident took place a few days earlier, on Saturday 28 June. As reported by the *Stamford Mercury* the following Friday, a horse had just drawn several men up a shaft of Stoke tunnel. As they arrived at the top:

'. . .the horse backed a little, when one of. . .[the men]. . . in too hastily attempting to get out, missing his hold, was precipitated down the shaft a depth of 70 feet. The singularity of the affair is that although the shaft is intersected throughout its depth with timbers crossing in various

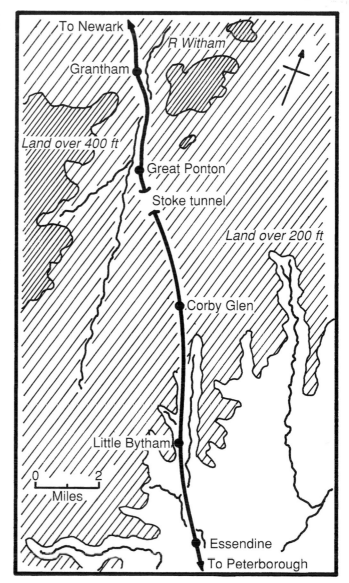

**Stoke summit today. The electrics rush up the gradient without noticing the 1 in 178, over the summit just behind the camera, and down at 1 in 200 into Stoke tunnel about a quarter of a mile beyond.** *C. V. Awdry*

directions, the man did not fall upon any of them, and the soil being soft at the bottom, he sustained no injury beyond a few bruises.'

Despite hopes in August 1851 that the line would be open to Grantham at the end of the year, it was not to be, and a month later an opening for the next March was being proposed. There was a heavy fall of snow on 3 November, and a strike for higher pay began on 2 December, only ending (peaceably) when troops arrived on the 11th. At last, in May 1852, Herepath was able to announce an opening date of 15 June, 'unless any unforeseen accident occur to prevent it'.

Alas, it did, and because of last minute problems relating to the BoT inspection, the opening was postponed at short notice. This annoyed the people of Grantham who had made preparations for the event, but they drowned their sorrows by having a party anyway! On Monday 28 June the GNR took formal possession of the line north of Grantham, the delay being a matter connected with Mr Jackson's contract - a Brick Tax (a short-lived tax imposed in 1851) had put him in financial difficulty - and despite a payment by the company of £16,753 he declined to hand the works over. He withdrew when police were drafted in, and the line was opened to Retford, quietly, for goods on 15 July, passengers on 1 August.

In keeping with its somewhat self-effacing image, Stoke bank begins quietly. From the south, climbing commences just north of Tallington, now marked only by a level crossing, with a mile and a half of 1 in 440. Then about 50 chains of level track heralds a mile and three quarters of 1 in 264 past Essendine, once a junction for both Stamford and Bourne, and beyond the station site a half-mile downhill pitch of 1 in 550 is the last fall for a little while. At milepost 90 the climb begins again, about 50 chains at 1 in 240, followed by half a mile of level. Four and a half miles

*Above left* **300 miles to Edinburgh: 'A3' 'Pacific' No 4472 *Flying Scotsman* powers up Stoke bank just north of Little Bytham with a special on 2 October 1966.** *P. H. Wells*

*Left* **'A4' 'Pacific' No 60022 *Mallard* nears the scene of its triumph of 1938 but travelling up the hill this time as it enters Little Bytham with an Ian Allan Special on 4 April 1951.** *P. H. Wells*

at 1 in 200 takes the line round a right-hand curve to Little Bytham, today only marked by the GNR goods shed now in private commercial use. It was at the foot of this pitch that *Mallard*, heading south of course, achieved its speed record in 1938. Fifty chains of level, half a mile at 1 in 330 and another level for half a mile brings the line past the site of Corby Glen, and the last three miles to the summit, at milepost 100, is at 1 in 178. At an altitude of 345 feet it was the highest point on the original Great Northern Railway.

From the north, climbing is steady from a mile and a half south of Claypole, with a mile and a half at 1 in 500 followed by two miles of 1 in 330 through Hougham. A further two miles at 1 in 200 takes the line past Barkston Junction before there is an easing to 1 in 440 for a mile through Peascliffe tunnel. A level stretch a mile long, then half a mile up at 1 in 240, a quarter-mile down at 1 in 330 and about 30 chains up at the same slope bring the line to Grantham station, the only one remaining open of seven on the section. There is half a mile of level off the platform end, but then five miles of 1 in 200 bring the line through Stoke tunnel to the top, some 28 chains south of the southern portal. The tunnel is exactly half a mile long, and is cut through the same oolitic limestone as we will meet later in the Cotswolds.

There were, as noted, seven stations between Tallington and Claypole - Essendine, Little Bytham, Corby Glen, Great Ponton, Grantham, Barkston and Hougham. All closed to passengers in the '50s, Barkston on 16 March 1955 and Hougham on 16 September 1957. Great Ponton lasted exactly a year longer, until 15 September 1958, and the three to the south of Stoke tunnel all succumbed on 15 June 1959.

The stretch has a dubious history so far as accidents

are concerned, with three each at Essendine, Little Bytham and Corby Glen, all between 1853 and 1896, and two at Stoke, in 1853 and 1854. Barkston had two in the 1870s, and there have been two at Grantham as well as the epic high-speed derailment there on 19 September 1906. Now trains rush faster than ever along the electrified East Coast route to Scotland - little can Thomas Jackson have dreamed that the line which he built would see such use almost 150 years later.

# The 'Northern Heights' (2): Elstree and Sandridge

Though it was able to make use of the Luton Gap through the Chilterns, the Midland really had no choice other than a hilly approach to the capital, and opened its London Extension as far as Brent for goods on 9 September 1867, just over four years after its authorisation. Passenger traffic was delayed, however, and began on 13 July 1868, running into St Pancras for the first time on 1 October.

Its gradient profile is a much more jagged affair, beginning with a short but sharp 10 chains or so of 1 in 106 to lift the line over the Regent's Canal. This is, in fact, the steepest pitch on the route, but grade for grade the climbing is probably tougher than out of King's Cross, Holloway bank always excepted. Beyond the canal and a short easing to 1 in 490, is a third of a mile on the level, which is followed by two thirds of a mile at 1 in 301 to Kentish Town.

Shortly after Kentish Town there begins a two-mile pitch at 1 in 178, which takes the line through Belsize Second tunnel, a mile and 73 yards long - it has a span of 25 feet and is brick-lined throughout. The Old, or Goods, tunnel is 95 yards shorter, and is the one originally built for the London Extension. Its first brick was laid on 27 January 1865 in a 'driving snowstorm and. . .a foot deep of half melted snow'. (F. S. Williams, *The Midland Railway: its Rise & Progress*). The clay, Williams tells us, was so hard that it required blasting by gunpowder, and 1,300 men and 100 horses worked round the clock. Five shafts were sunk, three of which were later sealed, leaving two for ventilation. The tunnel was completed in 1868 and has a horseshoe-shaped profile of 25 yards span, with a height of 26 feet from the crown to the bottom of the invert. It lies 120 feet below ground at its deepest.

At the north portal of the tunnel the gradient eases for a quarter of a mile to 1 in 282, and then goes down for 10 chains at 1 in 688 before hitting the half-mile up at 1 in 176 which takes the line past West Hampstead. Three quarters of a mile on level track herald a mile's descent at 1 in 200, past Brent Junction and the destination of all those erstwhile coal trains. Then, once across the 19-arch viaduct spanning the River Brent, comes another pitch up at the same slope for three quarters of a mile. An easing to 1 in 266 brings the line to Hendon and a half-mile descent before yet another climb begins, at 1 in 173 for half a mile, 1 in 176 for a mile, and a quarter of a mile at 1 in 160. There is a brief easing to 1 in 330 through Mill Hill, beyond which station a climb of 1 in 176 for half a mile, a quarter-mile level and another pitch of 1 in 176 for a little over two miles takes the line through Elstree tunnel. Both old and second bores are 1,072 yards long.

Beyond the north portal a quarter-mile pitch of 1 in 400 lifts the line to Elstree summit, and a similar gradient takes it down the other side towards a two-mile 1 in 200 to Radlett. A level-topped hump, reached by a quarter of a mile at 1 in 176, follows, before climbing begins yet again, this time over the chalk ridge. Three and a quarter miles of 1 in 176 lead through

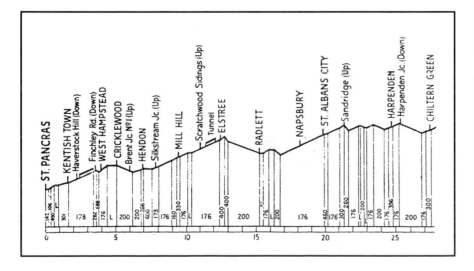

**Gradient profile, Elstree and Sandridge**

On greasy rails, Stanier '8F' 2-8-0 No 48221 blasts up the 1 in 176 from Elstree tunnel on 21 March 1953, hauling wooden-sided coal empties from Brent back to Toton. *Brian Morrison*

Napsbury to St Albans, where there is a brief easing to 1 in 460 for a quarter-mile. Then another, mile-long, pitch at 1 in 176, and a quarter of a mile at 1 in 300 bring the line to the summit at Sandridge.

During the Beeching era an idea was mooted for diverting long-distance trains to Euston, but the run-down of Marylebone improved traffic and the plan was dropped. Electrification of the suburban services helped, and they are now extremely busy. In 1983 HSTs were introduced for the long-distance trains, though 'long-distance' becomes relative when it is realised that (in the Winter 1991-2 timetable) Leeds is the longest of them, with but two weekday trains, while there is one which runs through to York on Saturdays.

# Sharnbrook

By the late 1840s the Midland Railway was realising that its coal traffic, reaching London by way of the LNWR from Rugby, was not getting the priority that the railway felt it should have been given. An alternative link between Leicester and Hitchin by way of Bedford was devised, giving access to London via the Great Northern; an Act for the work gained the Royal Assent first on 9 July 1847 but was abandoned. A further Act was obtained on 4 August 1853.

One of the obstacles was the ridge of oolite (our Stoke friend again), and in fact this line had to cross it twice, for having used a spur to lift itself out of the Ouse valley it then had to drop into the Nene valley

*Above* **BR 'Britannia' 4-6-2 No 70015 *Apollo* tackles the climb to Sharnbrook summit from the south. Note the double-track goods diversion lines, brought into use on 4 May 1884, at a lower level on the left. The train is a down Manchester express on 21 April 1960.** *K. C. H. Fairey*

*Left* **The down goods line was taken out of use on 18 October 1987, and by 13 May 1991 had been removed completely. This, of course, concerns the driver of HST No 43108 not at all, as he flashes southwards down the bank towards Bedford.** *C. V. Awdry*

and climb out again to a second summit at Desborough. The engineer was Charles Liddell, who estimated that the 62.5-mile extension would cost a million pounds.

Brassey gained the contract for construction, his partner and agent in this project being Stephen Ballard. Things did not go to plan; defections among the workforce meant that cuttings were made shallower than planned, and the result was a rather more variable line profile than had been anticipated.

Between Bedford and Sharnbrook there were six bridges across the Ouse, with viaducts near Sharnbrook village and over the Nene south of Wellingborough. These latter were both troublesome. That at Sharnbrook was designed with ten semicircular arches of 50-foot span, standing 40 feet at their highest. Two piers would stand in the river, which, on average was 20 feet deep here. Construction began in April 1854, and the first arches had been successfully

LONDON, MIDLANDS AND EAST

turned by August 1855. Liddell had reported in the previous July that 75 per cent of the brickwork, 60 per cent of the fencing and 40 per cent of the bridges were complete, but less than half the earthworks. He was still, it seems, optimistic enough to believe that the work could be completed to schedule.

But the work began to fall badly behind, and in January 1856, though confident that the completion would be in time, Liddell had to acknowledge that a mere four miles of railway had been laid. Ballasting near Sharnbrook began on 23 January. By May the engineer was at last admitting delays, and there were more labour problems during the summer. Construction of stations was begun in August, only to run into a shortage of bricks, despite the fact that private kilns had been set up at Radwell and Sharnbrook. Rails had been delivered, but remained unused because the earthworks on which they were to be laid were incomplete. To order nightwork would have been useless because Horne, the resident Engineer, was already unable to find enough men to work the day shift!

Then Horne died suddenly, in November 1856. Little work was done that month, but Brassey appointed Henry Harrison, his wife's brother, in Horne's place, and by concentrating manpower and working round the clock managed to get the high embankment between Sharnbrook and Radwell finished by the end of the year. At this stage Liddell was not expecting an opening of the line before March 1857, and the deep cutting between Souldrop and Wymington was giving trouble - spoil from the north end was carried to Irchester, but that from the south was dumped near Sharnbrook.

An inspection on 18 February 1857 showed that only the connection at the Hitchin end was missing, and Capt Galton expressed great satisfaction with Brassey's work, particularly the design and structure of buildings. The line opened for mineral traffic on Wednesday 15 April, for goods on the 22nd and to passengers on Thursday 7 May, a gala day in Bedford. Regular passenger services began the next day.

On leaving Bedford for the north the course along the Ouse valley is level enough at first, with a hump at Oakley involving short pitches of 1 in 174 in this direction and 1 in 146 down. Climbing in earnest begins about a mile and a half south of Sharnbrook, with short pitches of 1 in 180, 200, 158 and 100 for about a mile altogether. Then comes Sharnbrook viaduct, followed by a left-hand curve past the site of Sharnbrook station. Slippages impeded construction of the viaduct, and a firm foundation was only found for the piers at 25 feet. Inverts had to be provided after opening. From the viaduct a climb of 1 in 119 for three and one-third miles lifts the railway to a summit at around 300 feet above sea level. Twelve

chains or so of level brings the line to a two and three-quarter mile drop of 1 in 120, 1 in 162 past the site of Irchester station, 1 in 245 for a short while, and 1 in 163 past Irchester Junction and over the Nene viaduct. This, which spanned the LNWR Northampton to Peterborough branch line as well as the river, also gave trouble with slippage when the clay embankment pushed a complete abutment and wings forward. Not a brick was displaced, but substantial rebuilding was, of course, required. North of the river the gradient eases as the line curves into the flank of the valley, giving a gentle run to Wellingborough station.

In the southbound direction two easy and short downgrades of 1 in 518 and 209 lead to a 30-chain level, followed by a similar length of 1 in 420. Then the line is on to the 1 in 163, about three-quarters of a mile long, across the viaduct, and this eases to successive 25-chain pitches at 1 in 245 and 192 before the crunch comes with the 1 in 120 to the 60-foot deep summit cutting.

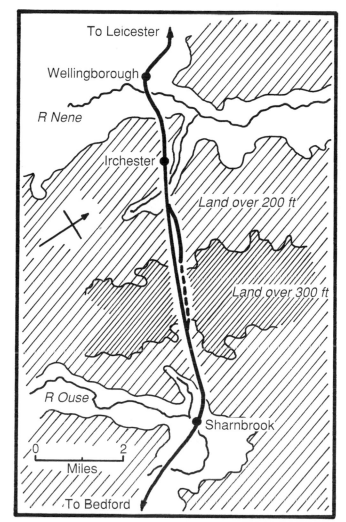

*Above* Stanier 'Jubilee' 4-6-0 No 45561 *Saskatchewan* passes Souldrop signal box with a down Sheffield express on 21 April 1960. This signal box, opened in 1920, had only six more years of life, being closed just before Christmas 1966. *K. C. H. Fairey*

*Left* Another 'Jubilee' at Souldrop on the same day, this time No 45639 *Raleigh* heading the 3.20 pm St Pancras-Bedford express. *K. C. H. Fairey*

Three stations were brought into use between Bedford and Wellingborough when the line was opened, but all are now closed, Oakley to passengers in 1958 and goods five years later, and Sharnbrook to passengers on 2 May 1960, goods in 1964. Irchester went through a number of name changes before finally reverting to its original, and closed to passengers on 7 March 1960, goods on 4 May 1965.

Water troughs were laid at Oakley in 1904 and served for 60 years. A new viaduct at Sharnbrook was inspected on 19 March 1880, after which traffic was diverted away from the original. A pier of the original had sunk, and the viaduct was rebuilt before being brought back into use. The goods line through the tunnel was 'rationalised' in the 1980s, and is now single.

In 1876, to mitigate the problems that heavy coal trains were having with the slog up this hill, a diversion was made on the east side, easing the gradient to 1 in 200 on both sides of the ridge, but at the expense of a tunnel 1,860 yards long near Wymington. Opened in about 1877, it is brick-lined throughout, with a horseshoe profile, a span of 25 feet and a height of 22 feet. There are five ventilation shafts. The small Johnson 0-6-0 engines of the day were now able to take 38 loaded wagons over Sharnbrook, instead of 31.

# Euston (Camden)

**E**uston is unique in that it is the only one of the termini so far discussed of which it can be said that it did *not* at first intend to use a steep ascent from its platforms. The London & Birmingham Railway, having taken its line in a curve south of the city's 'Northern Heights', was aiming for an easy entry with a terminus at Camden Town, a little to the north of the Regent's Canal. This was passed by Parliament on 6 May 1833, but before the line was open the plan had been changed: the L&B decided to pass above the canal and drop through a mile-long cutting to a site in Euston Grove; a climb for all trains leaving the station thereafter has been the result. Contractors for the section were Messrs Grissell & Peto.

In fact, there is a short downgrade from the buffers, which, in theory at least, helps to get a train on the move, but very soon it is on 1 in 70 for about 13 chains. The main part of the bank, something under half a mile, is at 1 in 112, but the climb is not over at the top of it, for a final 15 chains or so of 1 in 77 lifts the line to the top.

Little confidence was placed in the likelihood that the motive power of the day would be able to surmount the gradient unaided, so from 20 July 1837, the date on which the first train pulled clear of the platform, until 1844, all were cable-assisted up the slope. *The Times* of 14 July 1837 described the operation: 'On the trains arriving within a mile of London,' it wrote, 'the engine is to be taken off, and a rope, worked by stationary steam machinery, is to be attached to the carriages, and thus will be wound up,

The down 4.15 pm Euston-Liverpool express heads up Camden bank on 22 May 1949 in the charge of Stanier Class '5' 4-6-0 No 45418. It is thought that the 'plum and split milk' livery on the vehicles behind the first four was being tried out as an experiment at this time. *E. D. Bruton*

as it were, to their place of destination'.

It was not long before there was a mishap:

'. . .at the back of the terminus at the back of Euston Square, the engine having been disengaged, but the impetus still continuing at a considerable velocity, the men whose duty it was to check the motion by operating what are technically called the "breaks", not being sufficiently expert, or miscalculating their power, the carriages came with frightful force against the barrier wall at the extremity of the line, dashing it to stones, and causing a rebound which frightened all and damaged not a few.'

Correspondents to *The Times* were quick to register their disapproval.

Another accident is recorded in the *Leamington Courier* of 6 March 1852, when, three days earlier, there had been a brake failure on a descending train, which ran into the buffers, rebounded, and came back down the slope again to hit the buffers a second time. Mercifully, a black eye seems to have been the most serious injury on this occasion.

From 1844 until 31 December 1868 trains were piloted, the assisting engine leaving the train by slipping the coupling and running ahead into a convenient refuge. The points would be switched behind it, so that the train itself could proceed unhindered, but signalling staff had to be well alert to ensure that it did not follow the pilot into the refuge. From 1 January 1869 banking assistance was given in the rear, and this remained standard practice at Euston until diesel haulage took over.

# Marylebone

Ambition was the cause of the Manchester, Sheffield & Lincolnshire Railway's London Extension, and the ambition belonged mainly to its Chairman, Sir Edward Watkin. He saw the line, via a Channel tunnel, as a link with the Continent, and the company deposited a Bill for the 1891 session of Parliament.

It was set out in three stages - Annesley to Verney Junction, the Metropolitan Railway's outpost in Buckinghamshire, a section via the Metropolitan to West Hampstead, and finally West Hampstead to a terminus at Boscobel Gardens. However, it was thrown out in the face of stiff opposition, one of the main objectors being the MCC at Lord's. An Agreement and a tunnel were arrived at, and, having placated the other opposing parties in various ways (the cricketers did not come out losers) the MS&L tried again the following year, and Royal Assent was given to the Act on 28 March 1893.

Sir Douglas and Francis Fox were the Engineers appointed for the first two miles from the terminus, and the contractor for the 1 mile 71 chain section from Marylebone to Canfield Gardens was the well-respected firm of J. & T. Firbank, who took possession of the works on 31 August 1896. The tunnelling went on round the clock, because a proviso in the contract

**Gradient profile, Marylebone to Amersham**

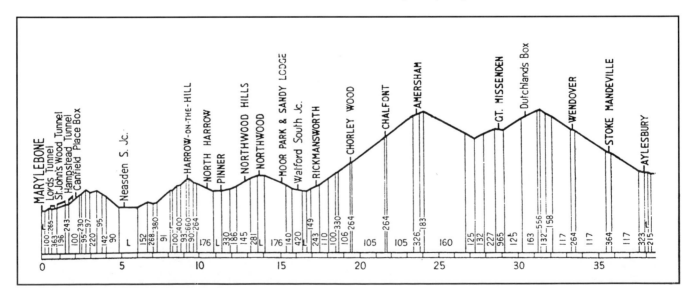

was that no disturbance should be made to the cricket at Lord's. The tunnel top was covered with much of the original soil, turfed with material from Morley cricket ground at Neasden, and the finished work was handed over on 8 May 1897, presumably in time for the new cricket season.

In 1897, with construction of the Extension well under way, the MS&L decided it needed a less provincial-sounding name, and changed, as A. A. Jackson puts it in his book *London Termini*, 'to the more resounding Great Central Railway from 1 August 1897'.

Off the end of the platform of the new station at Marylebone, built in a less than salubrious (at that time) area south-west of Regent's Park, is an uphill 300-yard stretch of 1 in 100. This lifts the line over the Regent's Canal on a bridge carrying 14 tracks, many of which went into the goods yard at Lisson Grove. A short downslope of 1 in 265 then takes the line into Lord's tunnel, at about the centre of which it begins to rise again, at 1 in 363, for a third of a mile. The southern portal of St John's Wood tunnel (1,279 yards) stands at the end of this pitch, at which point the gradient steepens to 1 in 196. Each of these tunnels accommodated seven tracks. Lord's was constructed by the cut-and-cover method, but St John's Wood is a combination of cut-and-cover and bore; a gap for ventilation was set between them.

At the northern end of the tunnel the slope eases to 1 in 263, as the West Coast Main Line is crossed on a girder bridge 118 feet long. After a gap of 125 yards the line plunges into Hampstead tunnel (691 yards), also covered way rather than bored tunnel. At the south portal the gradient steepens for three-quarters of a mile to 1 in 100, until it is again in the open and curving sharply to the left at Canfield Place. The GCR line runs parallel with the Metropolitan Railway from Canfield Gardens, but there is still a short pitch of 1 in 95 to come before the summit is reached, two and a half miles from the terminus.

Goods trains began to move along the London Extension on 25 July 1898, and the goods yard at Lisson Grove was opened on 10 April the next year. This was shortly after passenger facilities had been inaugurated, on 9 March, in the presence of, among others, a now ill Sir Edward Watkin, and three special trainloads of notabilities from Manchester, Sheffield and Nottingham. Public traffic began on 15 March, when fearsomely light loadings did not augur well for the line's future. From 1 July there were eleven weekday trains in each direction, a journey to Manchester taking five hours until the track had settled down.

Traffic was very poor to begin with, but Sam Fay (later Sir) was appointed General Manager in 1902 and began to wake things up. The time to Manchester came down to ten minutes under four hours, and other timings improved too. Goods came to be the important thing for the GCR, however, with, after the completion of the loop line in conjunction with the GWR between Northolt Junction and Grendon Underwood, an increasing suburban service. Indeed, it is this that now provides the only real reason for Marylebone's continued existence.

In 1960 BR began a run-down of main-line passenger services, and Marylebone went over entirely to suburban traffic on 4 September 1966. It has seen a number of steam specials in recent years, but even these appear to have gone now: multiple units up the bank under Lord's remain the sole order of the day.

# Amersham

The construction of the GCR's London Extension employed 300 men from May 1896 until July 1898. They used, says George Dow in volume 2 of his classic history of the Great Central, '13 locomotives, 6 portable engines, 23 steam travelling cranes and a steam navvy'. Times had changed in the 60 years since the London & Birmingham set its sights on London, and the speed of progress had changed significantly. Stephenson's men took five years to build 113 miles, while the GCR built just under 100 miles to Quainton Road and Ashendon in roughly half the time.

But though the GCR used extensively both of the gradients with which we finish this chapter, it actually built neither of them.

The credit for Amersham goes to the two companies related to the Metropolitan Railway - the Kingsbury & Harrow and the Harrow & Rickmansworth Railway. The first was authorised in 1874 to extend the Metropolitan & St John's Wood company's line for five and a half miles to Harrow, and this opened, worked by the 'Met', on 2 August 1880. The second was authorised three weeks after the first to build on to Aylesbury, but when this scheme was abandoned in 1877 the 'Met' took it over and built it under revived powers obtained on 6 August 1880.

The contractor for the section to Rickmansworth was Richard Hattersley, who had the Nowells as sub-contractors. Engineer was Charles Liddell, and the line was opened on 1 September 1877. At a general meeting the next January it was stated that there was 'no intention' of extending the line towards Aylesbury, but feelings had changed a year later, when the matter was again discussed and further building agreed.

J. T. Firbank was the contractor for this section, and the line, reported *The Times* of 23 January 1892, 'had been made very cheaply at a time when the price of labour and materials was low'. It could also, it opined, be worked very cheaply. It was opened on 1 September 1892.

The gradient profile of the section concerning us here proceeds in a series of gables - at Harrow on the Hill (naturally), with another, rather less abrupt, at Northwood. Watford South Junction was located almost at the foot of the dip beyond Northwood, and after a brief level section the line begins to tackle the climb into the Chilterns at 1 in 149 for a quarter of a mile, followed by 1 in 243 for half a mile, this pitch taking the line past Rickmansworth. A severe curve here prevented expresses making much of a run at the bank, and likewise restricted fast running on the descent. Successive half-miles at 1 in 110 and 100 are followed by a very brief easing to 1 in 330 before a three-quarter mile length at 1 in 106.

The easing to 1 in 264 through Chorley Wood is brief indeed, and soon the line is climbing at 1 in 105 and will continue to do so for the next two miles. There is another brief easing to 1 in 264, this time through Chalfont, before another pitch of 1 in 105, this time for one and three quarter miles. Half a mile of 1 in 326 through Amersham station, and a final few yards at 1 in 183, brings the line to the top, from which two and a half miles down at 1 in 160 bring it into a dip from which it must climb again. This is much more straightforward. Two lengths of between 50 and 60 chains each at 1 in 132 and 1 in 227 respectively lead to a short downslope (1 in 965) through Great Missenden, and successive miles at 1 in 125 and 163 are topped by a short 1 in 556 to the summit.

Travelling south, Aylesbury is at the foot of the climb, literally, for it begins at 1 in 323 from the platform end. A mile and three-quarters at 1 in 117 leads to an easing to 1 in 364 through Stoke Mandeville, and another two miles follow at 1 in 117. Wendover has an easing of 1 in 364 through the station and just over a mile of 1 in 117 yet again beyond it. At the end of this pitch there remain three-quarters of a mile to the top, and this distance is split evenly at 1 in 158 and 1 in 132. From the dip beyond Great Missenden, half a mile of 1 in 125 leads to the last two and a half mile stretch, at 1 in 160, to Amersham.

# Saunderton

The GCR fell out with the Metropolitan before it got to using its line to London, so it had to find an alternative. It reached an Agreement with the GWR that a line, administered by a joint committee, should run from Northolt Junction to High Wycombe, along the existing Great Western line thence to Princes Risborough, with a link between Ashendon and Grendon Underwood.

The original section of line north-west of High Wycombe, once broad gauge but one of the first parts to have been converted, climbed through a gap in the Chilterns at Saunderton. It had been an extension of the Wycombe (in early correspondence often spelled without the 'e') Railway, through Princes Risborough to Thame, ultimately reaching Oxford. Brunel was its Engineer, and his charge for professional services up to passing of the Act was £594 15s 6d. His own part of this was £201, the remainder being for assistants and an engraver for the plans. The line was built by the Tredwells, and during the summer of 1859 a dispute seems to have arisen about how they should be paid. Brunel made a suggestion to the solicitors (which, since there seems to have been no follow-up, may perhaps be assumed to have been adopted) in a beautifully written letter on 19 August 1859, which gives no hint of the ailing man who, just under a month later, would be dead.

E. F. Murray succeeded him, though he had to fight for the job - perhaps his most telling argument was that he had, in any case, done most of the work during Brunel's illness. He had worked with Brunel for 22 years on various projects, and Brunel clearly regarded him as reliable or he would not have survived so long. On 2 February 1861 Murray was able to write to the Directors:

'With the exception of one embankment the whole of the Earthwork has been finished from Wycombe to near Bledlow, a distance of about ten miles. . . In about three or four months that [Thame] Cutting and the whole of the Earthwork will be completed.

'All the brickwork for the bridges has been built, and the whole of the Iron Work and Timber has been fixed. A few culverts only remain to be done.'

Severe weather later hampered the work, and Murray asked that a special arrangement for carriage rates be made with the owner of a ballast pit at Cookham. The line opened on Monday 4 August 1862, with stations at Wycombe, West Wycombe, Princes Risborough and Thame.

The Tredwells had laid the line with bridge-rails, supplied by the Rhymney Iron Company, bolted to cross-sleepers. These were still in place at the turn of the century, when, following the Agreement between the Great Central and the Great Western, and the formation of the GW&GC Joint Committee, it became necessary to upgrade the line between Princes Risborough and Wycombe. The Committee was

authorised to widen the existing line north of Wycombe for 8 miles 16 chains to Princes Risborough. The contractor for the work was Mackay & Davies, of Cardiff, who began in June 1902. A new up line was put in, for about two miles diverging to the east of the original course, with an easier slope, a deep cutting through chalk and a short tunnel. The tunnel, which carried a minor road across the railway, was a source of some difficulty because of water, but the new line was opened on 2 April 1906.

From High Wycombe there is a short bank of 1 in 141 followed by an even shorter one at 1 in 380. Quarter of a mile on the level leads to a mile and a half at 1 in 179 and an easing to 1 in 550 through West Wycombe. Rather more than half a mile of 1 in 440 serves as introduction to the next two miles, at 1 in 164, and again there is an easing for Saunderton station, this time to 1 in 264. Half a mile at 1 in 164 and a half-mile level bring the line to the final short pitch, a third of a mile at 1 in 164, which tops the summit.

From the north the climbing begins just south of milepost 40, at the end of a level which began at Haddenham. Half a mile of 1 in 200 leads to two miles of 1 in 176, a brief level, and a mile and a quarter of 1 in 200 to Princes Risborough. Then, before the diversion, the line went up first at 1 in 264, then 1 in 161, before two-thirds of a mile at 1 in 88 gave way to three-quarters of a mile at 1 in 100. This, no doubt thankfully from the train crews' point of view, ended at the summit. Now a steady 1 in 167 from Princes Risborough, punctuated after about a mile by the tunnel, bypasses what is still the 'down' summit in deep cutting and emerges on the level half a mile beyond it.

Saunderton and West Wycombe were the only stations on this section, Saunderton having been opened on 1 July 1901. Slightly surprisingly, it is this one that has survived; West Wycombe closed to passengers on 3 November 1958.

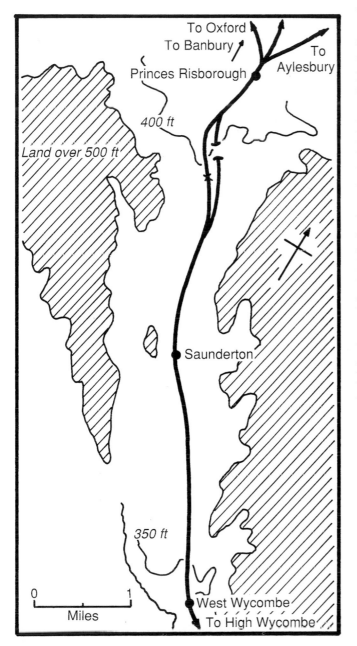

# 3
# COTSWOLD COUNTRY

## Masbury

In order to tap the coalfield which lay deep beneath the Mendip Hills, the Somerset & Dorset Joint Railway obtained an Act on 21 August 1871 authorising it to buy the Somerset Coal Canal Tramway, some six miles of which, between Radstock and Wellow, it used for a railway. More significantly, the Act also authorised a 25-mile line to run from Evercreech, on the old Somerset and Dorset line, to join the Midland Railway at Bath. The contract for building the line was given to Messrs Thomas & Charles Walker of Westminster for £352,000, though in the end the cost exceeded £400,000, not including rolling-stock, equipment and staff.

It was not an easy job. Extremely heavy works were involved, including four tunnels and seven principal viaducts, and it was made no easier by the threat of bankruptcy which hung over the project from the start. The geology involved was complex too - Devonshire tunnel, for instance, was cut through a waterbearing stratum of blue lias clay, below which lies a filtering bed of iron sandstone. Regular undulations of the strata affected the water supply of local residents. Because of the financial constraints, all the tunnels were built as cheaply as possible, to minimum dimensions, and the portals bear no decoration.

Work began in 1872, however, and proceeded apace, with 3,000 men employed. The Consulting Engineer was W. H. Barlow, who divided the work into three sections, the Bath section being put in charge of a Mr Lean; Mr Arthur Collins was Overseer for the whole contract.

On 1 February a Plymouth newspaper welcomed the project, and noted that 'the engineers have this week been surveying the route of the proposed line in the neighbourhood'. On 28 February the *Bath & Cheltenham Gazette* reported that the men had '. . .already

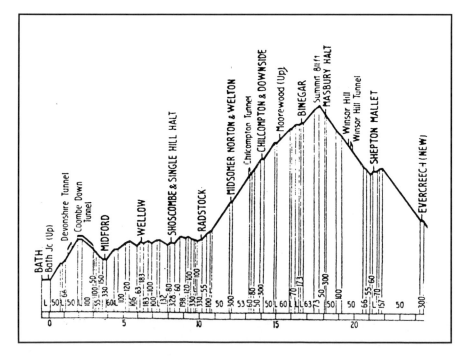

**Gradient profile, Masbury**

58

'West Country' 'Pacific' No 34043 *Combe Martin*, assisted by BR Standard Class '4' 'Mogul' No 76015, approaches the 811-foot summit at Masbury from the south on 1 September 1962. The train is the 10.05 am from Bournemouth West to Bradford. *Hugh Ballantyne*

In the opposite direction, the southbound 'Pines Express' passes the down Masbury distant near the summit on 30 July 1955. Piloting BR Standard 2-6-0 No 76012 is Fowler '2P' 4-4-0 No 40634. *Hugh Ballantyne*

begun to sink a shaft in the neighbourhood of Combe Down, and a large number of waggons, rails and other implements. . .have arrived. . .so that work will shortly be commenced'.

Three weeks later work had begun in earnest, and on 24 April the same journal observed that a new method of excavation was being used:

'Instead of excavating the whole width of the cutting at once, by working it down in notches, a small tunnel is driven underground and at intervals small shafts are sunk into it. A train is then placed at the bottom of each shaft down which soil is thrown and thus the work is continued until the small preliminary tunnel is reached.'

A navvy fight at Lyncombe Vale was noted at the end of May, and wet weather held things up in November and December, but on

27 February 1873 the *Bath Chronicle & Herald* reported that a tunnel, presumably Combe Down, had been 'pierced within the last days and the work is being rapidly pressed forward'. On 18 August that year four navvies died in a rockfall in Winsor Hill tunnel - a memorial fashioned from the rock which had killed them marks their ultimate grave, in Shepton Mallet cemetery.

But trouble was brewing. In April 1874 the contractor complained that he had not been paid, and threatened to withdraw the workforce. All work 'not absolutely necessary for the opening of the line for traffic' was suspended, and the contractor was persuaded to accept shares, debentures and Lloyds Bonds in part-payment. Work then went on round the clock, though there was another hiatus in May when difficulty in the acquisition of land was reported, and a difference arose between the S&D and the Bristol & North Somerset Railway about a crossing near Radstock. A reference to the Board of Trade was necessary, and this seems to have taken a while to settle, for it is not until 2 July that we read:

'It is understood that the requirements of the Board of Trade Inspector have been almost, if not quite, carried out, so that no doubt, very shortly, an official intimation will be made of the completion of this line for the use of the public.'

Luggage trains ran for several days before the official opening, which was on 20 July 1874, with church bells ringing at Wellow, a flag at Binegar, and crowds at Evercreech beneath a 'Success to the Railway' banner.

From the south side the climb was no less fierce than on the other, though it began comparatively gently. About three-quarters of a mile beyond the actual junction were ten chains of 1 in 66, followed at once by a third of a mile at 1 in 50. There was a brief easing to 1 in 300 through Evercreech (New), then almost two and a half miles of 1 in 50. This brought the line to Cannard's Grave summit, where the 45-foot deep cutting was almost two miles long apart from one short break.

Level or downgrades then led through Shepton Mallet station, but the respite was temporary, for a quarter of a mile beyond the station the line was once more rising, at 1 in 55. This gave way to 1 in 66 for about another quarter-mile, and then there was another pitch of 1 in 50, a mile and a half of it, which took the line through Winsor Hill tunnel, cut through solid rock. The original tunnel, later on the down line, was 242 yards long - the second bore was cut when this section of line was doubled in 1892, and was a good deal shorter at 132 yards. The gradi-

ent eased slightly to 1 in 100 then, for about 30 chains, but reverted to 1 in 50 again for another three-quarters of a mile, up to Masbury Halt. A very short easing through the station (1 in 300) gave on to the pitch of 1 in 50, about a third of a mile long, which led to the summit cutting, 811 feet above sea level.

The climb to Masbury from the other side began at Radstock with a quarter-mile of 1 in 55, and another of 1 in 100. A very brief level pitch led to a 1 in 50 a little over a mile long, a short 1 in 300 through Midsomer Norton & Welton, and another mile of 1 in 53. At the top of this section lay the twin bores of Chilcompton tunnel (66 yards), where the cutting was 44 feet deep through red and yellow sandstone conglomerate/limestone breccia - more attractively (and comprehensibly) known as 'plum-pudding stone'.

The tunnel was followed by successive short lengths at 1 in 60, 80 and 50 before an easing to 1 in 300 for Chilcompton station, a watering point for locomotives in steam days. The next two and a quarter miles were at 1 in 50, 60 and 70, broken only by a ten-chain or so level between each pitch. The 1 in 70 was short, about a quarter of a mile, and then the gradient eased through Binegar, where there were a couple of short level sections. Finally, half a mile of 1 in 63 and a quarter-mile of 1 in 73 led to the summit.

That, of course, was the main summit. There was also a fearsome climb up to Combe Down from Bath, starting immediately Bath Junction had been passed, with three-quarters of a mile of 1 in 50. Ten chains level and another ten of 1 in 66 led once again to 1 in 50, this time for a shade under a mile, and taking the line through the 440-yard Devonshire tunnel. As the north portal of Combe Down tunnel was reached, so was the top of the climb. Combe Down was 1,829 yards long, 350 feet below ground level, and its bore (13 feet 6 inches wide by 13 feet 9 inches high) was the longest unventilated railway tunnel in Britain. It was cut through Bath freestone, masonry and brick lining being only occasionally required. There was a quarter of a mile of level track in the first part of the tunnel, and the line then fell at 1 in 100 for three-quarters of a mile. Brief pitches of 1 in 50, 100, 55 and 150 led down to Midford, from where a switchback of short, sharp gradients continued to Radstock. Working an unfitted freight train over this section must have been a nightmare.

Much traffic came to the new line - too much! It was soon obvious that the single track was totally inadequate, as was the amount of stock provided. There were too few sidings and loops, and those that existed were too short. Neither was the revenue sufficient to cover costs, and since construction had used up all the money there was nothing with which to put matters right. The costly gamble was a failure. The story of how the company went to the Midland instead of the GWR has been often told - suffice to say here that a joint lease, for 999 years, to those two companies was agreed by the Board on 20 August 1875, with effect from the next 1 November; Parliament ratified it on 13 July 1876.

After early years of consolidation, the two lessees turned a line that had already acquired the soubriquet 'Slow and Dirty' into an efficient concern which was neither. It was amid much snow and sorrow, on 7 March 1966, that many saw the closure of the line over Combe Down, Masbury and Cannard's Grave summits.

# Sapperton

The Cheltenham & Great Western Union Railway, incorporated on 21 June 1836, had only a very brief independent life, and was one of the first undertakings absorbed by the GWR. The company had projected a line from Cheltenham to Swindon via Gloucester, but was in trouble almost before it had started. There was clearly widespread doubt among shareholders and others, so that during the summer of 1839 the Directors (one suspects) were moved to issue a statement to the press, which was taken up by both the *Wilts & Gloucestershire Standard* and the July issue of Herepath's *Railway Magazine*.

'Persons who have expressed their doubts,' it ran, 'of the intention of the directors to carry the line forward through Stroud &c to Gloucester, are at last fully satisfied of the sincerity of their promises, as a considerable number of landowners and others on that portion of the line have been served with notice to make their terms for the sale of their lands.'

The line's first section, from Swindon to Kemble (not the section including Sapperton summit) opened on 31 May 1841, and on that date the line began a seven-year lease to the parent company. The lease did not run its full course, for the C&GWUR almost bankrupted itself in fighting (successfully) a competing scheme which threatened its business, and applied to the GWR for absorption. With a certain amount of gratitude (or so one would like to think, since GWR business had been threatened by the competing scheme too), the Great Western took over the smaller concern from 10 May 1844.

The 16 miles between Standish, south of Gloucester, and Kemble took four years to build, largely because of the heavy earthworks involved - nine viaducts and a tunnel at, or should one say under, Sapperton village. The work was let in three contracts: Stonehouse to Sapperton, the tunnel section, and from the south-east end of the tunnel to Kemble. Francis & Thomas Tredwell got the first-named (Contract No 2), their quotation of £73,308 being amended to £72,500. The nine viaducts on the section were built in timber, one near Chalford being the longest-lived, though none of them survived for anything like as long as their Cornish counterparts. They were gradually replaced with masonry structures from 1859 onwards.

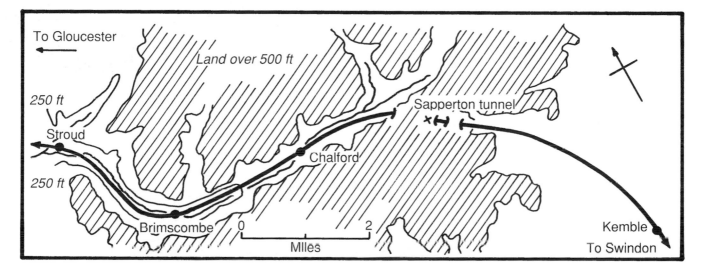

By July 1844 two-thirds of this contract was complete and ballasted, while Contract No 1, let to John & William Blinkhorn, was ready for permanent way. Contract No 3 was that for the tunnel. This had been projected as curved, but Parliament was unhappy about it, so Brunel produced a plan which had a short bend at the north-west end only. The contract was won by Jonathan Willans Nowell, at a price of £89,000. Nowell had earned Brunel's approval by his work on Wickwar tunnel, on the Bristol &

Gloucester line, which stood him in good stead here. He was of Dewsbury stonemason stock, taking up railway work with five contracts on the London & Birmingham Railway. After the Sapperton job he went into partnership with Eckersley at Standedge (see Chapter 5). Nowell began work at Sapperton in 1838, when nine shafts, each 220 yards apart, were sunk. Brunel reported in October 1841 that the heading was expected to be complete by the end of the year.

It never was. Faced with a shortage of money, the company asked Brunel to shorten the tunnel, which he did by increasing the approach gradients. Though this was to be a disadvantage so far as working was concerned, it did cut the amount of tunnelling by 500 yards, and part of this distance can be seen today in the three-chain section of open cutting between the short and long tunnels, made possible because the level of the line had been raised. The main tunnel is 1,860 yards long, with a span of 27 feet 6 inches. Brunel's report to the Board of Trade noted:

'The tunnel has been cut through the rock of the great and inferior oolites and fullers earth formation, with shale and beds of shaly limestone. The rock being of unsound quality with many wide and deep vertical and horizontal fissures, partly filled with clay or earth, it was deemed necessary to line it with masonry and brickwork throughout.'

His remark about 'unsound quality' sounds something of an understatement! In fact, Brunel's assistants, R. P. Brereton and C. Richardson, supervised the work, and the chief Engineer took little part in the operations. It was February 1845 before the tunnel was finished, and the remainder of the permanent way, laid throughout by George Hennett, was completed.

Standish Junction is where the Swindon line diverges from the Gloucester to Bristol line and heads south-east into the Golden Valley. In fact, there has been a steady rise all the way from Gloucester, the steepest section being a mile and a half of 1 in 104 between Tuffley Junction and Haresfield. Easier grades continue to Stroud, after

*Above left* Bankers for Sapperton were housed in a small shed at Brimscombe. Here, in unlined green livery on 26 September 1964, Prairie tank No 6106, now enjoying an extended life in preservation, awaits its next turn. *Hugh Ballantyne*

*Left* No 7029 *Clun Castle* hauls the seven-coach 14.00 Gloucester-Swindon train past Thrupp, east of Stroud, climbing up the Golden Valley towards Sapperton tunnel. The date is 25 August 1985, and the train is one of a series celebrating the 150th anniversary of the GWR. *Hugh Ballantyne*

which town two miles of 1 in 250 take the line up to Brimscombe Bridge, and there is a short 1 in 185 before the site of Brimscombe station itself.

Then, after a quarter-mile at 1 in 310, the hard work begins. A quarter-mile at 1 in 103 leads to half a mile of 1 in 75, followed in turn by a quarter of a mile at 1 in 70 and three-quarters of a mile at 1 in 74. There is short level section, slightly less than a quarter of a mile, then a similar distance at 1 in 75, before the heaviest part of the climb, three-quarters of a mile at 1 in 60. This ends at the mouth of the tunnel, where the gradient eases to 1 in 90, maintained to the summit and in tunnel throughout. A mile of 1 in 94 down takes the line into the open again, and this is followed by a mile of 1 in 100, after which easier slopes lead down to Kemble.

The line opened on 12 May 1845, which happened to be Whit Monday. It was laid with bridge-rail on longitudinal baulks to broad gauge, double track from the start, for Brunel was already seeing it as the start of a through line to South Wales by way of a bridge across the Severn. However, as noted above, the timber bridges were soon replaced with more durable materials, and the line was converted to standard gauge in 1872. The tunnel has lasted better - the vertical sidewalls and the haunch of the arch were built in stone, with the centre 20 feet of the arch in brick. A thorough programme of mechanical re-pointing was carried out during 1953-4.

Banking assistance has been habitual on the climb up the Golden Valley, thought of as one of the most difficult sections of the GWR to work. Bankers were housed at Brimscombe, in a shed built for the purpose in 1845, only for one engine at first, but it is thought that the allocation may have been doubled at the time of the gauge conversion in 1872. Bankers would remain uncoupled, and come off the train between the short tunnel and Sapperton Sidings signal box, where they would wait for a path back to Brimscombe. Occasionally they assisted in the other direction also.

Though the line between Kemble and Swindon has now been singled, the summit section remains double. Many stations have gone, only Kemble, Stroud and Stonehouse remaining open. Closed on 2 November 1964 were all the halts in the Golden Valley, at Ebley Crossing, Downfield Crossing, Bowbridge Crossing, Ham Mill Crossing, Brimscombe Bridge and St Mary's Crossing, together with the stations at Brimscombe and Chalford. Even in 1980 the gradient required most up freight trains to be banked, making the line a rather less than popular alternative to the Severn Tunnel route. The line saw some steam specials in recent years, but then seemed to go out of favour.

# Box and Dauntsey

In order to get his - or, more properly, the Great Western's - main line from Swindon to Bristol, Brunel had to cut through the Cotswolds, part of a range of limestone hills which stretches diagonally across southern England from Dorset to Lincolnshire. He rejected the route along the Kennet valley because he was seeking a route which could ultimately be a fast one; a line through Didcot and Swindon also made the arrangement of a branch to Oxford, to which the GWR was committed, an easier proposition. The eastern slopes of the Cotswolds are gentle and fairly easy to negotiate. On the west, however, they fall steeply towards the Severn estuary, and it was this fall which posed the problem.

A severe gradient was inevitable, and Brunel decided to drop down into the Avon valley at Bath by way of a tunnel at Box. Discussion of the controversy aroused by this has been lengthy elsewhere, and this is not the place to rehash it. Suffice to say that Brunel knew perfectly well what he was doing, and the other reputable engineers of the day supported his views. But the GWR Act was obtained only at the second attempt, and it was November 1836 before work on this part of the project was begun by the sinking of six permanent and two temporary shafts along the line of the bore. Even so, the tunnel was the last portion of the original GWR line to be finished, and even on the official opening day almost five years later was not quite complete.

The line rises steadily all the way from Bristol, but until four miles beyond Bath the ascent is very gradual, mostly at 1 in 1320. At this point the train is on 1 in 850, and approaching half a mile of 1 in 660, at the top of which is the site of Box station. A quarter-mile of 1 in 330 follows, and then a little over half a mile at 1 in 120 (the short 210-yard Middle Hill tunnel is on this pitch) leads to the two miles at 1 in 100 which carry the line through the dead straight bore of Box tunnel. There is a summit at the eastern portal of the tunnel, but this is not the high point of the route. That is some miles further yet, almost at Swindon, in fact.

So, more climbing remains to be done, but not for a while because the line slopes down for seven miles at 1 in 660 after Box summit level, past Thingley Junction and through Chippenham. Two and a half miles beyond Chippenham the line begins to climb at the same rate, 1 in 660, and continues to do so for four and a half miles. Dauntsey station has closed now, but it lay near the top of this pitch. Beyond the station site a final stretch of 1 in 100 for a mile and a half leads to easier grades, and the summit is reached half a mile before Swindon, after nothing more arduous than 1 in 660. It was while coming down Dauntsey bank that No 6015 *King Richard III* recorded a speed of 100 miles an hour, but if anyone reached high speeds through the tunnel, they haven't admitted it.

Three contractors, watched over by William Glennie, the Resident Engineer, were responsible for Box tunnel. The greater portion - all but a third of a mile at the eastern end - was given to George Burge of Herne Bay, while the east end went to a local contractor, Lewis Brewer of Bath. A condition of the contract was completion within 30 months, but it was soon obvious that this was a vain hope. In November 1837 water poured in through the limestone, the shaft was flooded to a depth of 56 feet, and a rapid evacuation had to be made. Work was suspended until a more powerful pump could be acquired - there was another inundation twelve months later, but this was more swiftly dealt with.

Work went on round the clock, but it was no easy task. The rock strata the men had to cut through were, from the western end, lias, blue marl, lesser oolite, fullers earth, upper oolite (Bath stone), and there were traces also of forest marble for good measure. Progress

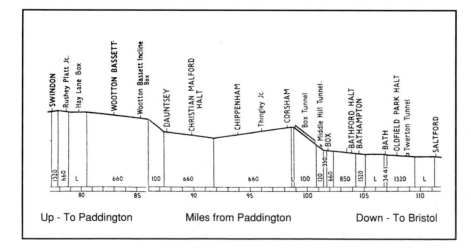

Up - To Paddington      Miles from Paddington      Down - To Bristol

**Gradient profile, Box and Dauntsey**

flagged, and the original workforce of more than 1,500 men had been increased to 4,000 for the last six months, to ensure completion.

The western portal, which can be seen from the Bath road, was finished with an imposing masonry portico, but the other, which is not overlooked, was treated plainly. The tunnel is 30 feet wide, with vertical side-walls, and stands 25 feet above rail level at the crown of the arch. The official length is 3,212 yards. In the March 1839 issue of Herepath's *Railway Magazine*, the Directors' report is quoted:

'At the Box tunnel no increased difficulties have been encountered, and the material through which the excavation is carried continues to present every favourable indication of the future easy execution of the work. The contractors have allowed parts of it to fall into arrear, as compared with the stipulated rate of progress. The directors have enforced the penalties, and the works have been proceeded with more efficiently.'

Penalties notwithstanding, work slowed even further when a wet winter caused parts of the embankment to slip. Brunel had expected this length to be the last completed, but in February 1841 he was able to report

that the works were now '. . .in such a state that by proper exertion their completion within the time required may be ensured; this exertion shall not be wanting on my part', he adds somewhat self-righteously.

There were heavy earthworks on the Chippenham-Box section - a long cutting and embankment on which work had begun during the summer of 1837. It made slow progress, being about half finished two years later. Rowland Brotherhood, later to establish an engineering works at Chippenham, had a ballasting contract over this section.

The official opening took place on 30 June 1841. Though the tunnel itself was finished, only a single line of rails - broad gauge baulk road, of course - had been laid through it, and Daniel Gooch, the GWR Locomotive Superintendent, tells in his memoirs of a near-miss when there was almost a head-on collision in its darkness. That really would have given the scaremongers a field-day!

Not a great deal has changed along this route since that day. The broad gauge has gone, of course, con-

**'Castle' Class 4-6-0 No 5023 *Brecon Castle* pulls past Box Mill Lane with an up stopping train. The train is on a gradient of 1 in 120 here, shortly increasing to 1 in 100 as it enters Box tunnel. The east portal of Middle Hill tunnel can be seen in the background.** *Hugh Ballantyne*

verted during the big operation of May 1892, but the line has remained the main route from Paddington to Bristol. Station rationalisation between Bath and Swindon has taken out those at Bathampton (3 October 1966) and Box, Corsham, Dauntsey and Wootton Bassett, all of which were closed on 4 January 1965. Banking is no longer necessary up through the tunnel, and the inhabitants of Box are no longer disturbed by the hard pounding of engines during the night.

# Severn Tunnel, Patchway and Badminton

The Great Western had exactly the same problem when it came to build its 'South Wales cut-off' via the Severn tunnel, though the task was tackled only indirectly. The tunnel was authorised by Parliament in 1872 and was a very long-term project, not opening until 1886, as part of a route from Bristol. Since the line was built after Brunel's day - he had died more than a quarter of a century before - it becomes

the first GWR example covered in these pages that was not originally built in broad gauge.

So far as the through route to Swindon from South Wales (10 miles shorter and a good deal quicker than that via Bristol) was concerned, the Severn Tunnel actually made the task of surmounting the Cotswolds more difficult, since the climb necessarily began below sea-level. The connection between Wootton Bassett and Filton Junctions, often referred to as the Badminton line, has heavy earthworks. Chief Civil Engineer for the GWR at the time was James C. Inglis, an Aberdonian born in 1851. Most of his civil engineering career was spent in England, and prior to joining the GWR in 1892 he had worked on harbours at Newport, Newlyn and Plymouth. He became General Manager of the Great Western in 1903, and was knighted in 1911. Resident Engineer for the tunnel was W. W. Grierson.

The contract divided the undertaking into five sections, and the contractor was Messrs S. Pearson & Son of Westminster. By March 1901 *The Railway Magazine* could report 'considerable progress', but it was a massive task. Five million cubic yards of excavation were involved - the bulk of the embankments slightly exceeded this - there were two tunnels, 88 bridges, four viaducts with a total of 32 arches, and seven stations, all in the 33.5 miles between Patchway and Wootton Bassett.

At the Wootton Bassett end Oxford clay gave a good deal of trouble. Somerford viaduct has 11 spans of 25 feet and one of 58 feet, the latter across the River Avon. The 506-yard Alderton tunnel is part of a very much bigger excavation involving 700,000 cubic yards of blue shale, though, mercifully, the

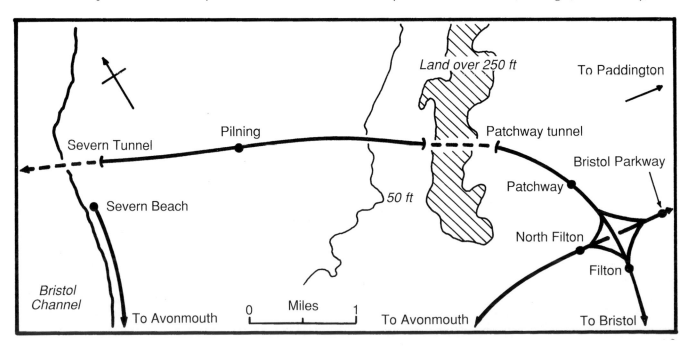

*Right* A 'King' going well - No 6019 *King Henry V* climbs past Pilning (High Level) with the 8.00 am Neyland to Paddington express on 10 February 1962. *Hugh Ballantyne*

*Below right* The up 'Red Dragon' approaching Patchway tunnel on 27 May 1959. The locomotive attacking the 1 in 100 is BR 'Britannia' 'Pacific' No 70023 *Venus*, and the steeper (1 in 68) gradient of the old line can be clearly seen in the background. *K. C. H. Fairey*

builders found the tunnel, which has two shafts, to be water-free.

Sodbury tunnel yielded about 410,000 cubic yards of forest marble; it has a vertical fall of 45 feet through its length, and water had to be culverted away beneath the trackbed. It is 4,444 yards long, the longest of the Cotswold group by some way. Seven shafts varying in depth from 90 to 280 feet were sunk to work it, and it is lined with locally-made red brick throughout, though the facings are in blue. The portals are made from limestone excavated from the approach cuttings, and the bore has a span of 27 feet 6 inches, a height of 20 feet 9 inches and a semi-circular profile.

The cuttings contained 1,835,000 cubic yards of coal shales, lias and mountain limestone. According to *The Railway Magazine* of July 1903, the contractors, in building the line, used '. . .fifty locomotives, seventeen steam navvies, 1,800 earth wagons, and three large, specially-constructed brickyards. Upwards of 4,000 men were employed on the works, and it is estimated that 50,000,000 of bricks and 20,000 tons of cement and lime were used.'

There is more 'down' within the Severn Tunnel on the Welsh side than there is 'up' on the English side, and the English bit is at 1 in 100 rather than 1 in 90. The gradient eases at Pilning, after three and a quarter miles, and there is even the luxury of three-quarters of a mile on the level. There followed (note the past tense) a little under a mile and a quarter of 1 in 68, finishing at the western portal of Patchway tunnel, which is straight and, for up trains, used to be on a slope of 1 in 90. A quarter of a mile at 1 in 80 led to a mile-long level through Patchway station, and thereafter the gradient eases considerably through Bristol Parkway and beyond. The 13 miles from Patchway to Badminton summit are graded at nothing worse than 1 in 300, and this section has not changed - the bit that has been altered is the length through the Patchway tunnels. That just described is now the down line, while the up has a new alignment, and a longer tunnel, with a uniform gradient of 1 in 100 from half a mile beyond Pilning as far as Patchway, a distance of almost three miles. The new tunnel is exactly a mile long, and was built as part of the Severn Tunnel works when the old single line to Portskewett was doubled - it opened in 1887.

The Badminton line was partly opened, between Swindon and Acton Turville (Badminton) for goods, on 1 January 1903, and throughout for all services on 1 July. Two-hour expresses to Bristol had been promised via the new line, but in the event actually took five minutes longer than that. The line's real advantage proved to be in the South Wales services, which improved greatly, and today it is now possible to reach Cardiff from London in under two hours.

Local services have suffered, however, for rationalisation has stripped the stations from the line. To begin with there were stations at Winterbourne, Coalpit Heath, Chipping Sodbury, Badminton, Hullavington, Little Somerford and Brinkworth - none survive for passenger use, though Badminton's red-brick station building is still there, and Chipping Sodbury is in use as a coal yard. All were closed on 3 April 1961 except for Badminton, which, perhaps because of the proximity of Badminton House, defeated closure until 3 June 1968. Near Filton Junction there is now a new station, however, Bristol Parkway, opened on 1 May 1972.

# Chipping Campden

**P**assengers travelling towards Oxford from Worcester are faced, as are those from South Wales, with the barrier of the Cotswolds. They do not look quite such a fearsome obstruction from here, but it takes a deal of climbing to cross them nevertheless.

The route across them was projected by the Oxford, Worcester & Wolverhampton Railway, which got its Act to do so on 4 August 1845. Brunel was the company's Engineer and the GWR a subscriber to the undertaking, so onlookers might have been forgiven for thinking it would turn out to be another broad gauge railway. The Act said it should be, and the GWR certainly hoped it would be, because it wanted a broad gauge link with Birmingham, but there was a body of opinion that thought otherwise and, to cut a very long and complicated story short, in the end it wasn't.

As with not a few concerns about this time, its cost was underestimated. The GWR had promised to help up to a certain limit, but there was a misunderstanding about this, a deal of wrangling, and when the Great Western noted that the railway was not being laid to broad gauge, it withdrew. It is perhaps a wonder the line was ever built at all, but in the end the two companies buried their differences and the GWR took over the OW&W (by then the West Midland Railway) in 1863. The crucial thing about the row, though, was that it sparked off Parliamentary debate as to what the gauge used by railway companies should be, which led, in its turn, to the ultimate demise of the broad gauge.

Early in 1847 2,800 men were at work on the line. Already there was trouble at the site of Campden tunnel (there was to be more), and the next year the money ran out. The prevailing financial climate did not allow the raising of more capital, despite the fact that, with magnificent irony, the line was almost finished. Except between Stourbridge and Dudley, and for a couple of unfinished viaducts, the shareholders were told in 1848, the formation was ready to have track laid. The cost of the remaining work, however, was estimated at £1.5 million, and the company asked the GWR for help. It declined.

In 1850 a scheme was evolved by which Samuel Morton Peto would complete the line between Oxford and Worcester, and Tipton and Wolverhampton, within 18 months. Since Peto was a major shareholder, it was naturally in his own best interest to see the line complete anyway. Railway politics do not concern us here, but about now there was a great deal of it. Finally the OW&W broke with the Great Western, and in 1851 work was resumed. Peto's agent for the contract was a Mr Watson, and Tredwell was one of the contractors.

Peto was a prominent Baptist from East Anglia who went into railway contracting quite early, and in partnership with Edward Betts built numerous lines, many of them for Brassey. He became an

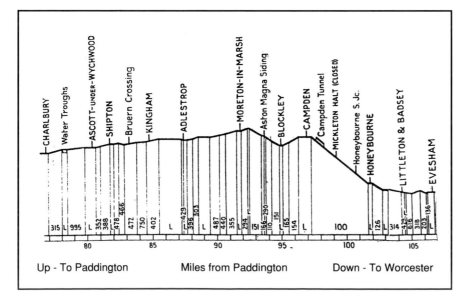

Up - To Paddington     Miles from Paddington     Down - To Worcester

**Gradient profile, Campden**

**A Dean 0-6-0 approaches Campden tunnel with a down train in about 1904. Single-line working is in operation while maintenance goes on, and platelayers wait in their hut as the train passes.** *Brunel University Library, Locomotive Photographs*

MP for Norwich in 1847, and was created a baronet in 1855; then, hit badly by the financial crash of 1866, he left Parliament two years later. He disliked the truck system intensely, and did what he could to suppress it, issuing a notice that he would not permit sub-contractors on the OW&W works to use it.

In 1846 the contract for the Campden length had gone to Messrs Williams, Ackroyd & Price. The trio fell out, and Williams then went into partnership with a minor contractor named R. M. Marchant. When building resumed in 1851 only Marchant remained. In June, when a dispute halted work once more, Peto took possession of the plant and works, though Marchant remained holding the tunnel and its approaches. Brunel intervened and Marchant was forced to withdraw. Poor Marchant came off very much the worst in this encounter - he was owed £4,300, and had, in addition, paid £10,000 for the plant at the tunnel mouth, which had now been taken off him. Brunel has often received the blame for Marchant's ill-usage, and there are conflicting stories about the 'Battle of Mickleton' as it has come to be called, but it is notable that Marchant himself put the blame on Peto rather than Brunel. A subsequent report stated that the company was now carrying on the works at the tunnel itself:

'These works are proceeding rapidly,' it went on, 'and if no unexpected impediment should occur there is every reason to hope that this portion may be completed as soon as the rest of the southern portion of the line.'

On 18 September 1852 the *Railway Times* announced that the tunnel was ready for opening. By the following November the paper could report that:

'The laying of the permanent rails will be commenced at Moreton-in-Marsh in a few days, so as to meet the Campden men downwards and the Charlbury men upwards. Should the weather prove favourable, we may expect to see an engine in that road within four months.'

The line was finished at last and it was hoped that it could be opened throughout on 21 April 1853 (various other shorter sections had opened meantime) and the *Railway Times* stated that the date 'has been definitely fixed for opened (sic) the passenger traffic from Oxford'. But it was, alas, a false hope. At the very last minute a slip, which caused the ballast to rise under pressure from both sides of the cutting at the north end of Campden tunnel, put paid to that idea. The line was packed from below, but despite these remedies the Inspector, Capt Galton, would not pass it for traffic - other works, notably the broad gauge connections, were still incomplete in any case. A formal opening was held on Saturday 7 May, but three more inspections were required before Capt Galton was satisfied, on 2 June. Public traffic began two days later.

From Worcester the profile of the line undulates, until, just before milepost 105 (from Paddington), the line rises towards Littleton & Badsey, regrettably no longer with us. After 1 in 429 past the site of the station, the gradient steepens to 1 in 314 for a mile and a quarter, there is half a mile of level track, and then three-quarters of a mile at 1 in 126. A level through Honeybourne gives on to the bank proper - 4 miles 25 chains at 1 in 100, leading through the tunnel and for about a third of a mile beyond, when Campden summit level, a mile long, is attained. Though not actually the highest point of the line, drivers could at least claim at this point to be over the worst.

Now the line goes down at 1 in 154 for three-quarters of a mile and 1 in 165 for half a mile, before a level past the site of Blockley station, when it begins to climb again. Two-thirds of a mile at 1 in 151, half a mile at 1 in 110, a short pitch of 1 in 290 and a slightly longer one of 1 in 166 lead to the final mile of 1 in 151 that brings the line to the summit, about half a mile short of Moreton-in-Marsh station.

Soon after the opening of the line a locomotive

derailed on the ascending approach to Campden tunnel, coming to rest against the side wall. No one was hurt, and the engine was quickly righted, presumably making its own way on without assistance. More than once the longitudinal baulks on which the rails were laid saved the day, as on the occasion when a horse-box derailed coming down the bank; instead of bouncing completely off the rails as probably would have happened on cross-sleepered track, it managed to rerail itself on the approach to Honeybourne station, just as disaster seemed imminent.

Latterday rationalisation has taken its toll, and the line now remains double only on the central section, between Ascott-under-Wychwood and Moreton-in-Marsh, and from Norton Junction to Worcester. Not many stations have gone, though one is perhaps slightly surprised to find that Chipping Campden is one of them - it closed on 3 January 1966, as did Blockley Halt. Both were, however, some distance from the places they purported to serve.

# Hatton

In the Great Western's ambition to reach Birmingham it was a case of third time lucky. They were pipped at the post by the Midland in the matter of the line from Bristol - see the next section dealing with the Lickey - and the upset with the OW&W has just been related. So it decided to build its own line.

The Birmingham & Oxford Junction Railway was incorporated on 3 August 1846, the contractors being Messrs Peto & Betts. 'Mr Hennet [sic] and Mr Tredwell' were also, in due course, at the opening dinner, which implies that they too had a connection with the works.

Work was begun early in 1847, but soon a shortage of money caused a slowing down for almost two years, and there was also a dispute in August of that year about land bought at Leamington 'not required for the purposes of the Act of Parliament', according to the *Leamington Courier* of 4 September. The line had originally been planned to pass west of Leamington, but deviation powers to pass through the town were obtained in 1848. Negotiations with the London & North Western Railway over viaducts in the Birmingham area took more time, but in August 1849 Brunel - who was, of course, Engineer - was able to report that the viaduct into Birmingham had been finished, and that the deep cutting at Harbury was well advanced.

It was 1851 before the Leamington deviation was begun, and although more hopeful reports now begin to appear, one wonders whether they were little more than a sop to shareholders. On 31 January 1852 a letter written to the Editor of the *Morning Herald* on 23 January was published in the *Leamington Courier*, observing, among much else, that:

'. . .The residents along the line have been led to believe that it would be opened early in the spring of the present year. I think you, Mr Editor, will, when you have perused the following observations, arrive at the conclusion. . .that it is not likely to be opened during the present year. . . The great Harbury cutting continues to slip in this wet weather, and counterforts and inverts are being put in at the worst places to hold any future slips off the line. . . The state of the works would lead to the supposition that there is no fixed intention of opening any portion of the line north of Banbury before the autumn of this year.'

The correspondent, who signed himself as 'A resident on the Line', was very nearly right, but Brunel had his problems, too; he wrote to the Chairman of the Leamington Commissioners:

18 Duke Street, Westminster
29th June 1852

My dear Sir,

The letter of Mr Haymes, on the part of the Leamington Commissioners, of the 8th of April, has been, I am sorry to say, overlooked by me. I sent at the time to my assistant, Mr Bertram, for some information on the subject, and neglected to reply to it. Our line through Leamington is so nearly similar to that of the London and North Western, that I have assumed the same extent of screening would be required in the one case as in the other, and propose to adopt what experience might prove necessary. From my own experience, in other cases, I believe that nothing beyond good high parapets, which we have, is ever desirable; but I shall be happy to give attention to any suggestion which the Commissioners may make

I am, my dear Sir, yours very truly,

I K BRUNEL

**Gradient profile, Hatton**

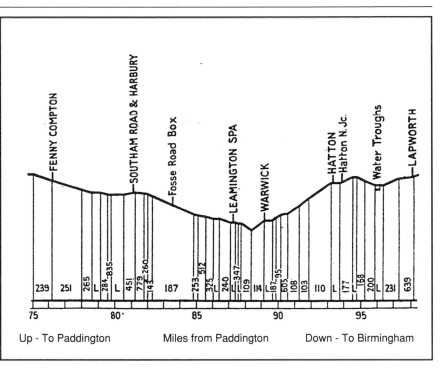

The Birmingham station at Snow Hill was not started until January 1852, by which time permanent way was being laid between Banbury and Fenny Compton. In February a domestic problem was reported in the *Leamington Courier* after a local publican had been fined 6 shillings with 14 shillings costs for allowing a fight among a group of navvies in the house, and for doing nothing to stop it. In fairness to the poor man, he might have come off a very poor second best if he had, so one can hardly blame him!

On 14 August the newspaper was expecting an opening on the first of the next month, but it was September before the line was ready for inspection. Capt Galton was happy with everything as far as the junction with the LNWR near Birmingham, and sanctioned opening to there. Public traffic began, for passengers only, on 1 October 1852, after an ill-fated first run by the Directors the previous day. Various accounts have implied that this journey was abandoned, but three local Leamington versions all agree that the special terminated there, somewhat late. Goods traffic began on 3 February 1853.

There were a number of substantial engineering works involved in the line, mostly at the northern (Birmingham) end. The cutting at Harbury, however,

No 4079 *Pendennis Castle* works hard on Hatton bank on 4 March 1967. The train was an Ian Allan special, the 'Birkenhead Flyer', and this was its down journey. *P. H. Wells*

is 110 feet deep and about half a mile long, with a short tunnel of 73 yards - a longer one had been projected, but cutting was substituted after a landslip in 1850. Three million cubic yards of marl and limestone were excavated from this spot, and the spoil formed most of the adjacent four-mile-long embankment. Hatton has a three-mile embankment, and the cutting here, not so deep as that at Harbury, yielded half a million cubic yards of marl.

The line runs mainly downhill from Fenny Compton, and a three-quarter mile pitch at 1 in 451 leads up to the minor summit just beyond the site of Southam Road & Harbury station. It is then downhill all the way to Leamington, a two and a half mile pitch of 1 in 187 being included past Fosse Road signal box. Leamington itself is on level track, but more downgrade follows, half a mile at 1 in 109 taking the line down to its lowest point, at which it crosses beneath the Grand Union Canal, and then over the River Avon on an iron girder bridge 150 feet long.

Three quarters of a mile at 1 in 114 takes the line out of this trough, ending at Warwick station. Half a mile of level follows, then 200 yards at 1 in 187 and a quarter mile of 1 in 95. This is actually the steepest pitch, but there is more climbing to come. An easing of a little less than half a mile at 1 in 605 brings the line to three-quarters of a mile at 1 in 108, then rather over half a mile at 1 in 103. This is followed by the main body of the bank, a mile and a half at 1 in 110, Hatton station lying just beyond a levelling out at the top. The top of this pitch, that is to say - the summit of the entire climb is still more than six miles away, but now, after half a mile of level track, the minor summit is reached via three-quarters of a mile at 1 in 177.

Two short downgrades follow the brief level at this point, and after half a mile more of level, the line angles upward again, at 1 in 231 for a mile, then at 1 in 639 for another, at the end of which it reaches Lapworth station and steepens to 1 in 258 for three-quarters of a mile. Sections graded at 1 in 271, 1 in 183 and 1 in 350, the first just over half a mile, the two others each just less, lead to the real summit, which lies about a quarter of a mile beyond Dorridge station.

Because of the proposed connection with the LNWR the line was laid in mixed gauge on longitudinal baulks, though the third rail was useless at first since it connected with nothing. At Leamington only broad gauge trains could enter the main station, the mixed gauge lines being diverted by a loop to the north-east side, and having platforms of their own. The mixed gauge rail was removed on 1 April 1869, but the line has remained double to this day.

There have also been few casualties among the sta-

tions - Lapworth, originally called Kingswood, was added after opening, in 1855, and Dorridge was first simply Knowle, then Knowle & Dorridge, and is now just Dorridge. Southam Road & Harbury is the only original station on this section to have closed, on 2 November 1964.

# Notgrove

Notgrove? Where's that? One might be forgiven for asking, but it does have a certain small claim to fame in that, at an altitude of 760 feet above sea level, it was the highest through station on the GWR - Princetown was higher, but that was a terminus.

Well, as may be deduced from the chapter in which it appears, Notgrove is in the Cotswolds, and lies some four miles west of Bourton-on-the-Water and six east of Andoversford.

The line that reached it was the Banbury & Cheltenham Direct Railway, which, though linking the towns, was not exactly direct in quite the sense we understand today. It began, in embryo only, very early, back in 1845 as a Northampton, Banbury & Cheltenham Railway, but that scheme's last advertisement appeared in September 1846 and nothing more was heard of it. But by 1855 a branch line had been built from Kingham (then called Chipping Norton Junction) eastwards to Chipping Norton. A branch the other way, west to Bourton-on-the-Water was opened in 1862, at which time an extension was projected to Gloucester. Nothing came of that, either. Various schemes were evolved through the 1860s, mainly centred around the desirability of getting iron ore from Northamptonshire to the smelters in South Wales; coal could be usefully carried in the reverse direction, which was not considered a disadvantage. Finally, on 21 July 1873 a company was formed to extend both the Chipping Norton and Bourton branches to Banbury and Cheltenham respectively, to make one line.

Work was very slow, and by 1877 the contractor at the Cheltenham end, Lawrence & Co., had gone bankrupt. A replacement was being sought, but in the meantime, reported the *Gloucester Journal* on 24 February 1877, 'the Company itself was doing what it could in unfavourable weather conditions.' The work was all suspended in 1878 at a time of countrywide financial instability, and did not restart until the autumn of the following year. Early in 1879 there had been a dispute with the new contractor, a Mr Terry, who had taken possession of some of the land but had done nothing with it. Then Terry died, and the third contractor was a Mr Lovatt, of Wolverhampton. He appears to have got things moving, for there was activity in the Dowdeswell valley, above Cheltenham, in October 1880, and on 1 January 1881, the *Gloucester Journal* was hopeful about the line being open 'in the course of a few months.'

For once this was not over-optimistic, despite the fact that the weather during the next three months was appalling. A 'second survey', made in the first week of May 1881, is referred to in the *Gloucester Journal* of 14 May, so we must assume, perhaps, that Colonel Rich, the Inspecting Officer, was dissatisfied with the first. He found no fault the second time around, but now a dispute between the Company and the GWR (which was to work the line) delayed the opening. This event finally took place, without ceremony, on 1 June 1881, the only leaning towards celebration being, reported the *Gloucester Journal* on 4 June, 'bunting and evergreens at the stations'. Engineers for the line had been Edward Wilson and a Mr MacIntyre.

Notgrove lies on the ridge between the valleys of the Windrush at Bourton and the Coln at Andoversford. Bourton is about 450 feet above sea-level, so a stiff climb westward was needed; the average gradient was 1 in 60, raised first on a high embankment to cross the Fosse Way and the River Windrush. After crossing the Windrush the line fol-lowed the river valley for a mile or so, climbing steadily meantime, until it was high enough to veer away to the west, above a small tributary of the river. It was now within a mile of Notgrove station, which was reached beyond a deep cutting spanned by the high three-arch bridge that carried the Andoversford to Bourton road. The gradient eased suddenly through the station, but then fell away again, more gently, towards Andoversford, where the line was joined in 1891 by the Midland & South Western Junction Railway at the end of its run from Andover and Swindon.

Andoversford's altitude is 550 feet. The fall from Notgrove had been easy so far - 210 feet in six miles is an average of 35 feet a mile, or roughly 1 in 151 - but from the platform end at Andoversford it fell at 1 in 70. Entering a deep cutting it plunged into the curved bore of Sandywell tunnel, still on a falling gradient. It left the tunnel in a deep wooded cutting, but soon ran on to the 12-arched viaduct that crossed the River Chelt and its deep valley. Charlton Kings stood on a slope of 1 in 77, which continued down to Cheltenham South & Leckhampton. Shortly after that the line joined the line from Gloucester by a 43-chain radius curve, ran through Cheltenham Malvern Road and came finally to its terminus at Cheltenham St James.

Cheltenham Malvern Road was built in 1908 to serve the Gloucester-Honeybourne-Birmingham line, and closed on 3 January 1966. Cheltenham South & Leckhampton had originally been plain Leckhampton, and Notgrove was Notgrove & Westfield to begin with. In his book on the line, J. H. Russell notes that the 'Cheltenham' name was added

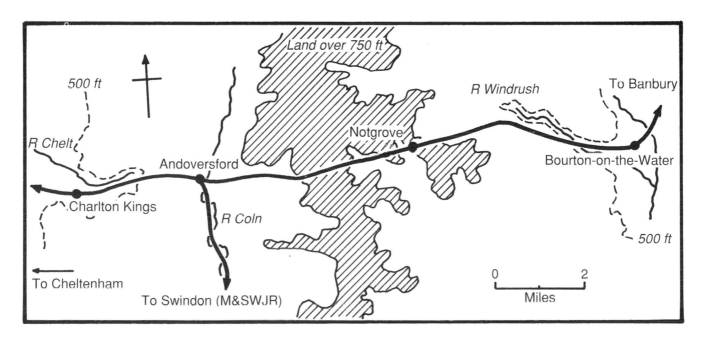

to that of Leckhampton so that in the heady days of the Welsh expresses Cheltenham could thus be added to the list of places served.

The line was standard gauge and single throughout to begin with, but was doubled between Andoversford and Cheltenham after the M&SWJR came on the scene. It remained single between Andoversford and Bourton, with a passing loop at Notgrove, throughout its life, which ended in total closure on 15 October 1962. Traffic on the M&SWJR had ended just over a year before, on 11 September 1961.

# Lickey

**N**ot strictly an incline in the Cotswolds, of course, but it is convenient to consider it at this point, hopefully without too much of a geographical wrench on the part of the reader.

The 'Lickey' was built by the Birmingham & Gloucester Railway, which received legal status on 22 April 1836. When the B&G was projecting its line in the early 1830s, three surveys were undertaken, one by Brunel (rejected on the grounds that it would avoid Cheltenham and Worcester) and two by Captain William S. Moorsom. One passed three miles from Cheltenham and nowhere near Worcester, while the other, a more roundabout route via Stourbridge and Kidderminster, served Worcester but not Cheltenham. On the grounds that directness indicated cheapness and because they considered Cheltenham more important, the Directors chose the former. It was undoubtedly the most expensive economy they could have made, for its very directness depended upon a steep climb into the Lickey Hills.

Moorsom was born in Whitby in 1804, and had been educated at Sandhurst, where he learned surveying. On this railway his method of crossing the River Avon by using iron caissons won him the Telford Medal, and he worked on many other lines. Here he decided that the incline up the Lickey should be split into two sections, one and a half miles at 1 in 54, and one and a quarter miles at 1 in 36, both worked by stationary engines.

It is built, Whishaw tells us, through 'strata intersected by. . .marl and lias clay'. Work began in November 1837, and when a partial opening of the line to Bromsgrove was anticipated it was hoped that the line up the Lickey and as far as Lifford would be finished later the same year. At a general meeting in February 1840, Moorsom gave his opinion that 'the railway may be opened to Lifford in October or November next. . .' By now, however, despite earlier optimistic noises about costs, Moorsom was also admitting that 'the cost of the undertaking would probably exceed the authorised amount. . .' He put this down to unforeseen events, such as the cost and quantity of engines and rolling-stock required, and of passenger accommodation at stations. Francis Conder, himself an engineer who published a volume of memoirs in 1868 (*Personal Recollections of English Engineers*, republished as *The Men Who Built Railways* in 1983), appears to have had a low opinion of Moorsom, not perhaps without reason.

A little later Moorsom was complaining of lack of money for the work, though he thought an opening would be possible by 1 July. Private trains ran between

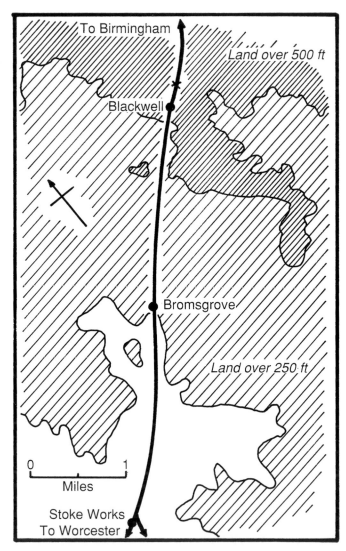

*Right* 'Big Bertha', the mighty 0-10-0 locomotive for which the Lickey incline is perhaps best remembered. She was built in 1920 for this specific job, and is seen here doing it at the rear of a Birmingham-bound train of 'blood and custard' stock near Bromsgrove on 17 July 1955. *Eric Sawford*

*Below right* Stanier Class '5' 4-6-0 No 44851 breasts the Lickey below Blackwell on 13 April 1959. Though the train is short a tell-tale whiff of steam from behind the last vehicle indicates that rear assistance is being given. *Peter Hay*

Cheltenham and Bromsgrove on 31 May 1840, and a formal opening was held on 24 June, with no celebration whatever. This section had been built comfortably within estimate but there was little comparison between the country covered and that still to be done. The Board made the fatal blunder of over-riding its Engineer and accepting the lowest tender for this work, rather than that nearest to the estimate - another false economy when the contractor went bankrupt and the work had to be re-let at higher cost. The line opened to Cofton Farm, a mile on the Birmingham side of Barnt Green and about eight miles from Birmingham itself, on 17 September 1840. When the finances were at last untangled it was shown that the building of the railway had exceeded estimate by £390,000, £55,000 of which had been spent in getting the Birmingham end finished ahead of time for traffic which was not there anyway!

Profits in the first half of 1842 were a mere £1,600. Things were about to be improved, however, for the three big Norris tank engines purchased from America to bank the incline were saddle-tanked, which considerably reduced costs. These were astronomical, no doubt because, as a contemporary circular issued by a group of shareholders remarked:

'. . .separation of the goods from the passengers [it had been usual to combine the two] . . . [required] two extra engines and trains each way for merchandise [with]. . .a diminution. . .in the traffic revenue.'

Geologically the northern end of the line passes through red sandstone. While this provided excellent building material, over 4.5 million cubic yards of material needed to be excavated by pick and shovel, and moved, as required, to nearby sites for embanking. Long cuttings at Moseley, Brede, Barnt Green, Grovely and Longbridge were necessary, that at Moseley being over 85 feet deep. Three (Grovely, Barnt Green and Longbridge) were found to be in a dangerous state by the BoT Inspector, who declined to pass the line as safe. But the B&G opened it anyway!

Grovely tunnel, later known as Cofton, was troublesome. The rock was unstable, so that the whole tunnel had to be brick-lined, and seeping water was a continual problem. The lining was trussed in 1841, but it didn't stop the water. It continued to be a nuisance until the LMS opened it out in the late 1920s; to avoid delays to trains, the up and down tracks were slewed so that the inner rails of each were 4 ft 8½ in apart, providing a 'central' line in case of emergency.

Moorsom used Brunel's longitudinal system rather than cross-sleepers, though his rails were set in chairs at 5-foot intervals, intermediate saddles giving supplementary support. The baulks were American yellow pine, 15 feet minimum by 12 inches by 14 inches, kyanised and cut diagonally. Whishaw tells us that cross-sleepers were used on embankments more than 5 feet high; the BoT Inspector apparently expressed a preference for the longitudinal system.

As noted, it was originally intended to work the Lickey by haulage, and stationary engines were being designed for the job when Moorsom decided that locomotive power should be used, if only to prove Brunel, Stephenson and Bury wrong. American engines were available, he maintained, which had produced spectacular results, so he opened negotiations with Norris of Philadelphia. This decision appears to have been made before Whishaw's book was written, for he comments:

'If this is satisfactorily effected it will save a vast original outlay in future works. We have long considered that the present system of making sixteen feet [per mile, or 1 in 330] the minimum is far from desirable. The advantages of working a railway thus graduated are not equivalent to the immense original outlay necessarily incurred by tunnels and overwhelming earthworks.'

The American engines were not an economical move, however - they pulled well, when they worked, but they consumed prodigious amounts of coke, which, since they had been designed for wood-burning, had side-results. The locomotive superintendent, William Creuzel, reported the 'Americans' as very much out of order. 'This is due,' he wrote, 'to the construction of their fireboxes, and their tubes being made of copper, which our fuel does not suit.' They were repaired at considerable cost, and gave good service, but it proved an expensive lesson.

The locomotive position went from bad to worse, but in July 1841 James E. McConnell took up his duties as Foreman of Locomotives. Bankers are expensive to run because they do productive work for only half of each journey, but McConnell set about improving the efficiency of the other engines to make banking less necessary. He succeeded, too. *Bristol* and *Hercules*, two of three new goods engines, were built to his own design, and he designed, planned and built *Great Britain* for heavy goods traffic, specifically on the Lickey. It emerged from Bromsgrove Works in the summer of 1845 to find that the B&G was now amalgamated with the Bristol & Gloucester as the Birmingham & Bristol Railway, which had, in turn, been leased by the Midland.

The Midland used 0-6-0s as bankers, until the only other engine specifically designed for the job came from Derby in January 1920, only the second type with 10-coupled wheels in British locomotive history. With several smaller tank engines 'Big Bertha' did her duty efficiently until superseded in 1956 by various Standard '9F' 2-10-0 locomotives. The LNER Beyer-Garratt No 69999 was tried from 1949, but was not much liked, and returned to Yorkshire after two years. There were various other experiments too, from every region except the Southern, but none were effective. Diesel banking came in due course, and now the HSTs hardly notice the climb.

This actually begins some 16 miles from Bromsgrove, after the Avon viaduct, but gently, at nothing more than 1 in 301. There is nothing steeper until the approach to Stoke Works Junction, where about 30 chains of 1 in 111 leads to two miles of 1 in 283. Then a quarter-mile at 1 in 105 brings the line almost to Bromsgrove station, and eases through it to 1 in 185 for about 14 chains. Now the incline proper is reached, almost two miles at 1 in 37.75. The site of Blackwell station is at the top of this pitch, but contrary to what seems to be popular belief, this is not the top of the climb - drivers still have another mile at 1 in 291 to negotiate before they reach the summit, at around the 600-foot contour, a third of a mile short of Barnt Green station.

# 4
# CAMBRIAN MOUNTAINS

## Drws-y-Nant

In many ways this exit from the Cambrian coast has notable parallels with its better-known counterpart at Talerddig. Maybe the main difference is that since it afforded fewer locations for photographers it was less well covered from that point of view, and the fact that it is no longer with us is another factor. But it is only slightly less steep, and despite being a little shorter was no less difficult to work.

The GWR yearned for an independent line which it could use for its holiday traffic to the Cambrian coast. It was not completely successful, as we shall see, but by supporting a small, nominally independent, company, it influenced a line from Ruabon to Llangollen. This technique it then extended in turn to Corwen and Bala, and finally to Dolgellau, where it met a Cambrian Railways branch from Barmouth Junction (Morfa Mawddach) and had to be dependent on that for the final few miles to the coast. To reach this point, however, the line had to cross the watershed between the valleys of the Dee and the Wnion, and it was the latter's narrow and steep valley which provided most of the climb.

**Thomas Brassey was responsible for building more than 1,000 miles of our railways, and he worked on many others things beside. Drws-y-Nant was one of his last lines, and the man and his works are commemorated in this bust in Chester Cathedral, near his birthplace of Bulkeley Manor.** *C. V. Awdry*

The Bala & Dolgelly (sic) Railway Act received Royal Assent on 30 June 1862. The line from Bala Junction to Dolgellau was 18 miles long, and its Engineer was Edward Wilson. Though shareholders were told on 2 September 1863 that contractors

had been invited to tender, the building contract was not actually let to Brassey & Field until 1866, shortly before the financial crash in May of that year. W. Field, who worked with Brassey on many contracts, both as partner and agent, was a partner here, and there were two agents: Day, who often acted in that capacity though there appears to be no record of his ever having been a partner in any of Brassey's projects, and Drennan, whose only other job for Brassey seems to have been on the Enniskillen & Bundoran Railway, in Ireland. Payment of part of the £230,000 agreed was to be made in shares, as indeed part of Wilson's salary had also been.

In February 1867 Wilson reported that '. . .the formation of six and a half miles of the line has now been completed and about one mile of permanent way finished. The whole of the cuttings are in hand, and the masonry in the culverts and bridges is in a forward state.' Six months later work had slowed down, but a comment in a letter from Wilson to the Directors indicates that Brassey had drafted in extra men to push things along.

At a shareholders' meeting on 23 July 1868 it was stated that 'the line has been inspected by the Government Officer, and will be ready for opening on the 1st August'.

This was nearly correct. Lt Col Hutchinson had not been greatly impressed during his inspection, and on 5 August *The Times* reported that the line

had actually opened on 4 August 1868. 'It was to have opened on Saturday,' it went on, 'but the Government Inspector, having insisted on some improvements, these were attended to by the contractor as speedily as possible, and the line was open for traffic on their completion.' The station buildings at Dolgellau were still unfinished on opening day.

Approached from the Llangollen side the summit is reached more or less gradually. There is a stiff pull out of Llangollen, now once more resounding to steam thanks to the preserved Llangollen Railway, but once through Berwyn tunnel it was an easy enough journey to Bala Junction, having nothing steeper than 1 in 150 to contend with. Even beyond there, along the lakeside, there are no problems until a mile beyond the private Flag station, where a short but sharp pitch of 25 chains at 1 in 71 began. The gradient eased to 1 in 471 along the straight to Llanuwchllyn station, but immediately beyond the platform this gave way to about 70 chains of 1 in 63. A series of short pitches followed, at 1 in 161, 545, 126 and 309, none longer than 25 chains. This was the respite, for now came ten chains of 1 in 64, fifteen of 1 in 81 and finally about 70 of 1 in 64, which gave on to the short summit level.

From the Dolgellau end, climbing really began in a short pitch of 1 in 108. According to the official gradient profile this length actually includes the station, with leveller stretches on either side, which

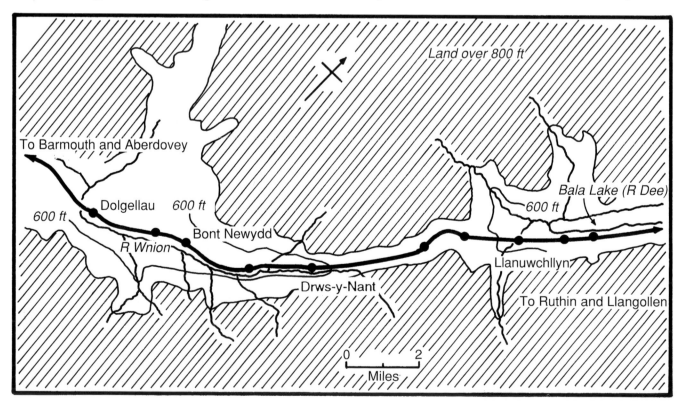

seems odd. However, be that as it may, two pitches of 1 in 181 and 187, each a quarter of a mile long, soon follow, with a similarly lengthed easing to 1 in 213 and a 10-chain down at 1 in 117. Seventy chains of 1 in 110 heralded the beginning of the bank proper, and this was followed by a little over a mile at 1 in 91. An easing to 1 in 200 at Bont Newydd was so brief as to be almost unnoticeable, and a mile and a half of 1 in 50 came next, with 25 chains of 1 in 66 to follow and 10 chains each of 1 in 73 and 66 for good measure. An easing to 1 in 132 for a quarter-mile led only to another steep mile at 1 in 62 and 63, but things eased off very slightly for the approach to Drws-y-Nant. The 50 chains including the station had five short pitches at 1 in 218, 64, 129, level and 144, the level at the platform being the shortest. A quarter of a mile at 1 in 62 came next, followed by 70 chains of 1 in 65 and three-quarters of a mile at 1 in 59. Finally, a fractional steepening to 1 in 58 brought the line to its summit at about 760 feet above sea level, not quite ten miles out from Dolgellau, whose station lay on the 50-foot contour.

It was a useful route to the sea, but never a prosperous one - the lines flanking it saw to that. Between the wars the GWR made efforts to encourage both local and holiday use by opening halts and introducing camping coaches, and it was used by Radio Land Cruise trains during the 1950s, but once car travel had become the norm the writing was on the wall, and, like King Nebuchadnezzar, the line was found wanting. Dr Beeching recommended closure, which was set for 18 January 1965, but he was forestalled when fierce storms caused a washout at Llandderfel, between Bala and Corwen, a month earlier and closed the line as a through route from 14 December 1964.

# Talerddig

A venture to link the Dyfi valley with a proposed railway westwards from Oswestry was launched in Machynlleth on 20 December 1856. It must have been an act of some faith on the part of the promoters, for at the time of the meeting the putative Oswestry & Newtown Railway had not even had its first sod cut - indeed, this event was still nine months in the future. There was another proposal on the table too: a line from Llanidloes to Newtown, which was not to open until September 1859. But nothing daunted, the new line planned to branch from the Llanidloes route at Moat Lane, near Caersws, and take a course up the valley of the little River Carno. This led directly to the main obstacle, the watershed between the Severn and the Dyfi, which, it was intended, would be crossed at the village of Talerddig. At first a tunnel was planned at the summit of the climb, and the works were estimated at a cost 'not exceeding £125,000'.

Notwithstanding this confidence, support in some quarters was variable, but the Parliamentary Bill became an Act on 27 July 1857, and the first general meeting, under Sir Watkin Williams-Wynn's chairmanship, was held on 22 August. Thereafter progress seems to have stagnated a little - there were difficul-

**Gradient profile, Talerddig and Llandre**

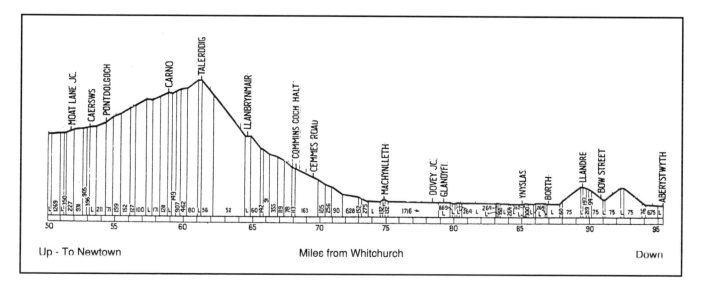

Up - To Newtown          Miles from Whitchurch          Down

ties in buying land, and, in any case, what was the hurry when none of the contiguous projects were finished? But at last, on 27 November 1858, the first sod was cut at Machynlleth by Countess Vane. The brothers Benjamin and Robert Piercy were appointed Engineers under J. Cubitt as Engineer-in-Chief, though he appears to have done little more than lend his name to the enterprise. The contract for construction was let to Messrs Davies & Savin for £130,000.

The tunnel at Talerddig was still planned at this time, and it may have been only when work reached that spot that the decision to open it out to a cutting was taken. It was clearly a wise move, whenever it was made, for the site furnished a large quantity of building stone, which was used extensively in bridge and railway construction throughout the length of the line. Much of this was of excellent quality, though some layers proved very friable and were to give rise to problems of stability both during and after construction.

The distance noted in the Specification for the Works of 1860 as '23 miles or thereabouts. . .' from Moat Lane (known as Caersws Junction until 1862), was divided into two sections for construction purposes - nine miles from the junction to Talerddig, and 14 from

*Left* 'Manor' Class 4-6-0 No 7822 *Foxcote Manor* - now enjoying an extended life in preservation - emerges from the rock cutting at Talerddig on 1 September 1962, and heads fast down the 1 in 52 towards Machynlleth. *P. H. Wells*

*Below* Harder work though for sister engine No 7819 *Lydham Manor*, struggling towards the summit with a well-loaded 'Cambrian Limited' special on 22 September 1991. The run had begun at Aberystwyth and terminated at Shrewsbury. *Hugh Ballantyne*

The 12 noon Aberystwyth-Shrewsbury and Wolverhampton stopper enters the up loop at Talerddig behind ex-GWR 'Dukedog' Class 4-4-0 No 9004 on 26 September 1953, slowing ready to give up the single-line tablet. A down train is already held in the station, so it may get through and away first. It will be noted from the signals that down trains were able to use either loop. *E. D. Bruton*

there to Machynlleth. It was estimated that building the specified single line of railway would take a year, though it was actually to be 19 months before the first locomotive would make the journey. Strict instructions were laid down as to the quality of the works, and the solidity of the structure today, after more than 130 years, bears, as G. Briwnant-Jones has written, 'silent testimony to the standard of workmanship and quality of materials used in its construction'.

The Talerddig line was surveyed by George Owen, and the main problem was the 'big rock'. Work began there on 4 June 1859, and continued for two years. Over that period 200-300 men worked on the site, and when the 115-foot deep cutting was finished it was, at the time, the deepest in the world. Given the primitive nature of the equipment available, it was a remarkable achievement. Not that the cutting was the only problem - there was a bog to negotiate as well, and this was solved when a tributary of the River Carno was diverted to the other side of the watershed, thus flowing thereafter into the Dyfi.

Each 22-foot length of rail (65/70 lb per yard) was spiked to light larch sleepers which had been previously grooved to receive them. The men working on the contract (probably 1,000 or more) seem to have

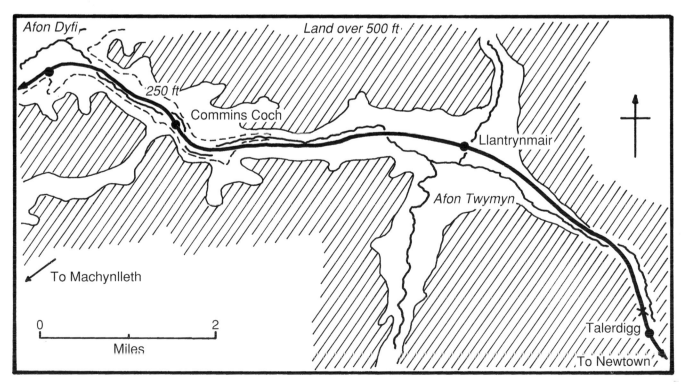

been a fairly mobile force, moving about the linear site as required. Incidents of drunkenness and misbehaviour seem to have been fewer than on other railway sites, and it has been suggested that this may have been because many of the men were recruited locally and so would have been able to return home at weekends. Not that there was a complete lack of misdemeanour, and the company took appropriate policing precautions.

The *Oswestry & Border Counties Advertiser* announced that the line was open on 21 November 1859 'for general traffic', but the company then had neither locomotives nor carriages and would have had difficulty in maintaining a service. Though the eastern section was said to have given few problems, there were delays due to the weather, land purchase and the decision to open out Talerddig tunnel. However, in August 1860 the Engineers told the Board that an opening to Llanbrynmair, 13 miles from Moat Lane, would be possible by the next spring. They were also confident, at the time, to be finished in time for a summer service to Machynlleth in 1862.

Alas for optimism. At this point things began to go wrong. The contractors, Davies and Savin, split their partnership, Savin going his own way while David Davies saw the Talerddig job through. On 21 September 1862 a correspondent of the *Oswestry & Border Counties Advertiser* managed to reach Llanbrynmair, but only by rail as far as Talerddig, on a 'ballast engine'.

The approach from Moat Lane was the easy side. There was heavy engineering on the other, and the press to get the work finished was halted when a bridge at Commins Coch, three and a half miles below Llanbrynmair, collapsed six days before the initial run through to Machynlleth was scheduled. It was a temporary timber structure, which gave way on being crossed at too great a speed. With the driver dead, and its only engine in the river, the company might have been forgiven for postponing the proposed run, but not a bit of it. The locomotive was recovered, by no means irreparably damaged, the bridge was rebuilt, and the same engine steamed into Machynlleth on 1 May 1862 as promised. A grand opening was held on 3 January 1863, but this was the railway only - buildings there were not, and the girder for the bridge at Machynlleth lay on the station platform. The line cost £9,000 per mile to build, a figure that compares well with others, and Davies gave a dinner for his foremen, with a £50 purse to Richard Metcalfe, his engine driver, to whom he was grateful for the speed of construction.

Approaching from the London side, trains had a comparatively easy time, largely because the line at Moat Lane is a fair height above sea level already, and the climb from here is a mere 243 feet against 645 feet on the other. There is a pitch of 1 in 71 for half a mile up from Pontdolgoch, almost a mile of 1 in 100 a little later, and a three-quarter mile length of 1 in 80 to the summit. Otherwise the steepest sections are at 1 in 127 and 128.

The other side is another matter, however. Short pitches of 1 in 275 and 152 begin a mile out of Machynlleth, and are followed by a mile and a quarter of 1 in 628. Then comes three-quarters of a mile at 1 in 90, easing to 1 in 256 for half a mile before another half-mile of 1 in 105. The next one and three-quarter miles is at 1 in 163, and it takes the line through Cemmes Road and round a right-hand curve to forsake the Dyfi valley for that of the Twymyn. The pitch ends at Commins Coch, and is followed by short lengths at 1 in 113, 78, 119 and 355, the last three each about half a mile long.

Now comes half a mile at 1 in 91, and when this eases to 1 in 142 it is no more than a breather, for then three-quarters of a mile of 1 in 60 bring the line to a level at Llanbrynmair. From here on it is tough going, and one has great sympathy with drivers who had to restart trains from here. Almost off the platform end the gradient is 1 in 52, and it stays that way for the next two and a quarter miles. Road, rail and river are compressed into a narrow gorge, and suddenly the line swings across the road to take the other side of the valley. As it does so the gradient eases but the drivers didn't get excited - it was now 1 in 56 for the best part of a mile. Then beyond an overbridge comes the deep cutting, a left-hand curve, the top of the hill (693 feet above sea level) at Talerddig station and great relief all round.

The permanent way and works have stood the test of time, though an accident was caused by heavy flooding in 1868, when the driver of an early morning Machynlleth-Newtown goods at Carno found river water washing over his footplate. He was anxious about the safety of the Severn bridge at Caersws, but, after careful inspection, crossed it without trouble. Later in the day, however, it collapsed beneath a train, killing the crew, and it was found that floodwater had undermined the bank behind the bridge abutment. Another train was held at Pontdolgoch in the nick of time when it was found that the bridge there was also unsafe.

The Newtown & Machynlleth did not enjoy independence for very long, becoming part of the Cambrian Railways' system on 25 July 1864, and thus into the GWR group in 1922. Only Caersws of the original stations between Newtown and Machynlleth remains open, though a passing loop is retained at Talerddig. Today's 'Sprinters' have no difficulty in surmounting the bank, which in steam days involved regular double-heading. Moat Lane Junction closed for passengers when the Llanidloes line did, since it was an interchange point only, on 31 December 1962, though that route was retained for goods while the Chlwedog Reservoir was being built. The other stations - Pont Dolgoch, Carno, Talerddig, Llanbrynmair, Commins Coch and Cemmes Road - survived until 14 June 1965. The line is worked under the RETB (Radio Electronic Tokenless Block) system now, which replaces fixed signals with a direct signalman/driver radio link, and though there were teething troubles at first, things seem to have settled down. There have even been steam specials over the bank in recent years.

# Llandre

No one, I think, would ever suggest that the two gables, like twin pyramids, between Borth and Aberystwyth, are major gradients, yet they presented some problems to train crews, not so much for their severity as their situation. They originated as part of the Aberystwith (sic) & Welsh Coast Railway's connection between Machynlleth and Aberystwyth, authorised for building on 22 July 1861.

The line to Borth was built by Thomas Savin, who then, in February 1864, fell foul of the company Chairman, G. H. Whalley, over the matter of his (Savin's) method of financing the work. Whalley, who was an impulsive Irishman and a magistrate for three surrounding counties, was also the MP for Peterborough and had been elected Chairman of the company on its formation. The contretemps could have been serious, as the future of the extension line to Aberystwyth was threatened, but after a while Whalley and three other Directors resigned.

Benjamin Piercy, the Engineer, was asked to resign also, but refused, so he was dismissed. Piercy, then approaching his 37th birthday, had been trained in his father's office, and worked under Robertson on the Shrewsbury & Chester Railway. He was involved with many Welsh lines, and this was by no means his last - he later became connected with Barmouth Bridge. He died in 1881 while in India, still in harness, at the age of 61.

His replacement at Llandre, appointed in March

1864, was Henry Coneybeare. Coneybeare (some references spell him without the first 'e') was born in Brislington on 22 February 1823, and educated at Rugby and Kings College, London. He spent three years working at a locomotive works in Newcastle, then went out to India on the staff of the Great Peninsular Railway. He returned to England in 1855, where he opened what was to become an extensive freelance practice in railway engineering.

A clause in the A&WCR's Act stipulated that in the event of non-completion of the line by 1 August 1864, the Newtown & Machynlleth would be empowered to take over and finish the job - the deadline was beaten by seven weeks, on 11 June. On 9 June *The Times* had reported:

'The company's line from Borth to Aberystwyth has been completed, and the Government Inspector, Captain Tyler has been over the railway. A few matters remain to be carried out, and then the line will be opened for passenger traffic.'

There is some uncertainty as to when the opening date for this actually was. The first train over the line has been said to have arrived in Aberystwyth at 3.15 pm on 23 June, though other authorities give 1 August as the opening date. A Directors' report of August 1864 simply states that the line is open, without stating a date. The assembled company was treated to a civic welcome, and there was an address to the builders, Savin and Thomas, his partner, and the first pile of a new pier was driven. All then repaired to the Belle Vue Hotel for a banquet.

Leaving Borth, those first passengers must have wondered where they were heading, because the railway curves inland from the station to use a small valley which cuts behind the high cliffs separating the Dyfi flats from the Rheidol valley. The line is level for a mile, at which point is reached 15 chains of 1 in 60, giving way to a mile and a third of 1 in 75. This brings the line to the top of, as it were, the first pyramid, where there is a level and Llandre (originally Llanvihangel) station. The descent begins in short pitches of 1 in 197, 219 and 94, before giving way to about 70 chains of 1 in 75 through Bow Street station, almost at the foot of the bank. It must have been a fearful place for a restart in damp or icy weather.

After a short level section the line climbs again, for a little over a mile at 1 in 75 to the 16-chain level at the top of the second pyramid. One and a quarter miles down at 1 in 75, a sharp right-hand curve once across the main valley road, and a quarter-mile at 1 in 76 bring the line to the valley floor. The narrow-gauge Vale of Rheidol Light Railway approaches from the left, and from Llanbadarn level crossing a shade under a mile at 1 in 675 descends to Aberystwyth station.

Both intermediate stations on this section closed to passengers on 14 June 1965, but the line to Aberystwyth itself is kept reasonably busy. In the Winter 1991/2 timetable there were eight down and nine up trains daily, with five up and six down on Sundays. Most run through to Shrewsbury, but some simply connect at Machynlleth with services to Barmouth and Pwllheli. Most steam services out of Aberystwyth now use another hill, to reach Devil's Bridge, but there has occasionally been a steam service on the big railway too, surmounting the twin peaks at Llandre.

# Trawscoed

No prize is offered for knowing where this was, but the reader could be forgiven for having been unaware of it - as, indeed, the writer confesses he was before undertaking the research for this book. And he found, on investigation, that it lies - or rather lay - on the watershed between the headwaters of the Teifi and the Ystwyth valley.

The lack of success of the Manchester & Milford Railway, which built it, has been often told and needs no repetition. From its inception it was going to have a substantial climb to surmount the high ground between Strata Florida in the Teifi valley, over the pass at Eisteddfa Gurig, and down to Llangurig in the Wye valley on the other. But that never came to anything. What had been intended as a branch to Aberystwyth became the main line, and that was as far as the M&M got.

The line to Aberystwyth was finally authorised in 1865, and a construction contract was agreed with Davies & Beeston - the same Davies we have already met on Talerddig, with a new partner. By February 1866 the line from Pencader Junction in the south was open to Lampeter, and at the general meeting good progress on the Aberystwyth line was noted. Twelve months later, with the line now open to Strata Florida, attention was concentrated on the last section by a force of 450 workmen. At this time only two and a half miles of permanent way remained to be laid, though some earthworks and bridges were not finished, and no signalling had been installed. But by August all was ready for inspection, and the line was opened for traffic on 12 August 1867.

Celebrations were muted, though Davies gave a banquet at the Belle Vue Hotel, Aberystwyth, and the navvies enjoyed a dinner the following day. It was, apart from the tiny Van Railway in 1871, the last rail-

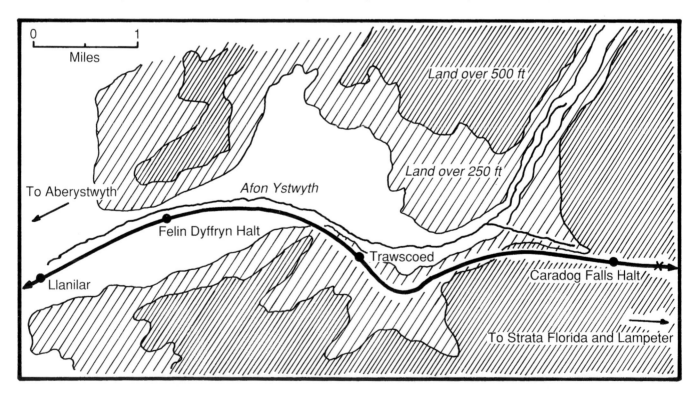

'43xx' Class 'Mogul' No 7334 draws into at Trawscoed platform with a light train heading for Aberystwyth on 29 May 1961. Note the sharp increase in grade to 1 in 111 and then 1 in 51 beyond the train. *Peter Hay*

way he was to build: he had had too much capital tied up in this company for too long.

'I feel,' he said at the banquet, 'when I am riding up through the cutting [Tanycraig, at the summit of the line], that these old rocks will tell a tale of Mr Beeston and me when we are gone.'

Trains travelling to Aberystwyth were faced, from the restart from Strata Florida station, with a sharp left-hand curve around the head of Tregaron Bog. There was a very short pitch of 1 in 79, followed at once by successive 10-chain pitches at 1 in 53 and 1 in 44. Then, after half a mile of 1 in 46, came about five chains of 1 in 55 and 20 chains of 1 in 367 to the top.

From Aberystwyth it was very much another story. A mile from the station there was a hump with 1 in 56 on the facing side and 1 in 51 on the other. At milepost 47½ (from Pencader Junction) there began a succession of short pitches at 1 in 55, 39, 42 and 47 - these led to 15 chains of 1 in 131 and a level through Llanrhystyd station. The next two and a half miles were comparatively easy, if irregular, and at Llanilar station a mile of 1 in 211 began. The slope increased progressively over the next mile to 1 in 174 and 166, and then eased again for half a mile at 1 in 207. A third of a mile at 1 in 179 led to the really hard work. It began near milepost 33 with a very short pitch of 1 in 85 followed by two 20-chain lengths at 1 in 45 and 41 respectively, and a quarter-mile at 1 in 44. There was then an easing to 1 in 62, 1000 and 111 through Trawscoed station; hardly surprisingly it was a difficult place to work, and runaways were frequent throughout the life of the line.

Seventy chains at 1 in 51 met the driver just beyond the platform end, and then half a mile at 1 in 43. A short 1 in 41 and slightly longer 1 in 46 brought the line to half a mile of 1 in 41, with another half-mile of 1 in 43 to follow and 50 chains of 1 in 42 after that. If their engine was still in one piece the crew could relax then, for they had reached the top, after three and a quarter miles of 1 in 51 or steeper. The vertical climb was about 300 feet, an average which makes it more severe, in its final section, than even Taleiddig.

It was never a lucrative undertaking. An Official Receiver was appointed in 1880, and the line was leased to the GWR from 1906, before that company took it over completely under an Act of 2 June 1911. Passenger traffic over the whole line ceased on 22 February 1965, and goods on 30 September 1973. The bay which its trains used at Aberystwyth remains in use, however, by the narrow-gauge trains of the Vale of Rheidol Light Railway - and drivers on that line have their climbing problems too.

# Llangunllo and Sugar Loaf

Like most railway companies within reach of South Wales (and one or two which weren't) the LNWR had ambitions towards that area of the Principality. West Wales had promising mineral deposits ripe for exploitation, in addition to which Swansea was, at that time, regarded as the most likely port to be developed for transatlantic traffic.

The route began with the Knighton Railway, branching from the LNWR/GWR Shrewsbury to Hereford line at Craven Arms. This was extended in

stages, first via the Central Wales Railway and further by the Central Wales Extension Railway as far as Llandovery, where it met lines projecting towards it from the Swansea area. There are two summits on this line, at Llangunllo on the CWR and Sugar Loaf on the CWER.

The former was the earlier, being authorised on 13 August 1859 as a line 19.75 miles long, beginning at an end-on junction with the Knighton Railway. The construction contract was let to Richard Hattersley with John Morton, who, earlier, had been closely connected with work on the GNR. Bad weather prevented a prompt start to construction, but work began at the end of March 1860, with the hope that Pen-y-Bont (about four-fifths of the line) would be complete by August the next year. By August 1860 shafts for the 645-yard tunnel at Llangunllo (Llwyncoch) had been sunk and earthworks at either end were almost complete.

At this point the company's money began to dry up, and this, combined with problems in the work, slowed progress. By the spring of 1861 work had begun on Knucklas viaduct, and another shaft had been sunk in the tunnel before bad weather intervened again. Hattersley began to be concerned about his payment, and he ultimately (and successfully) took his case to arbitration. By August 1863 the viaduct was finished and track was laid as far as the tunnel, the bore itself being completed in September. The line eventually opened to the public on 10 October 1865, though many of the architectural details were unfinished and some stations were simply temporary shelters. The line was worked by the LNWR under an Agreement of 1862.

The climb towards the first summit actually begins before Knighton station, but immediately beyond the platform it steepens to 1 in 194 for a mile and then 1 in 151 for a half-mile. Four miles at 1 in 60 forms the main part of the bank, punctuated by Knucklas sta-

tion, about a mile up it. A pitch of slightly under half a mile at 1 in 100 takes the line through the tunnel, which has a curved bore, and the summit is reached a few yards beyond the southern portal. At 980 feet above sea level it is the highest point on the route.

From here the line falls at 1 in 100 through Llangunllo station, and there is a mile and a half at 1 in 122 before a sharp half-mile at 1 in 80 leads to a minor summit. Llanbister Road lies just beyond, on a downslope (in this direction) of 1 in 90, and the line goes on falling, on easier gradients for the most part, to a point a mile and a quarter beyond Dolau, where a level almost a mile long begins. A short 1 in 362 leads up to another summit, at which the slope changes to 1 in 80 down and takes the line into Pen-y-Bont tunnel, 440 yards long. Two-thirds of the way through, the gradient steepens to 1 in 74, and this continues for a little more than a mile and a quarter. The line is now following the Ithon valley, and has but another two miles to run before reaching Llandrindod Wells on a rising gradient of 1 in 110.

The CWER was incorporated on 3 July 1860, for 27.25 miles of railway from Llandrindod to Llandovery, and Henry Robertson was appointed its engineer. Robertson was born in Banff in 1816, began his career at Port Glasgow, under Locke, and was made a Member of the Institution of Civil Engineers on 5 June 1849. He was responsible for many railways in North Wales, where he settled, and was elected Chairman of several of them, notably the three leading to this line. Later he became Liberal MP for Shrewsbury for two periods, from 1862-65 and 1874-80, and a JP for Merionethshire and Denbighshire, dying at Llandderfel in 1888, aged 72. We shall meet him several more times in this chapter.

An elaborate sod-cutting ceremony took place on Thursday 15 November, and work was put in hand at Llandovery and at the Sugar Loaf summit next day. After that, though, evidence of progress becomes conflicting. Newspapers of March 1861 indicate that work was well in hand, and yet it is not until 2 September 1863 that *The Times* reports:

'. . .the directors have entered into a contract for the construction with Mr R. Hattersley, who has commenced the works and will carry them out with as little delay as possible.'

The works were *not* speedily done, however, for it was the best part of five years after the Directors' pious hope quoted above before Lt Col Rich was able to inspect the line. It cost much more to build than had been estimated, and unstable rock and water both caused problems in Sugar Loaf tunnel. The contractors had difficulties too in the descent down the valley from the tunnel; Cynghordy viaduct required virtual rebuilding, and in 1867, before the section was completed, the company had to obtain an Act extending the time allowed for building the line.

At last, on 1 June 1868, Directors and officers made their first journey along the whole line, and an official opening ceremony was held. It was yet another four months, however, before it opened to the public on 8 October, and shortly afterwards both the CWER and CWR companies were absorbed by the LNWR under an Act of 25 June 1868.

From Llandrindod the line continues to rise at 1 in 110 for the best part of a mile before falling for three-quarters of a mile at 1 in 74. There is then a rise of half a mile or so, this length including a short pitch of 1 in 80, then a descent at 1 in 302 is followed by two and a half miles at 1 in 74 to cross the Wye near Builth Road. The Irfon valley south-westwards is now taken, towards Llangammarch and Llanwrtyd. Southward lies the high moorland area of Mynydd Eppynt, which dominates more and more as the line, rising steadily but not consistently for seven miles, crosses two viaducts over the River Irfon, near Garth, and approaches a point half a mile beyond Llangammarch station. From here two short levels are interspersed with slopes of 1 in 80 and 1 in 100, the latter slightly over a mile long. Another level, at a little over a mile, brings the line to Llanwrtyd, where the River Irfon's valley veers north, leaving the railway to continue on and up, along the valley of the little River Cledan. As the mountains crowd in to east and west, the third of a mile beyond the station is at 1 in 70, and the next two and a quarter miles, at 1 in 80, lead to the summit. This, 820 feet above sea level, is a short distance before the north end of the tunnel, a 1,000-foot curved bore cut through a spur of Sugar Loaf Mountain.

At the top the gradient changes abruptly to a downslope of 1 in 70 through the first 800 yards of the tunnel. At this point it becomes 1 in 60 and con-

**'Black Five' No 45283 blasts up the 1 in 60 that leads from Cynghordy to the southern portal of Sugar Loaf tunnel with the 10.25 am Swansea Victoria to Shrewsbury train on 10 June 1960.** *Hugh Ballantyne*

tinues thus for four and a half miles, giving north-bound trains by some way the most difficult climb on the entire route. The line runs down the valley of first the River Wyddon and then the River Bran, which, at Cynghordy, is crossed, still on 1 in 60, by the 18-arch viaduct of brick and sandstone which gave so much trouble. It stands 100 feet above the water, but, though higher, seems less impressive than Knucklas viaduct at the other end of the line.

This route remains as one of the few rural lines in Wales still open, albeit as a basic railway, singled and with passing places at Knighton, Llandrindod, Llanwrtyd, Llandovery and Llandeilo. BR, to its credit, makes an effort to encourage its use. Sugar Loaf Halt, built with two platforms at the summit of the line, was originally for railway purposes only, but it was opened to the public during the summer of 1991 on Sundays in connection with the 'Heart of Wales Rambler' service. The weekday service (Sept-May 1991/2) is of four trains daily in each direction, with an extra one on Saturdays.

# Torpantau (Seven-Mile Bank)

**S**outh Wales, the valleys and the docks were the places where people were making money during the 1850s. Brecon, though cut off from this wealth by the little matter of the Brecon Beacons, saw no reason why it should miss out, so a railway was promoted to cross the mountains to Dowlais, near Merthyr Tydfil, with the obvious hope that it might stretch further south in due course.

On 1 August 1859 the B&M (it very rarely gets, or got, its full name of Brecon & Merthyr Tydfil Junction Railway, for obvious reasons) was incorporated. That October it was estimated that the cost of the line would be £5,000 per mile (it actually cost more than three times that amount), and on 29 November *The Times* announced that the Board had 'entered into arrangements with responsible contractors for the construction and completion of the line.' The contractors concerned were Messrs Davies & Savin, who not only undertook to complete the line in two years, but to supply rolling-stock and plant

also. Davies saw the B&M as a north/south trunk route through Wales, but when his partnership was Savin was dissolved it was Davies who left. Savin took his brother-in-law, John Ward, as partner, and they set to work on Wednesday 18 January 1860, when first sods were cut at either end of Beacon (or Summit) tunnel. At that time it was hoped that the line from there to Merthyr could be complete by the end of the summer.

Joint consulting engineers were Henry Coneybeare (later Consulting Engineer in his own right) and J. C.

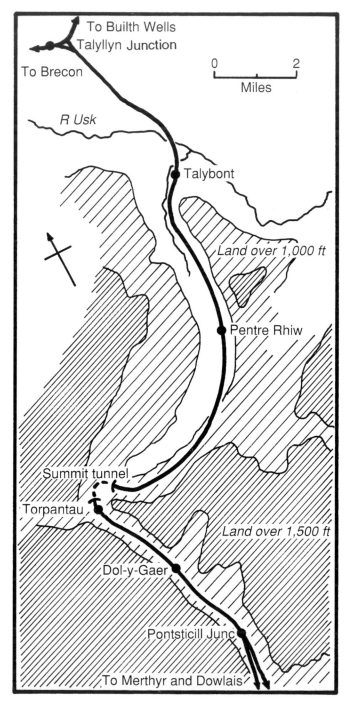

Birkinshaw, who seemed overly optimistic about the problems they would meet in the mountains. In August 1860 the shareholders were told that because of a decision to double the line, the cost would be increased. The Engineer also told them that a 'considerable portion of the line near Dowlais was ready for ballast and permanent way. . .' Twelve months later the contractor's works were within six miles of Brecon, and in March 1862 an opening to that town was anticipated by the following August.

But the building went slower than expected - how often already have we met that expression in these pages, and this will not be the last time - but the bore of the tunnel was through by 11 January 1862, and a trial trip over the line was arranged for 28 August, from Pant, north of Merthyr, to Talyllyn, east of Brecon. Freight workings began in April 1863 after an inspection by Capt Rich on 12 February, and there was a grand ceremonial opening, with banquet and the full works, on 1 May.

A crow flying between Brecon and the line's summit at Torpantau would have needed to travel only seven miles, but the train had to cover twice that distance. The climbing really began at Talybont, however, a mere seven miles out, where, because of sharp slopes at either end of the platform, the passing loops were extended at each end in case drivers had difficulty controlling their trains. Immediately on leaving the station, there was six and a half miles of unmitigated slog at 1 in 38 along a shelf cut in the eastern flank of Glyn Collwyn. An idea of what this entailed could be seen from the towpath of the canal,

where the old railway bridge, still in situ in 1992, crossed at an angle more appropriate to a road than a railway. The farms and dwellings served by Pentre Rhiw, about halfway up the hill, are mostly now beneath Talybont reservoir, but perhaps the most important duty of the signalman here was to man to points to the runaway siding that ran up the hillside into the trees. Hereabouts the line began to trend to the right (west), and by the time it reached the tunnel was actually heading north-west! Half a mile below the tunnel the gradient had eased to 1 in 68, and it reached its 1,313-foot summit at the west end of the 660-yard, sharply curved bore having climbed 925 feet in 7.25 miles.

The line, still swinging south, immediately ran into

Not strictly on the Seven-Mile Bank, but it does give some idea of the bleak nature of the countryside above Dowlais. A '56xx' Class 0-6-2T leaves Dowlais Top station with the 12.45 pm to Cardiff Queen Street on 5 September 1959. *Hugh Ballantyne*

the station at Torpantau. Hardly a buzzing metropolis this, and the line hurried on downwards, winding along the hillside for three miles at gradients of 1 in 47 and 1 in 55. At Pontsticill Junction the branch to Merthyr, built with LNWR aid and opened on 1 August 1868, diverged from that to Dowlais. The Merthyr line involved six and three-quarter miles of almost continuous 1 in 45/50 and two big viaducts, at Pontsarn, 455 feet long and 92 feet high, and Cefn Coed, 770 feet long and 115 feet high. Both still stand, though they have not been used for rail traffic since 4 May 1964 - the passenger service ended on 13 November 1961.

The B&M's best years were the first two decades of this century, and it came to its climax during the First World War, when it was used as one of the routes by which coal from South Wales reached the Navy at Scapa Flow. In this respect at least it achieved the 'trunk route' status which Davies had foreseen.

Almost inevitably 'Wild Runs' were quite frequent down the bank, often with spectacular results. A breakaway at Torpantau let a rake of wagons run back to collide head-on with a passenger train at Dolygaer: somewhat miraculously, no one was killed. It was a different story with the wild run of December 1878 though, when a double-headed coal train, with a third engine coupled behind the brake-van, ran out of control down the seven-mile bank. At an estimated speed of 60 mph it came off the rails at a curve half a mile south of Talybont and plunged down a 16-foot embankment, killing all the crewmen bar the fireman of the pilot and the driver of the banker.

The Company was grouped with the GWR from 1 January 1922. Under BR the banks closed as noted above, but part of the route at least survives. The trackbed passed first to the Forestry Commission, but the stretch from Pant to Torpantau was then privately leased and is now used by the narrow-gauge Brecon Mountain Railway between Pant and Pontsticill. This company hopes eventually to be able to lay rails through the tunnel to a station high above Glyn Collwyn, a spot with arguably the best view in Wales. So, possibly, the Seven Mile Bank may ring once again to the sound of steam engines. David Davies would have been delighted.

# Llanvihangel

In the early 1840s a grandiose scheme was promoted that would link Worcester with the iron-foundries of Merthyr Tydfil. It is difficult to see just what Worcester could have offered in exchange, and perhaps the general public thought so too, since the project foundered. What came out of it, though, was a line between Newport and Hereford, built by the Newport, Abergavenny & Hereford Railway incorporated in 1846.

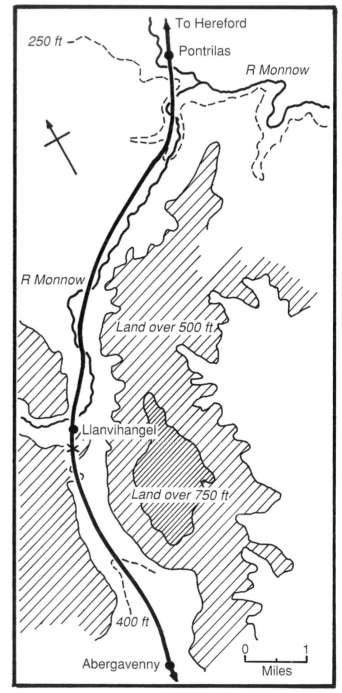

It began by buying the trackbeds of two tramways, but a money crisis in 1847-51 halted further progress. The LNWR tried to buy the undertaking, but Parliament prevented it: even so, when the line opened throughout (on 16 January 1854) the North Western worked it, and continued to do so until the company was absorbed by the Oxford, Worcester & Wolverhampton as part of the newly named West Midland Railway in 1860.

The company's Engineer was Charles Liddell, who reported in March 1851 that he expected the cost of the line to be £287,000 if laid single, £352,000 if double. On 29 March the *Railway Times* observed that:

'The Newport, Abergavenny & Hereford has made a good impression among landowners, who, much to their credit, have engaged to sell their land at its agricultural value, and in many cases to take the price in shares or in debenture.'

By the summer of 1851, however, the shareholders were becoming restless, for nothing seemed to be happening, but the Chairman reassured them at a meeting on 1 August that contracts would be prepared 'in a month's time'. An advertisement inviting tenders for rails appeared in the *Railway Times* on 22 November and 6 December, but nothing else seemed to happen that year. On 31 January 1852 that journal announced that the contractors for the whole line, 43.5 miles long, were to be Rennie, Logan & Thompson, of Newport, who expected to complete their work in less than two years. In fact, the stipulated completion date was the end of September the following year, and the anticipated total cost was half a million pounds.

By March 1852 work was well under way, as indeed it needed to be. In May Messrs Bailey & Co, of Nant-y-Glo, contracted to supply 21 tons of rail per day for two months from mid-July, and the next Directors' report was optimistic:

'. . .since the last meeting the works have been carried on by the contractor with great energy and rapidity. . . Of the

total quantity of 1,600,000 cubic yards of earthwork, 750,000 cubic yards have been done up to 27th July, being at the rate of 150,000 cubic yards per month. The average number of men employed daily on the line amounts at present to about 2,300.'

By October 1852 land had been bought for a station at Hereford, easily connectable with the Shrewsbury & Hereford line, also building at the time, and which the NA&HR was depending upon for through traffic. Liddell reported in February 1853 that bad weather had delayed progress, but that about three-quarters of the earthworks had been completed and two-thirds of the masonry. About eight miles of single line had also been laid and completed.

In mid-July it was expected that the deadline would be met, and the Chairman reported to a meeting on 31 August that 'the line of railway from Newport to Hereford was now completed, and Mr Rennie had passed over it on an engine a few days ago'.

It was announced that both routes would be publicly opened for traffic on 1 November, but there was a delay on the S&H line. A formal opening was held on 6 December 1853, but then a serious slip in the deep cutting at Llanvihangel caused a postponement of regular services along the whole line until 16 January 1854, though the Newport-Pontypool section opened on 2 January. Other than the earthworks on the banks, the only heavy engineering works were the bridges across the Wye at Hereford and the Usk at Penpergwm. The permanent way was laid in Barlow rail to standard gauge, with double track. The line between Pontypool and Newport, opened as single

**This was the first main-line run for many years by 'Modified Hall' 4-6-0 No 6998 *Burton Agnes Hall*. It took place on 31 May 1986, and the engine is here seen piloting No 5051 *Drysllwyn Castle* and the 'Red Dragon', from Swindon to Hereford, up Llanvihangel bank.** *Hugh Ballantyne*

track in 1852, was doubled in 1854.

Between Newport and Hereford lies a surprisingly uneven course along the Welsh border, which would, no doubt, have been easier had it not been felt necessary to deviate from the Usk valley to serve Pontypool as well as Abergavenny. The main summit is at Llanvihangel, which the line had to cross to get out of the Usk valley, but before reaching there northbound trains have a stiff pull up to Pontypool (the former Pontypool Road) from the start. Having set out along the Usk valley from Newport, crossing the river twice, the line swings sharply to the left beyond Caerleon, to follow the River Lwyd towards Cwmbran. The climb begins half a mile beyond Caerleon with a half-mile pitch of 1 in 148, with a very short level to the site of Ponthir station. A mile and a half of 1 in 120 follows past Llantarnam, beyond which is a short level and just over a mile and a half of 1 in 106. Two and a quarter miles of 1 in 95 lead to the summit easing at Pontypool, after which there is a two-mile drop at 1 in 104, a hump before Nantyderry, and another fall for almost a mile and a half at 1 in 80 towards Penpergwm, where the line is back in the Usk valley again, at least as far as Abergavenny.

Now begins the climb proper, as the line seeks to climb out of the Usk valley once more, with 1 in 100 and a level in short pitches. Almost a mile of 1 in 154 eases to 1 in 181 for another three-quarters of a mile, and steepens to 1 in 153 for just under another mile. The line trends away from the Usk and there is a short level through Abergavenny, then half a mile of 1 in 85 and one and three-quarters of 1 in 82. The final one and three-quarters to the top is at 1 in 92, which is the last climbing of any consequence before Hereford.

In the other direction things are little easier, for just more than a mile out of Hereford climbing begins at 1 in 220, 287 and 143 for successive half-miles. About 70 chains of 1 in 92 eases to a mile and a half of 1 in 104 to the first summit, after which the trend is generally downhill for a mile beyond Pontrilas, until 15 December 1941 the junction for the Golden Valley Railway to Hay-on-Wye. Now the line hugs the left bank of the River Monnow as a mile of 1 in 216 steepens to a mile and a half of 1 in 170 before a brief 1 in 300 down - about 10 chains. Then a mile of 1 in 204 is succeeded by about 70 chains at 1 in 100, near the top of which lies the site of Pandy station. Half a mile at 1 in 99 and a mile and a quarter of 1 in 100 lead to the final half-mile of 1 in 512 which tops the summit.

A long list of disposed-of stations litters this route. Those between Hereford and Abergavenny - Tram Inn, St Devereux, Pontrilas, Pandy and Llanvihangel

- closed to passengers on 9 June 1958, as did Penpergwm, Nantyderry and Lower Pontnewydd. Llantarnam, Ponthir and Caerleon survived until 30 April 1962, and now that stretch of line between Pontypool and Newport has closed in favour of the duplicating line via Cwmbran. The line is, however, still well-used as the main route between Cardiff and Manchester, and has been a popular route for steam tours in recent years.

# Church Stretton

The Shrewsbury & Hereford Railway was authorised on the same date as the NA&HR, 3 August 1846, and was almost the same length too, at 51 miles. Yet another parallel was a delay in starting work, though that could be said of a good many lines during this period.

The line's Engineer was Henry Robertson; though tenders were being advertised for in June 1847 in respect of a 'joint station at Shrewsbury', he was prevented by financial problems from letting the construction contract. The first general meeting was held in Chester on 4 August 1847, but thereafter things appear to have congealed until the end of 1850, when Brassey not only undertook to build the line, but also to run it. He appears to have had no partner in the venture, though Field is noted as being his agent for the project. The contract offered nothing notable in the way of engineering problems, though Dinmore tunnel was to occupy a good few man-hours.

By 8 March 1851 work had begun, and a start was made on the tunnel in October that year. A *Railway Times* report of 18 October noted 'rapid progress along the whole length', and remarked that the 'gradients throughout the line are superior to almost any other line; with a solitary exception they are not more than 1 in 100'. On 22 May it was announced that Messrs Bailey & Co, of Nant-y-Glo, had undertaken to supply 21 tons of rails every day for the next two months.

The line between Shrewsbury and Ludlow was opened on 20 April 1852, but the next information about the rest of it comes a year later, when, it was announced, the Ludlow-Hereford section was almost finished and would be open for traffic on 1

**Gradient profile, Church Stretton**

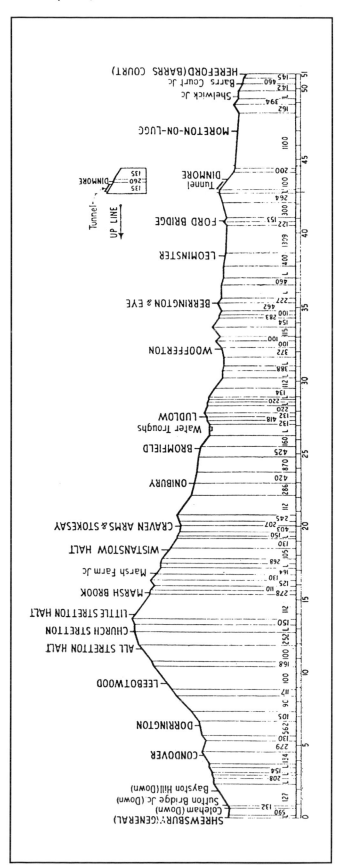

September. It wasn't though, because on 3 September came another report that the 'works on the line between Ludlow and Hereford are progressing to completion, and in all probability the whole line will be open for traffic late in October'.

This was highly optimistic, for in July the *Railway Record* reported that the progress of the works between Ludlow and Hereford 'is confined to the costly and heavy tunnel at Dinmore hill, [where] men are at work at both ends. They expect to meet in the middle in about a month.' One is forced to conclude that they didn't, for it was more than a year before the *Railway Times* told its readers, on 15 October 1853:

'The great work on the Shrewsbury line has been the Dinmore-hill tunnel. This undertaking is 1,060 [the official length is now given as 1,056] yards long, 18 feet high and 16 feet wide, and in its construction 3,250,000 bricks were used. The largest "heading" which has ever been driven is in this hill, and it [the tunnel] can be seen straight through. The whole has been 2.5 years in the making, during which time the mining has been of the most arduous character, in many places being equal to solid rock.'

In fact, the line opened throughout on 6 December 1853. Brassey's 'running' contract was altered to a nine-year lease from 1 July 1853, and he made such a success of it that by 1860 he was paying the company, at a rate of 4 per cent plus half the profits, enough to allow it to pay ordinary shareholders a dividend of 6 per cent. In 1862, when his lease expired, he was able to hand over a flourishing concern, which became LNWR/GWR joint property later that year.

The course of the line, heading north from Hereford, presents no major problem to an engine driver other than about a mile and a quarter of 1 in 100 up through Dinmore tunnel - that is until 1893, when the up line was diverted through a new bore at the somewhat easier slopes of 1 in 135 and 1 in 200. There is a hump to be got over at Ludlow, but a mile and a quarter beyond the station come 70 chains at 1 in 160 to Bromfield and easier slopes for the next three and a half miles. A mile beyond the site of Onibury station begins a pitch at 1 in 112, a mile and a half long, which leads to a fall to Craven Arms. Short pitches thereafter at 1 in 403, 150 and level lead to three-quarters of a mile at 1 in 130 and a similar distance at 1 in 105. Then more short pitches, none longer than half a mile and several considerably shorter, at 1 in 268, level, 164, 130, 125 (down), 110 (up) and 268 lift the line to the one and three-quarter miles of 1 in 112 which bring it to the summit.

From the other direction, however, it is a much

more serious affair, which starts almost as soon as Shrewsbury is left behind. A mile and a half of 1 in 132/127 leads to short pitches of level interspersed with 1 in 208 and 154. Three-quarters of a mile at 1 in 134 brings the line past Condover, and this pitch is followed by a down at 1 in 279. It is the last for a while, as 1 in 132 eases to a mile of 1 in 562 through Dorrington, steepening again beyond for about 50 chains of 1 in 105 and a mile of 1 in 90. Then comes half a mile of 1 in 117 and a one and three-quarters at 1 in 100 past Leebotwood. After a quarter-mile easing to 1 in 168, the slope returns to 1 in 100 for a further mile, and there is another mile at 1 in 252. Finally, a 30-chain level pitch becomes 1 in 150 for the last 30 chains to the summit.

In 1862 arrangements were made for doubling the hitherto single line between Hereford and Ludlow, though it remained single through the tunnel. The stations on this line have suffered from closures, Moreton-on-Lugg, Dinmore, Berrington & Eye, Bromfield, Onibury, Marshbrook, Leebotwood Halt, Dorrington and Condover Halt all having had their passenger services withdrawn on 9 June 1958. Ford Bridge had succumbed quite a while earlier, on 5 April 1954, while Woofferton, the junction for Tenbury Wells, lasted until the branch service finished on 31 July 1961. The line is still well used, however, and has seen a number of steam railtours in recent years.

# Gresford

There was once a railway called the North Wales Mineral Railway. It ran from Wrexham to a quay on the Dee estuary near Saltney, its original purpose being simply to 'open the Rhuabon and Brombo [both sic] mineral fields' and to form a link between coalfield and waterside. By the time it was open, a line through to Ruabon and Shrewsbury had been mooted, and the original extension company (the Shrewsbury, Oswestry & Chester Junction) had amalgamated with the NWMR to form the Shrewsbury & Chester Railway. One might reflect that we have the fact that the line was originally projected as a mineral line to thank for its course. Had it been conceived from the outset as a line between Chester and Shrewsbury it

might have followed the Dee valley instead of taking to hills, there would have been no need to surmount Marford Hill by Gresford bank, and it would not be appearing in these pages.

The NWMR's Engineer was Henry Robertson, and he laid out his route to include a gradient almost four miles long of 1 in 82.5 up the east side of the valley of the River Alyn from Rossett to Wrexham, with the village of Gresford in the middle, that same Gresford whose bells are named as one of the seven wonders of Wales. The contractor was Brassey, Mackenzie & Stephenson, with an agent named G. Meakin.

At the first meeting of shareholders, reported in the *Chester & North Wales Chronicle* of 6 September 1844, it was explained to them that:

'The line will. . .be a single line of way, but with land and bridges for a double line. A great proportion of the land. . .has already been arranged for on favourable terms. Tenders will shortly be received for the execution of the works, and the

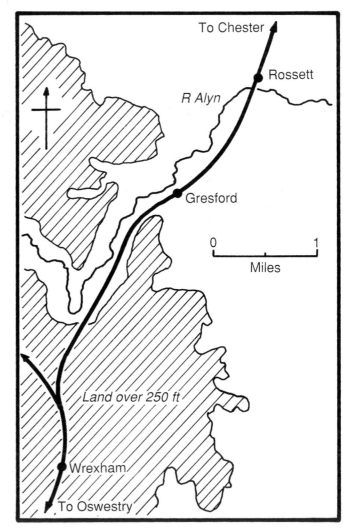

94

directors calculate that by the ensuing autumn the line will be open for traffic. . .'

This, as ever, was optimistic, for it was 11 months before the company advertised for 'a person qualified to superintend the carriage department and the building. . .of carriages'. In September 1845 the Engineer reported that three-quarters of the earthwork had been removed. The material in the cuttings was chiefly sand and gravel, and was, he said, 'most favourable for the economical maintenance of the way'. Masonry and bridgework was well advanced, and on the 'completion of the embankment at Marford Hill, now rapidly closing, the permanent way will be quickly extended to the river Dee'. It had been decided to lay double track instead of single, and opening was now hoped for by the end of the next June.

By February 1846 a single line of track had been laid and used, and the contractor was busy laying a second set of rails. The stations at Rosset (sic) and Gresford, and the wharf on the river Dee, 'are in a very forward state', reported the *Chester Chronicle*. By October, though the stations on the Wrexham/Ruabon section were incomplete, the line was considered ready for its Board of Trade inspection, duly made by Maj Gen Pasley on 21 October 1846. An opening was announced in the above journal's issue of 30 October, for the following Wednesday, 4 November.

A special trip over the line was made by Directors and guests on the 2nd, and the line opened to the public without fuss, as announced. The *Chester Chronicle* afforded the event no more than a single paragraph in its issue of 6 November, though, to be fair, there had been extensive coverage of the company's General Meeting in the previous week's issue. Despite the easy cuttings, the line cost £315,000, or around £14,000 per mile, including the branches at the Wrexham end.

The climb can strictly be said to begin a few yards south of Balderton, with a mile at 1 in 200. There is then a downgrade of just under a mile, this time at 1 in 360, before 70 chains or so up at 1 in 264 starts the climb proper. An easing to 1 in 412 through Rossett is brief, and from just beyond the platform end the line climbs steadily at 1 in 82.5, curving slightly to the

**There was still double track on Gresford bank on 23 March 1977 as 'King' Class No 6000 *King George V* (with one Bulmers Pullman car behind the tender) storms upgrade with the 'Cathedrals Express', running between Chester and Hereford.** *Hugh Ballantyne*

right to contour round the hill on which Gresford stands. Beyond the site of the station, however, there is a sharp twist left, and the top of the bank is two miles further on.

This is not, in fact, the summit of the route, which occurs at the site of Wynnville Halt, some 25 chains short of Ruabon station. To reach this point the line continues on a somewhat jagged profile, with short pitches of 1 in 100 or thereabouts, alternating with downs (both at 1 in 200) or levels. This summit, at 375 feet above sea level, is some 75 feet higher than the top of Gresford bank.

Thankfully this line is still with us, forming a useful part of the system. It has been singled between Wrexham and Saltney Junction, and has suffered station rationalisation, none of the stations shown on the RCH maps of 1903 between Chester and Wrexham surviving save those two. It was no clean sweep, however - the last to open, Balderton, on 1 July 1901, was the first to go, on 3 March 1952. Eight years passed before the next went, Saltney, on 12 September 1960, and Gresford Halt saw its last passengers on 9 September 1962, closing next day. Services to Rossett ceased on 26 October 1964.

Now diesel multiple units maintain a passenger service of 16 up and 15 down trains daily between Wrexham and Chester (winter 1991/2), with six each way on Sundays. 'Welsh Marches Express' steam rail-tours have used the route regularly recently.

# 5
# ACROSS THE PENNINES

## Hopton

The Cromford & High Peak Railway, the first line to make a crossing of the Peak District, was incorporated just before the Stockton & Darlington opened and began its operations shortly before the Liverpool & Manchester. There were some very steep pitches in the line's course, notably Hopton incline, which, at 1 in 14, became the steepest solely adhesion-worked sec-

tion of railway in the United Kingdom.

This incline barely qualifies for these pages, but it did run a passenger service for 20 years, albeit a fairly rudimentary one. In any case, the idea behind the scheme was actually not passengers, but a wish to link the freight traffic on the Peak Forest Canal at Whaley Bridge with that on the Cromford Canal. In fact, it was first conceived as a canal link, but the heavy works likely to be involved, and the difficulty, sometimes, of finding water in the limestone hills prompted the substitution of a railway.

Not that this is intended to indicate any great technological advance, for Josias Jessop, engineer of the 33-mile line, simply used the current thinking in canal terms and built long, more or less level sections linked by inclined planes instead of flights of locks. The inclines were worked by cable, and horses took

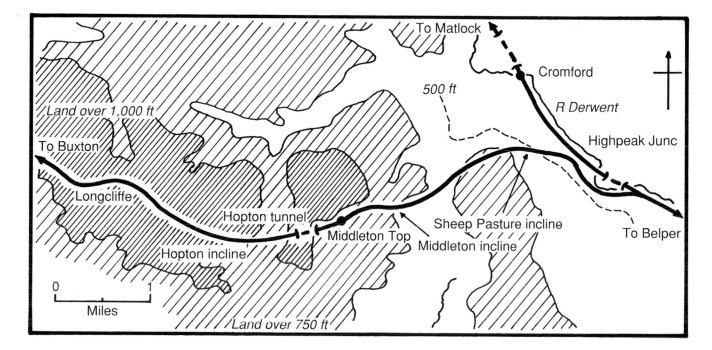

care of traffic on the level sections, which held tight to the contours at the expense of some very sharp curves, notably one at Gotham, a lonely spot 750 feet up in the hills.

And this is how it might have stayed, for the line was isolated until 1853 when a junction with the Midland's line to Rowsley was put in two miles south of Cromford station. Four years later a link was also made at the Whaley Bridge end, by a junction with the Stockport, Disley & Whaley Bridge Railway. The company had been re-incorporated on 26 June 1855, and at this point the LNWR began to take an interest, hoping that the line might give it a new route to London. Steam engines (small ones, naturally, in view of the curves), began to appear on the Derbyshire uplands. A passenger service between Cromford and Ladmanlow (near Buxton) opened on 30 June 1856, and was extended to Whaley Bridge, probably during the next year.

The North Western leased the line under an Act of 1862, but alas for its hopes, the passenger service came to nothing. It was never anything more elaborate than a carriage coupled to the goods trains, and as a journey might take up to six hours it was obviously quicker, after 1867, to use the Midland route between Whaley Bridge and Cromford. The service ceased, somewhat abruptly, but voluntarily, in 1876 after an accident between two goods trains in mist, in

which a fireman was killed. In his report, Col Yolland suggested that if passengers were to be carried, as he had been informed, on some trains, then the company should submit itself for inspection in accordance with the Regulation of Railways Act of 1842. In fact, the company had already questioned the future of the passenger service, which was reputedly failing, no doubt for the reasons mentioned above. It clearly made better economic sense to drop the passenger traffic rather than upgrade the line, so it ceased officially at the end of April 1876.

A service both more useful and long-lasting was the conveyance of tenders of water to factories, quarries, farms and cottages in the district. This perhaps seems odd in an area that has no shortage of rainfall - the problem was (and still is, for that matter) in retaining it, since the water tends to soak away almost instantly through the porous limestone. And it was, after all, the factories and quarries upon which the railway depended for its livelihood; well they served it too, for the final section did not close until September 1967.

The North Western absorbed the C&HPR in 1887,

**Hopton incline on 4 May 1934. LMS 0-4-0T No 7527 is about to reach the point at which the gradient steepens from 1 in 20 to 1 in 14. Note that the fourth vehicle in the rake behind the engine is a tender, no doubt one of those by which the railway maintained water supplies to the businesses along the line.** *H. C. Casserley*

and the section between Ladmanlow and Shallcross was abandoned five years later. On 27 June 1892 the stretch between Parsley Hay and Hurdlow, together with a short length between Hurdlow and Hindlow, was re-opened for goods as an Ashbourne to Buxton link. A passenger service began on 1 June 1894, leaving only Parsley Hay to Cromford of the original line. Middle Peak to High Peak Junction (Cromford) closed on 9 April 1967, and the branch was served from the Parsley Hay end only until the following September, when it closed completely.

Of the inclines themselves, there were three in the 14.5-mile stretch between High Peak Junction and Parsley Hay. The first was Sheep Pasture, about a mile from the junction, which had a ruling gradient of 1 in 9 and was cable-worked. Cromford shed stood at its foot. At the top was a mile of level going before Middleton Incline was reached, a quarter of a mile long at 1 in 8 and also cable-worked. Middleton Top shed was at its summit, and from here there are magnificent views to the south and east. The original winding engine, dating from 1825, survives here, preserved and restored to working order. Beyond here the line bore left, contouring for three-quarters of a mile or so before plunging into the short Hopton tunnel. This burrowed through an outcrop of limestone and, with no brick arch, suffered from damp. Beyond lay the embankment which led to Hopton incline - this too was cable-worked at first, but was modified in 1877 to allow locomotive working.

This was the summit of the line, for it now fell towards Longcliffe, thereafter contouring for some three miles at 110 feet and then falling gently before swinging sharp left, right, right again then left round a deep re-entrant at Gotham. Maintaining its height, the line reached, after another five miles or so, Parsley Hay. Sadly, steam no longer takes this journey, but the route is not lost to us, for now the trackbed forms the High Peak Trail.

# Peak Forest

During the period of railway expansion in the mid-1840s it occurred to the Midland Railway that every other company within, as you might say, spitting distance of Manchester had a line going there,

and why was the Midland missing out? As with most others, crossing the Pennines was a problem, but they had managed, so why not the Midland?

The Manchester, Buxton, Matlock & Midland Junction Railway, an independent company though strongly backed, one suspects, by the Midland, was authorised piecemeal under six separate Acts between 1846 and 1848. But these only took the line to Rowsley. The Act for the section in which we are interested here had to wait until 30 June 1862.

The line from Rowsley went first to Buxton, but there was a junction at Peak Forest which took a line east of the town to make a link with the Manchester, Sheffield & Lincolnshire Railway's line near Bugsworth [Buxworth] bridge. Its Engineer was W. H. Barlow, and the contractors were Eckersley & Baylis.

It was not an easy line to build, involving two tunnels, one of them very long, many deep rock cuttings and a substantial viaduct at the Chinley end to carry the line across a steep, narrow valley to the MS&LR. This viaduct was completed on 8 June 1865, when a 'last stone' ceremony at the site was performed by Barlow, using, says the *Buxton Advertiser* of 17 June, '. . .a handsome silver trowel, which was presented to him by the contractors for the consummation of his work. A party of 24 gentlemen afterwards repaired to the King's Arms for luncheon.'

But there was still a good way to go. The line opened first, for goods only, on 1 October 1866, and closed a month later. As the *Buxton Advertiser* for 2 February 1867 put it:

'The line. . .had not been in use for a few weeks ere a serious landslip occurred in a viaduct and embankment at Bugsworth, which necessitated a deviation and the construction of a viaduct and new embankment of about a quarter of a mile in length. The contractors. . .applied their large resources with great energy, and had as many men as it was possible to find room for employed on the works night and day, as many as 400 being at work at one time.'

What had happened was that, after heavy rain, 16 acres of land had slid into the valley and a bridge and a five-arch viaduct were destroyed. A quick diversion was organised, including a 1,000-foot timber viaduct, two skew bridges and a deep rock cutting. Capt Rich inspected the new work on Tuesday 29 January 1867 and passed it for traffic. The line re-opened for goods on 24 January 1867, and carried its first passengers on 1 February.

From the Derby side the line rises in a series of steps, beginning at Lee Wood tunnel, a mile and a

Bakewell station, looking south, as Fowler '4MT' 'Crab' No 42873 trundles a long rake of loaded mineral wagons northwards and prepares to tackle the mile of 1 in 102 that follows the easing through the station. The date is June 1958. *Hugh Davies*

half south of Cromford. From this point a mile of 1 in 299 is followed by a mile and a half at 1 in 177, which takes the line through both Cromford station and Willersley tunnel. Matlock Bath station is near the top of this pitch, and short stretches at easier grades lead through the High Tor tunnels to Matlock, the present BR terminus of the line.

Beyond Matlock was a fall at 1 in 170 for half a mile before easier upgrades took over for the next three and a half miles. A quarter of a mile at 1 in

102 led up to Rowsley, and 50 chains of 1 in 184 thereafter brought the line to the foot of one and two-thirds of a mile at 1 in 102 through Haddon tunnel. Beyond was another step, down for 25 chains at 1 in 145, but this was a brief respite only, for another pitch of 1 in 102 then began, continuing for 50 chains. There was a brief section at 1 in 229, with Bakewell station at the end of it, and then another mile at 1 in 102, ending in an easing to 1 in 178 at Hassop. More 1 in 100, for a mile and a quarter this time, a brief easing to 1 in 151 for Great Longstone station, then half a mile at 1 in 114 to the south portal of Headstone tunnel. Here there was another step, down at 1 in 107 for half a mile and over the famous viaduct against which Ruskin grew so hot in its days of building, before a sharp half-mile rise to Monsal Dale at 1 in 125.

Beyond the station the gradient steepened to 1 in 120 for a short distance, then still further, on to a pitch of 1 in 100 that lasted for just under two miles and took the line through Cressbrook and Litton tunnels, 471 and 515 yards long respectively. At the top of this stretch was the final step, a quarter of a mile down at 1 in 100 to a level through Miller's Dale, where, just beyond the viaduct, the line rose for almost a mile at 1 in 101. This was through the Chee Tor tunnels, where, soon after building had begun, a navvy was killed when struck by a contractor's wagon. At the northern portal of the second the slope eased slightly to 1 in 111 for 25 chains. A similar distance into the next pitch, at 1 in 90, was Peak Forest Junction.

On the Peak Forest route

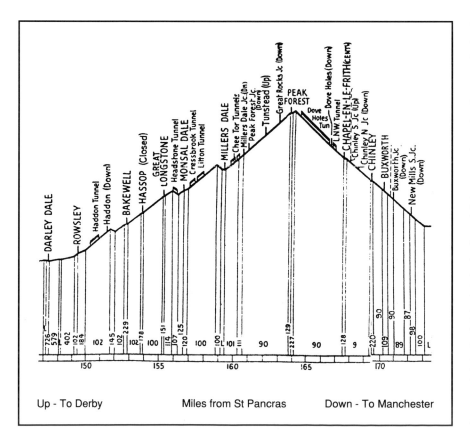

Up - To Derby          Miles from St Pancras          Down - To Manchester

**Gradient profile, Peak Forest**

**Ex-Midland 4-4-0 Compound No 41152 heads south across Monsal Dale viaduct with a short passenger train on its way down from Peak Forest on 15 May 1953.**
*H. C. Casserley*

there are (this section still carries freight) another two and a half miles of 1 in 90, about halfway along which is Great Rocks tunnel, 161 yards long. Then comes a 10-chain easing to 1 in 129 and a final 10 chains or so of 1 in 227, bringing the line to its 985-foot summit.

From the Manchester side the climb is simpler to describe, beginning at Cheadle Heath with a mile and a half of 1 in 100. A mile and a quarter of 1 in 140 comes next, then half a mile at 1 in 110, a quarter-mile at 1 in 120 before a half-mile easing to 1 in 200 leads to Hazel Grove. Then three-quarters of a mile of 1 in 100 takes the line to the north portal of Disley tunnel, and just before entering it the gradient eases to 1 in 132. The tunnel pierces the 600-foot ridge between the Goyt and Mersey valleys, and was opened in 1901, when the Midland built its own diversion from New Mills South Junction, whence they had shared GCR track to Manchester, to Heaton Mersey. It is 2 miles 346 yards long, brick-lined throughout, with stone portals, and with a 27-foot, horse-shoe shaped span. Nine shafts were used in its construction, which took two years.

There is three-quarters of a mile of level beyond the tunnel, but then a similar distance up at 1 in 100 and a quarter-mile at 1 in 98 leads to New Mills South Junction. Another quarter-mile at 1 in 87 continues the climb, easing almost unnoticeably to 1 in 89 for the next three-quarters of a mile to Buxworth Junction. Another imperceptible easing to 1 in 90 for half a mile, and half a mile at 1 in 109 brings the line past Buxworth, and it steepens to 1 in 90 again for the next three-quarters of a mile to Chinley. A brief 1 in 220 through the station is superseded by another two miles at 1 in 90, with the Sheffield line diverging to the left at Chinley Junction, about halfway up the pitch. Chapel-en-le-Frith stood at the head of a short pitch of 1 in 128, and then comes the final three and a half miles at 1 in 90 which leads to the top by way of Dove Holes tunnel.

This is cut through Cow Low, which stands some 265 feet above the bore, and was not an easy tunnel to master. Contractors, knowing the nature of the underlying rock, were reluctant to quote for its building, the lowest tenders (from Messrs Rennie) coming out at £179,595, substantially higher than the MR estimate of £139,986. In the end the MR undertook the job itself and reckoned it saved more than £43,000 by doing so. The resident Engineer was James Campbell.

Various underground streams needed to be overcome, after which eight shafts were sunk and the bore was begun from the lower, or north-western, end. About a third of the work was through mountain limestone, but a surprising quantity took in also old red sandstone and shales, the sandstone in particular being hard to work. Like Disley, the tunnel's lining is in brick with stone portals and wing-walls; it is 1 mile 1,224 yards long, and has a horseshoe-shaped span of 26 feet. An underline culvert carried away excess water, which, in steam days, supplied the water columns along the line down to New Mills. The vertical fall from one end of the tunnel to the other is 99 feet 6 inches.

The line had not been open long before there was another collapse, this time in Dove Holes tunnel, on 19 June 1872. Yet another, a more serious one, occurred on 2 February 1940, also in the tunnel. But an indication of the importance of the line is given by the fact that despite these the line did not lose its passenger service until 1 July 1968, and it is still well used to serve the many limestone quarries in the area.

The stretch between Buxton and Matlock is now the subject of a preservation scheme by Peak Rail. There is activity in the yard at Buxton, while the first stretch of a working line opened on 15 December 1991, between Matlock and Darley Dale.

# Cowburn

As early as February 1864 the *Sheffield Independent* was wondering why businesses in Sheffield, to get to Manchester, a mere 36 miles away as the crow flies, had to make a detour via Woodhead. 'In these days of greater skill and practice in the overcoming of natural obstacles,' it remarked, 'engineers pronounce works to be feasible from which the Stephensons and Brunel shrunk: and we may hope the time is not distant when we may perforate the Peak and wind through its valleys if we do not climb its hill.'

Yet it was to be another 20 years before a company projected a scheme to remedy this by building a more direct line through the Hope valley; it was called the Dore & Chinley Railway, and it obtained its Act on 28 July 1884. Nothing loath to having an alternative route between its Sheffield/Derby line at Dore and its Peak Forest line at Chinley, the MR happily subscribed (up to £100,000 was authorised by an Act dated 25 July 1885), and when the engineering problems became too much for the small company, the larger one took it over, absorbing it from 24 July 1888.

The line branches west from the MR main line at Dore, and between there and Chinley is a little over 20 miles long. Unfortunately, 25 per cent of it was

required to be in tunnel, and it was this that stymied the original company.

There were, it must be said, more problems than mere finance that stood in the way of construction. Percy Pickard was the resident Engineer, and during the construction of Totley tunnel he had to cope with outbreaks of scarlet fever, diphtheria and smallpox. Little wonder that the navvy camps were put under quarantine. Oh, and just for good measure there was a typhoid epidemic too! Hardly surprising, perhaps, that the contractors had difficulty not only in obtaining labour but in retaining it. Mind you, they weren't the only ones complaining, because in March 1889, according to the *Buxton Advertiser*, local lime quarry owners were blaming a scarcity of workers on 'the railway work available in the neighbourhood'.

On Monday 4 November 1889 Henry Ennis, a navvy on the works, was charged with drunkenness. Having pleaded guilty, he was fined 3 shillings, the amount found on him, including costs. Next day Richard Green, working on the Dore tunnel, was killed by a fall of earth. It was to be another three years before the bores from either end met, on 19 October 1892. After it all, Thomas Oliver, of Horsham, the contractor for the eastern ten miles of the line, including Totley tunnel, was given a bonus of £14,300 for his work.

Work on Cowburn tunnel began in 1890, but this too was not without its mishaps - Thomas Griffiths and George Smith, looking for work in March 1891, were knocked down by moving wagons in the working, while that November a Thomas Finch was 'hit by a stone propelled by a shot in the tunnel'. John Price Edwards won the contract for the Cowburn end - he failed after three years, but the company kept him on as a supervisor, and later repaid his debts.

The line was opened on 6 November 1893 for goods, and excursion trains began to use it on 13 May. The stations, built by Walker & Slater for a total cost of £11,500, were used by passengers for the first time on 25 June 1894. At last the *Sheffield Independent*'s plea was granted, and the Peak had been 'perforated'. It remains so to this day.

A mile and a half of 1 in 100 lifts the line from Dore to a few yards inside Totley tunnel, where it eases to 1 in 176 for half a mile before steepening to 1 in 150 for the next mile and a half. Still in tunnel, a level section now begins, continuing for two miles, by which time the line is once more in the open and half a mile beyond Grindleford station. There is a down for about 50 chains of 1 in 200, followed by a similar length of level to Hathersage, then 25 chains down, again at 1 in 200. Fifty chains up at 1 in 200 leads to

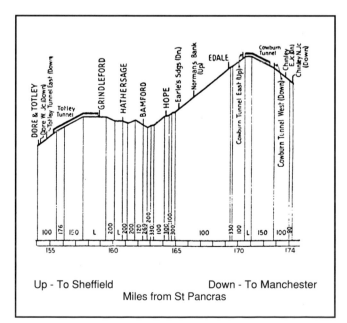

Up - To Sheffield          Down - To Manchester
Miles from St Pancras

**Gradient profile, Cowburn**

the top of a hump, the line descending on the other side first at 1 in 120 for 50 chains, then at 1 in 269 for half as far.

Now climbing begins again. A quarter of a mile at 1 in 200 leads to a similar length easing to 1 in 330, then steepening for 70 chains at 1 in 100. An easing to 1 in 300 carries the line through Hope station, and this pitch is followed by short lengths at 1 in 100 and,

again, 1 in 300. The next four and a half miles are at 1 in 100, at the end of which stands Edale station, with a brief easing to 1 in 330 just beyond it. Another mile at 1 in 100 lifts the line to the summit level, which begins at the east portal of Cowburn tunnel

**Class '8F' No 48723 labours up the 1 in 100 towards Cowburn tunnel with an Earl's Sidings-Stockport cement train on 1 May 1968.** *Les Nixon*

and continues for half a mile. Now the line falls at 1 in 150 for a mile and three quarters, and a further mile and a quarter of 1 in 100 brings it to Chinley Junction, where the Peak Forest line comes in from the south, or left.

So what of the tunnels, which, as we have found, make up a quarter of the route? Totley, when it was built, was second only to the Severn tunnel (completed seven years earlier) in length, though at 3 miles 950 yards was still some way behind the latter's seven miles plus. It was, by a substantial amount, the longest tunnel on the MR. Because of its depth, shafts, five of them, were only practicable at the shallower, eastern end. Working conditions were less than ideal, not only because of the air problem, but because inrushes of water repeatedly occurred. Coal and shale were the main formations encountered, and building took more than four years: the tunnel is brick-lined throughout, using some 30 million bricks.

Cowburn tunnel is shorter, only 2 miles 182 yards, but it lies deeper than Totley. One shaft only was sunk, and that was 900 feet deep, down to a circular side-chamber on the north side of the bore. A contemporary account tells that the limestone and millstone grit through which it is cut was so hard that drilling was difficult, even with the comparatively advanced equipment that was by then available. The profile is horseshoe-shaped, with a span of 27 feet and a height from rail level of 22 feet 6 inches; lined with brick for the most part, there is some stonework.

The line is still busy, of course, forming a well-used route from Sheffield to Manchester, providing perhaps a counter to those who would argue that the later-built lines are the ones that have been weeded out.

# Woodhead

The genesis of the line through the Pennines at Woodhead was a need to link Manchester and Sheffield by something which provided a swifter contact than the canal system. An early scheme involving inclines powered by steam engines was not pursued, and a similar fate befell an idea, published as being by George Stephenson, of surmounting the summit at Rushop Edge using limestone quarried in the locality to weight an incline, thus using building stone on its way down to power passengers on their way up.

Charles Blacker Vignoles was born in Ireland on 31 May 1793. He began an army career, but joined Rennie in 1825 in building the line to Brighton. He was engineer of the first railway in Ireland (opened on 17 December 1834), and in 1837 was to introduce the flat-bottomed rail which was named after him. Now he was sponsored by businessmen in Manchester, Sheffield, Ashton-under-Lyne and Stalybridge to survey a new railway route. Locke made a survey too, and both presented reports, on 14 October 1836.

They disagreed, of course, and it was decided to lengthen the proposed summit tunnel from two miles to three. Westbound, the route was to follow the valley of the River Don to Deepcar, where, via a tunnel through the ridge at Thurgoland, it was to cross a tributary and use its valley through Penistone to Dunford Bridge. This was the summit of the climb - at the eastern portal of the tunnel the line would begin to descend at 1 in 201, maintaining this slope for its entire 3 miles 22 yards. The climb from the other side was rather less strenuous.

On the grounds of expense it was decided to bore only one tunnel, though land had been bought for a dual bore. The summit, by virtue of the longer tunnel, was now 943 feet above sea level. Locke described the project as one 'of great mercantile importance', and it was authorised, with very little trouble, to the Sheffield, Ashton-under Lyne & Manchester Railway on 5 May 1837. A first sod was cut by Lord Wharncliffe at the west end of the proposed tunnel on 1 October 1838, and the line had been staked out before the following spring. Land proved cheap to acquire, mainly, no doubt, on account of the bleak landscape that the line was to pass through.

The first contract was let to John Smith, Eckersley & Worswick, and shafts were sunk by the SA&M on the centre line of a twin-bore, with driftways. By the summer of 1839 a further contract for the section between Broadbottom and Dinting had been let to Miller & Blackie of Liverpool, but even at this early stage money problems began to pinch. Planning fell behind schedule, Vignoles claiming that the specifications, gradients, working drawings and so on took months longer than intended.

Nicholas Wood was asked to report. Then Vignoles, having taken shares in an effort to get work started, found that he could not pay his calls, and resigned in December 1839 from an impossible position. Locke was appointed in his place as Engineer-in-chief from 2 January 1840, at an annual salary of £750 initially, to be increased by £250 when work extended beyond the tunnel and the line to the west of it.

As when Locke took over on the London & Southampton (Chapter 1), he put work in the way of Brassey, allotting him a 19-mile contract, and the work

rate at once began to improve. Henry & Co, the contractors for the Etherow viaduct, were replaced by Smith & Hattersley - Richard Hattersley worked at Standedge, and we have already met him in Central Wales, by which time he had branched out on his own account. This viaduct was to be 506 feet long, crossing the valley at a maximum height of 136 feet. Its foundation stone was laid on 5 March 1842, and it was open by the end of that year. Dinting viaduct was almost three times as long, at

GCR 'Director' 4-4-0 No 550 energetically approaches Woodhead tunnel from the west in the days just prior to the Grouping. *H. C. Casserley*

1,455 feet, but not so high, crossing a tributary of the River Etherow at 121 feet, and the nearby road at 90 feet. It was, wrote the Rev Oliphant Vignoles, C. B. Vignoles's son 'carried out by Mr Locke according to his predecessor's [Vignoles's] design, with a few modifications rendered necessary by the shortness of funds'. This consisted

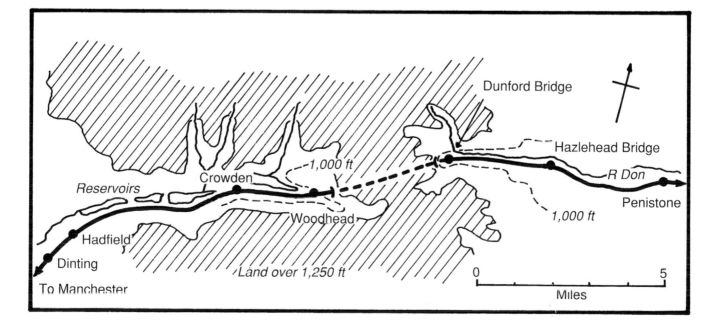

**Woodhead station, with the tunnel beyond, as an eastbound LNER express, headed by a Class 'B17' 'Footballer' 4-6-0, heads towards one of the original single bores.** *H. C. Casserley*

of a laminated timber superstructure carried on masonry piers.

On 8 November 1841 Locke reported that he did not expect the cost of the line to be more than 10 per cent above Vignoles's estimate, but that the tunnel would cost £207,000 instead of £106,000, principally because more powerful engines would be required to keep the shafts free of water. Three days later the first 8.25 miles of line was ready, and the Directors made a first experimental trip from Manchester to Godley. This section was duly passed by the Inspector, and brought into public use without ceremony on 17 November.

The section from Glossop to Woodhead was officially opened on 7 August 1844 (to the public next day), and 800 workmen on the Dinting and Longdendale contracts were given a free quart of ale. By June the next year the line to the tunnel was nearing completion, and was opened without formality on 14 July. Each workman was given free refreshment to the value of 1 shilling, and the *Sheffield Iris* waxed lyrical on the decorations and appointments 'of some of the most splendid carriages that have ever adorned a line of railway'.

The tunnel itself was inspected on 20 December 1845 by Gen Pasley, preceded, said the *Manchester Guardian*, 'by a wagon bearing six men with torches, which were held to the roof and sides. . .', and was formally opened two days later. A 'substantial collation' awaited the official party at Cutlers Hall, Sheffield, while all those engaged on building the tunnel were given a bonus of £1 and enjoyed some portion of a bullock that had been roasted on a rail. The line opened to the public on 23 December.

A single bore to take two tracks had been intended, but a single-track bore had been substituted. No doubt this saved money at the time, but, as with the Lickey, was it really such an economy in the long run? But it was unquestionably a magnificent engineering achievement.

At 3 miles 22 yards it was the longest tunnel in the country at the time of its completion. It was built on a slope of 1 in 201, through millstone grit, broken by shales, slate, clay and milder beds of sandstone. The building technique was to work from each end towards the middle, and outwards from each of five vertical shafts. The centre-line of the bore was transferred from the surface by means of wires suspended in the shafts, and the accuracy of the method was proven by the fact that there was never more than three inches of deviation. The task of building lasted six years and, though the statistics tend to be somewhat vague, as many as 1,500 men were said to be at work on the tunnel alone. By 1842, when Hattersley and Nicholson (he of Standedge) were appointed to complete the work, only about 1,000 yards remained to be bored. Nicholson took the eastern end and the greater part of the work, Hattersley the other.

The first rails, keyed into chairs on stone sleepers, were 16 feet long, of wrought iron, weighing 75 lb per yard. The climb was reasonably fair in distribution, just over half the 41.5 miles between Manchester and Sheffield facing trains from Manchester. It began with a shade under a mile of 1 in 382, and a shade under two miles of 1 in 173, before things became more serious with three-quarters of a mile of 1 in 100. A mile of 1 in 133 and easing gradients brought the line into Guide Bridge and half a mile beyond it. Then 15 chains of 1 in 77, followed by three-quarters of a mile of 1 in 97 disposed of the steepest pitches on the route in either direction.

Next 1 in 185 to Newton and 1 in 143 for a mile and a half beyond took in Godley Junction, and a mile at 1 in 462 led to Mottram, known over the years as Mottram & Broadbottom, and plain Broadbottom. A mile and a quarter of 1 in 122 carried the line across Etherow viaduct, but Dinting viaduct, beyond this pitch, lay on the level. Dinting station, at the east end of the viaduct, was at the foot of two and a quarter miles of 1 in 100. This was followed by five miles of 1 in 117 to the western portal of the tunnel, the whole of which was graded at 1 in 201. The summit of the climb lay at the eastern portal, exactly 22 miles from Manchester.

From Sheffield the rise was less broken, climbing beginning half a mile out with four miles of 1 in 132. Five miles of 1 in 120 followed, taking the line up towards Thurgoland tunnel, traversed on a two-mile pitch of 1 in

131. A mile of 1 in 160 came then, with a three-quarter mile steepening to 1 in 100 through Penistone and a 10-chain easing to 1 in 452. A mile and a half of 1 in 130 led up to Hazlehead Bridge, and the final pitch of two and a half miles to Dunford Bridge and the summit was at 1 in 135.

No sooner had the single bore been completed than it became obvious that it was inadequate. So in 1847 a second single bore was begun beside the first, being completed five years later. Its length was the same as its twin, but no shafts were necessary thanks to a series of 25 side-arches built into the original bore.

The pair became notorious among enginemen as smoky 'hellholes', and when electrification was considered for the route their deterioration was taken into account and a new double-bore was planned beside them. Work began in 1949, but a severe fall in 1951 took six months to clear, and the original construction estimate of three years was exceeded by a third. The new tunnel cost £4.25 million, and was formally opened on 3 June 1954 (to traffic on 14 June), when the original two tunnels were closed. It was slightly longer (44 yards), and the gradient was altered to 1 in 129 within it, to a summit at 960 feet and a subsequent fall at 1 in 186 towards Dunford Bridge.

Despite closure, usage of the old tunnels was not over. Power cables were run through the second bore in November 1969, at a conversion cost of £2.72 million. Yet a mere three months later the route was closed to passengers (except on the Manchester/Glossop/Hadfield routes which remain open today), and goods traffic followed them into oblivion on 20 July 1981.

# Standedge

**I**n 1844 a proposal was made for a railway linking Huddersfield and Manchester. The Huddersfield Canal, which already tunnelled through the Pennines at Standedge, became vested in the railway company, which used the same site for its own way through the barrier, hoping to gain from the experience won during the construction of the canal tunnel.

The company was incorporated on 21 July 1845, with powers to build two single-bore tunnels - Locke and Alfred S. Jee were the engineers. The construction contract for the first bore was undertaken by

Thomas Nicholson, who began work on 1 November 1845. By August 1847 1,200 yards (rather less than a quarter) had been completed, and he finished the work three years after starting. No shafts were sunk, adits being opened into the canal tunnel for the disposal of spoil. The tunnel is straight and level (watertroughs were later added at the west end) and is 3 miles 62 yards long. To build it Nicholson used 1,953 men, 1,200 horses, 40 barges and four locomotives, and it cost £201,608 0s 3½d. This included £30,605 for the approaches, a sum he disputed with the LNWR - which had taken over the original company in 1847 - and Nicholson lost heavily on the deal. The first train travelled through on 2 June 1849, and the line was officially opened on 13 July.

To reach this point from the Huddersfield side, one actually begins climbing a mile or so before reaching Mirfield, though the steepest pitch for a while is the 1 in 267 which begins west of the station. At milepost 28¾ (from Manchester) is Spen Valley Junction, and here also begins a short upgrade at 1 in 102, which soon eases to 1 in 147 for two and a quarter miles through Bradley. It steepens to 1 in 101 for half a mile, eases to 1 in 279 through Huddersfield station, but then steepens again to 1 in 96 through Huddersfield, Gledholt and Paddock tunnels. At the west portal of Paddock tunnel the slope eases slightly to 1 in 105, continuing at this pitch for two and three-quarter miles. A half-mile-long easing to 1 in 112 leads to the final stretch of three miles at 1 in 105 which brings the line to the summit level, just beyond Marsden and some half a mile short of the north-eastern portal of the tunnel.

From Manchester the journey up to Standedge begins with the infamous 1 in 59, 47 and 118 of Miles Platting bank, but thereafter things ease a little until Clayton Bridge, where there begin successive miles at 1 in 135 and 1 in 100. Short varying pitches follow, including a few yards of 1 in 75 up to Ashton-under-Lyne. Stalybridge is passed at 1 in 781, but then short lengths of 1 in 203 and 125 lead to Stalybridge tunnel, through which the gradient is 1 in 145. Now the hard graft starts - two miles of 1 in 125 through Mossley tunnel, and beyond Mossley station a mile-long easing to 1 in 150 is followed by another mile of 1 in 125. A mile and a quarter of 1 in 175 ends soon after Saddleworth, giving way to 1 in 125 for the final mile and few yards to the summit level, which begins just before the south-west portal of the tunnel.

The quantity of traffic approaching the tunnel very soon turned it in to a bottleneck, and in 1865 plans for the second bore were deposited. Thomas Nelson won the contract to build it, with a tender of £121,500, and fired his first blast on 16 April 1868 at the Marsden end. A year later he had completed

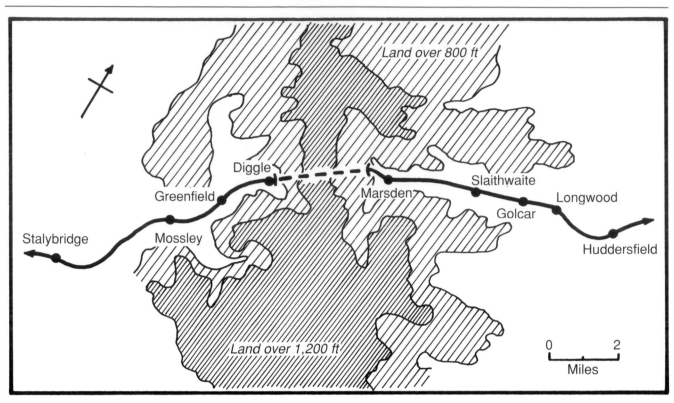

1,026 yards, and by October 1870 it was possible to walk through. Indeed, passengers had to do this for a while when an accident to a train at the Marsden end resulted in the running line being blocked by 50 tons of salt. While it was cleared passenger trains terminated at each end of the tunnel, and travellers made the link on foot, through the unfinished new bore. One feels that there must, even then, have been ways of travelling between Yorkshire and Lancashire without the necessity of a three-mile hike through an incomplete tunnel, and one suspects that many were tempted to take it.

The new tunnel lay to the south of the original, and 21 adits were made to connect the bore with the canal. As before, spoil was taken out this way; Nelson finished the job six months ahead of schedule, and it was opened on 12 February 1871. It was but 17 years before further traffic growth prompted the LNWR to project a new, double-bore tunnel 'north of all existing tunnels', as the Act has it. The company undertook the construction for itself, and a first sod was cut at Marsden on 5 August 1890. Two miles had been dug within twelve months, but part of the roof collapsed on Easter Monday 1892, and thereafter things began to go wrong. The company withdrew from the construction operations, leaving the three foremen, Williams, Lees and Thomas, to complete the work under contract.

The new tunnel, officially given as two yards longer than the previous ones, was inspected on 1 August 1894, and was opened officially on the 5th of the month. It has a span of 27 feet, and is not entirely straight, for there is a slight eastward curve at the north-east end. As with the single bores, water pick-up troughs were added - it is, after all, the longest level section between Leeds and Manchester - beginning about 120 yards in from the Diggle end.

The tunnels remained in the ownership of the LNWR until the Grouping of 1923, when the LMS became responsible for them until Nationalisation, 25 years later. The two single bores gave service until October 1966, when they were taken out of use. On Sundays for six months in 1970/71 the double-bore was closed for track relaying, though because of the 'possibility of snow and ice disrupting the alternative road services while the tunnel is closed, work will be suspended from mid-December to mid-February,' said the press-release. The route today is still very much a trunk one, and the history of the climb to Standedge, and its tunnels, is still being written.

# Werneth

Oldham expanded fast through the 19th century. A population of 12,000 in 1801 had increased six-fold 60 years later, and that figure had almost doubled in 1901. It needed a rail link but it stood on a hill, so the only way to get there was upwards.

On 1 July 1839 an Act of Parliament authorised the Manchester & Leeds Railway to '. . .make and maintain a branch from and out of the said Manchester and Leeds Railway to Oldham, commencing in or near a certain field in the Township of Chadderton. . .and terminating at Mumps within the Township of Oldham. . .on a Piece of Open Ground on the South Side of and adjoining or near to the Turnpike Road'.

The one and three-quarter mile line was planned by George Stephenson, the engineer in charge being Thomas Gooch, and it would cost, it was estimated, £45,000. Work began on 29 July 1841, and though no major engineering features were required, the main problem quickly resolved itself into a question of how the engines were going to get up to Oldham station

The 4.54 pm local from Middleton Junction to Rochdale approaches the summit of Werneth bank on 12 August 1953, hauled by Stanier Class '5MT' No 44736. The photograph gives a clear impression of the steepness of the incline. *Peter Hay*

(as it was then called), which lay some 180 feet above their starting point.

The first plan was that two locomotives, linked by a rope which ran round a pulley, would counterbalance each other, one coming up as the other went down. This idea was discarded in favour of the counterbalance being provided by ballast wagons, and this was the system used on opening in 1842. A brake-van was included in the ballast-train combination, so that runaways were usually averted, and the method worked satisfactorily for eight years.

Some time between 1848 and 1851 the name of the station at the top of the incline was changed to Werneth, but what was perhaps more significant was that at some time around 1849 locomotive power had so increased that speculation began as to whether an engine could climb the bank unaided. They could, and from June 1851 they did.

The line curved sharply away from Middleton Junction towards the east and remained level for some way, crossing meantime the Rochdale Canal and various roads. About a mile from the start the gradient began at 1 in 27, and continued to the platform approach at the line's destination. To begin with, of course, Werneth was a terminus, a cliff behind the bufferstops seeming to preclude further progress, but in 1847 the line was extended via two tunnels to a new station at Oldham Mumps. Lancashire & Yorkshire tank engines chugged merrily up and down the slope for many years, until, in 1960, passenger services were phased out, superseded by the easier and more direct route from the south via Failsworth. The last steam train, an enthusiasts' special, mounted the incline on 17 September 1960, and the line closed completely on 7 January 1963.

Now little of it remains. The upper section of the gradient has been given over to housing, but the canal bridge is still there, and the course of the lower end of the line can be traced to the site of the demolished Middleton Junction.

# Summit

From very early days there was a desire to build a railway between Manchester and Leeds, and when a company was formed in 1825 it projected a route that followed the course of the Rochdale Canal. An initial report published on 15 November 1830 describes a line differing considerably at either end from that actually built, and remarking:

> 'There will be no necessity in any part of the Line for Tunnels, or any Inclined Planes over which Locomotive Engineers cannot work with advantage.'

Thomas Gooch, the elder brother of Daniel, who was George Stephenson's Assistant Engineer in this project, did a survey, but the first Bill failed. The company was reconstituted in 1835, and Stephenson was again appointed Engineer, his new route envisaging two inclines four and four and a half miles long and a 1,705-yard tunnel ten miles from Manchester. Royal Assent was gained on 4 July 1836 and the route was finally determined and authorised on 5 May the next year. Gooch was again appointed Assistant Engineer, and estimated a cost of £156,800 for the tunnel. A tender of

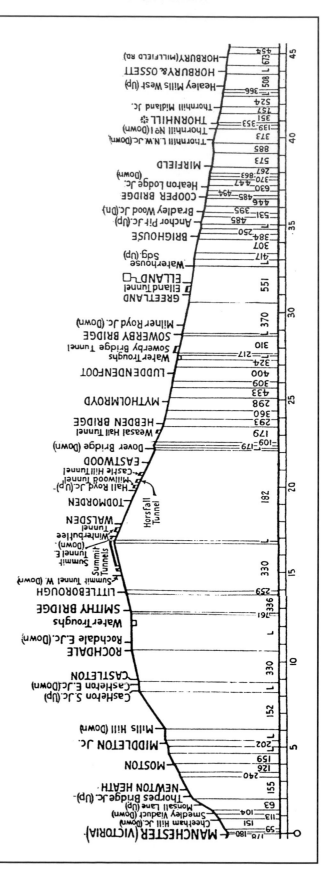

Gradient profile, Summit

£107,000 was accepted from John Evans and James Copeland, who won the contract on the strength of their work at Watford Gap on the London & Birmingham Railway. Here, it appears, they must have been less certain of what was involved, since they ran into financial trouble, and Copeland ended up in prison for debt. The pair were replaced after 19 months of work, and since the end cost of the tunnel was £251,000, they probably thought themselves well out of it.

Work on the Manchester-Littleborough section began on 18 August 1837, and Daniel Gooch himself worked for a time on the Rochdale section. A man called Barnard Dickinson was appointed Assistant Engineer for the tunnel, and work began with the sinking of No 10 shaft on 17 April 1838: it was completed by 8 November. There were to be 13 others, of which the deepest was No 9 at 341 feet. At this point, however, other work languished and Gooch advertised for alternative tenders.

'The tunnel at the summit of the country is not being proceeded with as rapidly as the contractors ought to do, and some change must be immediately made as regards the number of men employed and the general management of the work'. So said Herepath's *Railway Magazine* in May 1839, though it was but echoing an engineering report of two months earlier that noted that the Todmorden contract and Gauxholme viaduct were both behind, largely owing to 'not getting the land in time. . .'

John Stephenson, who was no relation to George, took over the Evans & Copeland contract on 18 March 1839. He was 47 years old at this time, and had begun an engineering/contracting career on the Stockton & Darlington Railway in 1824, becoming a friend and advisor to George Stephenson. In partnership with Brassey and Mackenzie he later built the North Wales Mineral Railway (see Gresford, Chapter 4), and died in 1848, while visiting the North Midland Railway.

On the Summit contract the driftway was half through by September that year, but things were not going fast enough for completion to time. Neither was the schedule helped by dissension among the bricklayers, paid at 6s 6d a day, who caused so much trouble that some were sentenced by the Rochdale magistrates to 3 months' imprisonment.

As if to add insult to injury, the tunnel was almost finished when, in December 1840, part of an invert failed. Both this and the sides had to be rebuilt, delaying the opening by about a fortnight. The last brick was keyed in on 11 December; there was a celebratory collation at the Summit Inn, while the workmen, reported the *Manchester Guardian* of 14 December, were 'regaled inside the tunnel'.

At the time of its completion it was the longest tunnel in the world, at 1 mile 1125 yards. Whishaw tells us

that it was cut through 'shales, rock, clay, bin [?] &c', and for the extraction and removal of this material the miners were paid from 4s 6d to 6s 6d per 10-hour day, and about 1,000 men were employed on the job. During early 1840 progress was at about 5 feet 3 inches a day, but in the spring and summer this more than doubled to 14 feet 1.25 inches, presumably after 24-hour working was introduced. The brickwork varies between five and ten rings depending on the strata, and the height of the tunnel from the springing line of the invert to the soffit of the arch is 21 feet 6 inches. The north end has a 60-chain radius curve, while at the south end there is a 49-chain curve for a distance of 12 chains. The line opened throughout on 1 March 1841.

But the Manchester & Leeds Railway had not waited until the tunnel was finished before opening its line. Ready revenue was much more important, and what was described as an experimental opening was held on 31 May 1839, after which the *Manchester Guardian* reported on 1 June:

'The rails laid down are, we believe, about 60 lb to the yard; they are of unusual form, being what are termed straight rails, having only one flange, and are laid with that flange upwards, thus T. They are laid to such a width, that, in the event of the

The south portal of Summit tunnel - the gradient at this point is 1 in 330, but the tunnel is a long one, with a curve at each end. It was also substantially enough built to survive a fierce blaze in 1984 when a train of tankers caught fire near the north end. *C. V. Awdry*

extension lines uniting the Leeds, and Liverpool and Manchester Railways at Hunt's Bank station, the same engines, carriages or wagons may proceed forwards..

The problems inherent in a change of gauge, already apparent at the extremities of the Great Western system, were clearly being noted already in this part of the country.

The official opening, reported by the same journal, but quoted in abridgement by John Herepath a month later in the August issue of his *Railway Magazine*, highlights a less happy incident:

'After leaving Mills Hill. . .in rising an incline towards its bridge over the Haywood Branch Canal, where the heaviest gradients occur. . .[the engine] at length, after a few expiring snorts. . . came to a dead stop about seven miles and a half from Manchester.

'The cause of this was afterwards found to be the complete choking of the engine with mud from the foul water used.'

Another water problem occurred some years later, when on 8 February 1852 an aqueduct carrying the River Roch across the line immediately south of the tunnel mouth burst 'owing to the great accumulation of water from rain during the night. The line,' went on the *Leamington Courier* of 14 February, was 'inundated so as to prevent several of the morning trains from passing along it'.

Experience so far in this book has indicated that the steepest rise across the Pennines is from west to east, but this is not wholly the case here. To be sure the steepest gradients *are* on the west side, but they are comparatively short pitches only, while trains approaching from the Yorkshire side have a continuous climb of almost 29 miles. The first two miles from Manchester are hard going, at 1 in 59, 151, 113, 104 and 63, this last about 55 chains. It is followed by a mile and a quarter of 1 in 155 through Newton Heath, and the next three-quarters of a mile, at 1 in 240 and 126, brings the line to Moston. About 50 chains of 1 in 159 and 25 chains level are succeeded by a short 1 in 220 and another three-quarters of a mile of level. The line has now reached Mills Hill, referred to above, and the next two miles are at 1 in 152, not actually the steepest part of the line, but the train must have expired about halfway up it. The pitch is followed by a level half-mile to Castleton, and the next mile and three-quarters to Rochdale is all at 1 in 330. Now comes a level for a little over two miles, with a climb of 1 in 336 from Smithy Bridge for a mile, 1 in 259 through Littleborough and the final two and three-

quarter miles at 1 in 330. This takes the line most of the way through the tunnel, the summit, 537 feet above sea level, occurring as the line levels for a short while a few yards beyond the northern portal.

Travelling west is something more arduous. Climbing begins about two and a half miles out of Wakefield, with 1 in 454 and 673 to Horbury & Ossett, which is actually sited on half a mile of level track. The next mile is at 1 in 508, with Healey Mills at the top of it, and then a section of short gradients, none steeper than 1 in 351, to Thornhill. Beyond Thornhill is a short pitch of 1 in 139 and a mile of 1 in 373. A downgrade follows, a little over half a mile of 1 in 885, before a mile of 1 in 573 lifts the line to Mirfield. More short pitches raise the line further to Heaton Lodge Junction. The section from here to Milner Royd Junction, near Sowerby Bridge, is now open for freight traffic only, passenger trains to Manchester via the Summit tunnel now running by way of Halifax.

There are many short lengths of broken grade on this section, the line rising steadily but easily at nothing steeper than 1 in 250 for a short way near Brighouse. A two-mile pitch of 1 in 550 leads through Elland and its tunnel, and a little less than two miles of 1 in 370 bring the line up to Sowerby Bridge, whose station is on a level. Sowerby Bridge tunnel comes at the top of a mile of 1 in 310, and pitches, none longer than about 55 chains, of 1 in 217, level, 324, 400, 309, 433, 298, 360 and 293 lead to Hebden Bridge. Beyond lies a section of 1 in 179, which includes the delightfully named Weasel Hall tunnel, and a few chains at 1 in 109, before the line suddenly dips for a short way at 1 in 179. From this point the climb is unchanged at 1 in 182 for the next five and a quarter miles, past the junction for the line to Blackburn over Copy Pit summit, across Todmorden's imposing viaduct and through its station, to the top.

# Stainmore

The Romans used the Stainmore Gap for a road long before the railway reached it, of course, and even had a camp and fortlet near the summit - a bleaker spot for duty it would be hard to imagine.

The line through the Stainmore Gap was promoted '. . .to connect the Ports of the North Sea with those of the Irish Sea, and to unite the manufacturing districts of Durham, Northumberland and Cleveland, with those of Lancashire and the West'. Thus read the prospectus of the South Durham & Lancashire Union Railway, a promotion of the Stockton & Darlington Railway. An Act was obtained on 17 July 1857 and tenders were accepted at once. By 8 August the line had been staked out, several pieces of land had been bought, and a Working Agreement had been made with the Stockton & Darlington Railway. On 25 August, at Kirkby Stephen, the Duke of Cleveland cut the first sod 'with the usual festive auxiliaries,' as *The Times* put it.

The Engineer was Thomas Bouch, with A. L. Nimmo, another Scot, as his Resident Engineer. Bouch was, of course, later to be knighted for his work on the Tay Bridge, only to fall into ignominy along with the bridge. There were large bridgeworks on this line too, with a major viaduct on either side of the summit, at Deepdale (740 feet long, 161 feet high), and the one for which its designer is best remembered, at Belah, 1,040 feet long, and at 196 feet high the loftiest viaduct in England. Crumlin, in South Wales, was the highest in Britain, by just one foot.

Work went on quickly and comparatively uneventfully, though the locals complained about the poaching proclivities of the navvies, to counter which the Chief Constable of Westmorland and Cumberland suggested the provision of four policemen, paid for by the railway. The Directors would agree to only one, whom they paid a guinea (£1 1s) a week plus 1s 6d boot allowance and 1 shilling for oil. This compares with the pay of the navvies themselves, who got from 3s 1d to 3s 4d daily and could thus earn around £1 in a six-day week. Masons did considerably better at 5 shillings a day.

On 26 February 1859 the half-yearly meeting was told that about a third of the work between Barnardcastle (sic) and Tebay had been executed; the Deepdale viaduct was finished, and the bridge over the Tees was 'in course of completion.' Six months later there was progress at both Beelah (sic) and Tees, and an opening was expected during autumn the next year. On 4 October 1860 *The Times* could report that the first section of the railway had been formally opened by the Directors on 27 September, the proceedings being followed by a dinner at the King's Head Hotel, Barnard Castle.

The piers of Belah and Deepdale viaducts each had six one-foot diameter columns set in parallel rows of three, which were strengthened by cross-bracing at five-foot intervals. There were also horizontal and diagonal tiebars of wrought iron. A base width of 50 feet narrowed to rather less than half that at the top, carrying the wrought iron girders which bore the track - Belah had 16 spans, Deepdale 11. Masonry abutments supported the ends. The viaducts cost £31,630 and £20,687 respectively, and the ironwork for them was carried out by Gilkes Wilson. Belah's foundation stone was laid by Henry Pease on 25 November 1857, and though official records state it was built in four months, a legend persists that it was done in 43 days. Either way it was no mean achievement.

In spite of the difficult terrain the line, which had cost £666,879 3s 9d was passed by the Inspecting Officer on his first visit. It opened for mineral traffic on 4 July 1861, with a formal opening on 7 August, carrying passengers from the next day. On that day

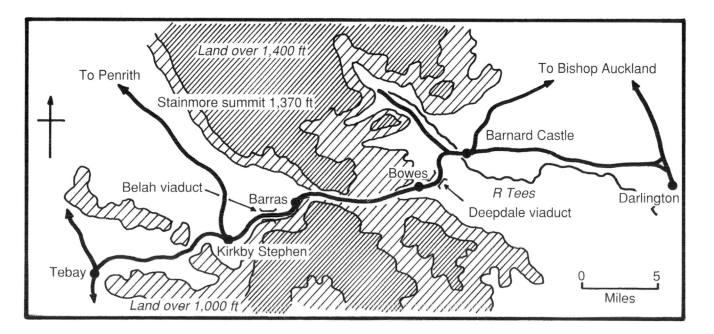

*The Times* observed that 'the undertaking would have been completed much earlier but for the wet summer of 1860 and the severe winter of 1860/1'.

The steepest climb was from the west, and began just before milepost 39 (measured from Darlington) with two and a half miles at 1 in 72. The gradient increased to 1 in 60 for the next four miles, this pitch crossing Belah viaduct, after about two-thirds of its distance. The line was in cutting for much of this section, emerging on to a north-facing shelf as the gradient eased slightly at Barras station. The houses it served lie below the line, which then curved right and began to climb again, at 1 in 59 for the two and a half miles remaining to the top, 1,370 feet above sea level.

From the east the climb was easier in terms of gradient, but longer by about four miles, with a higher vertical rise. It began at 1 in 71 after crossing the River Tees three-quarters of a mile beyond Barnard Castle, a pitch which continued past Tees Valley Junction and round a wide loop through Lartington. A brief easing beyond the station - possibly so as to cross under the road instead of on the level - brought the line to a two and a half mile pitch of 1 in 69. This took the line over Deepdale viaduct, round a sharp right-hand curve and under the main road, after which the gradient eased to 1 in 82 for the remaining mile to Bowes. An even easier stretch followed - 1 in 3,900 for a mile - but it then steepened to 1 in 154 for a mile and a quarter. Now came the final push to the top, with a mile and a half at 1 in 93, three miles at 1 in 68, and a last half-mile of 1 in 98 to the summit.

The nominally independent company that built the line did not survive for long. It was worked from the outset by the S&DR, which absorbed the smaller company from 1 January 1863 - not, incidentally, surviving itself for much longer, for it was taken over by the NER six months later. Track was laid single at first, with space for doubling, which was done between Bowes and Stainmore in 1867 and on to Barras seven years later. As had been intended it was always primarily a freight route; at the turn of the century mineral trains used the line round the clock, though paths were found for six passenger trains each way. But freight declined after the Second World War, and Summit siding, at Barras, closed entirely on 1 December 1952. Diesel railcars took over the passengers in 1958, apart from excursion and troop trains (to Warcop), and the line closed on 22 January 1962. The two iron viaducts were demolished the following year.

Winters can be bleak on Stainmore, once England's highest railway summit. Many are the stories of stranded trains, one of which became the subject of a film, 'Snow Drift at Bleath Gill' (British Transport Films), a classic of its type.

# Goathland

Goathland's 1 in 49 bank is clearly not a Pennine route, yet it falls just as inappropriately into the next chapter too, and since to omit it merely on those grounds would be unthinkable, here it is.

In 1831 Whitby considered its trade was being restricted by lack of communications and that it needed a railway. Discussion had been going on for two years, principally as to whether an outlet via Pickering or Eskdale would be preferable. George Stephenson, asked for his comments in 1832, came down in favour of Pickering, and reckoned that a line could be built for about £2,000 per mile. An Act of Parliament was obtained for a Whitby & Pickering Railway on 6 May 1833, and a survey was made by Stephenson.

His Resident Engineer for the work was Robert Swanwick, who had been born in Chester in 1810. He was, at this time, articled to Stephenson, for whom he later became second-in-command after Thomas Gooch. He worked on the W&PR with Stephenson from 1832 to 1836, and was given its supervision from July 1834.

The line followed the Esk valley to begin with, but, on reaching Grosmont, curved southward to enter the valley of the Murk Esk via a short tunnel. It had been planned to follow the valley of Wheeldale Beck past Mallyon Spout and Wheeldale Lodge, where a long tunnel would open the way to the south, but this idea was abandoned and an incline to Goathland substituted - which is why, gentle reader, you are here.

The first sod was cut on 10 August 1833 by the company Chairman, Robert Campion, and good progress was made. The tunnel at Grosmont - or Growmond as it was then known - was given an attractive castellated portico, but beyond came the incline. The line to it lay to the west of the present railway, crossing the beck several times before reaching Beck Hole, or Beck Holes. This was the foot of the incline proper, the line turning south-east and climbing for 1,500 yards at a maximum gradient of 1 in 10. Operations on it were made with the aid of a wheeled watertank, which, when filled at the top, counterbalanced the train to be hauled up.

At the top of the incline lay Fen Bog, which was 20 feet deep and occasioned no little difficulty to the constructors of the line. Large baulks of Baltic fir were pile-driven into it, and eventually a firm foundation was achieved by a combination of these, bundles of heather encased in sheepskins, whole trees and moss-covered hurdles. Having negotiated this hazard, the line then passed behind the present Goathland station, and rejoined today's route near Summit signal box, some mile and three-quarters further south. It was laid with 15-foot lengths of 40 lb fish-bellied rail on huge stone blocks two feet square. These were laid diagonally, possibly to give support to the rail along a longer length of their surface. The line opened to Grosmont on 8 June 1835, and throughout on 26 May the following year, but it had cost a great deal more than the sum Stephenson had estimated, and the company was to feel the effects of this for some time.

'In point of inclinations,' wrote Francis Whishaw, 'it is a very difficult line.' Quite soon that became

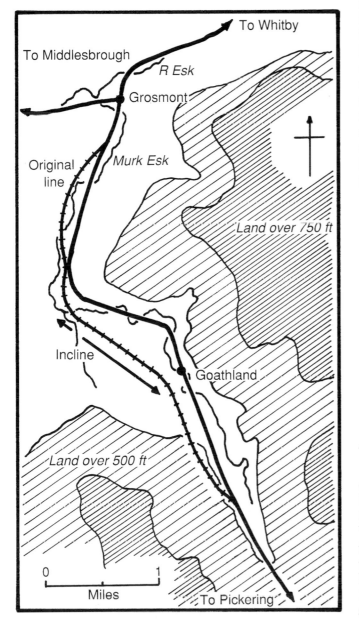

obvious to the owners too: the incline was causing a bottleneck, but there was little money with which to do anything about it.

George Hudson was a popular visitor to Whitby, however, and one of 'his' companies was the York & North Midland Railway. An amalgamation was agreed, and on 30 June 1845 that concern obtained an Act authorising it to take over the W&PR and rebuild it for locomotive haulage. Heavier rails were laid, the track was doubled, a new tunnel was cut at Grosmont, new stations were built, and deviations were made. Yet, although it was largely the cause of the problems, all the incline got was a wire cable instead of a hemp rope.

It was not until 1861 that relief arrived: the North Eastern Railway, having taken over the Y&NMR, was authorised to avoid the incline by building a four and half mile deviation. This climbed to Goathland on a 1 in 49 slope and was both difficult and expensive to build, for it included seven bridges across the Murk Esk, the removal and replacement of two farmsteads, and a new road bridge. A half-mile long rock cutting required blasting, which caused rockfalls so frequent that watchmen had to guard the line. Seventeen months before it was finished, however, disaster struck. On 10 February 1864 the cable on a passenger train broke while it was descending the original incline. There was a graphic description in, of all papers, the *Buxton Advertiser* of 20 February.

> 'When probably 150 yards on the descent the rope suddenly broke, and the train was left to its career down nearly a mile of incline of which the gradient is 1 in 14 [sic - it would actually have been 1,350 yards or so at 1 in 15]. The velocity likely to be attained under such circumstances may be more readily imagined than described, especially when the rails were frozen and slippery, which rendered the two brakes of the vans comparatively useless. At the foot of the incline the line curves rapidly to the right, crossing the Ellerbeck in Beck Hole. Round this curve and over the bridge the train shot with terrific speed and a few yards further [on] left the rails and rolled into the ditch.'

Two passengers were killed and 13 injured.

The new deviation line opened on 1 July 1865 but closed almost exactly a hundred years later, on 8 March 1965, allegedly losing £50,000 a year. Happily it is still with us, however, for in 1967 the North Yorkshire Moors Railway Preservation Society was formed, which managed to negotiate an agreement with BR, re-opening the line between Grosmont and Ellerbeck, just beyond the summit of the line, in 1970. Now trains run regularly to Pickering, and steam through Newtondale is a reality once more.

# 6
# BORDERS AND GALLOWAY

## Grayrigg and Shap

A through railway route between England and Scotland was suggested as early as 1801, though no constructive proposals were put forward until around 1835. For a while from then on it was considered that one line would be sufficient, and it was on 21 October 1835 that Locke was directed 'to see if there was a practicability of a line to Carlisle'.

He made a quick inspection, coming back to suggest a line following the Lune valley, making a short tunnel under Shap Fell and using the valley of the River Lowther for a descent. Three years later Job Bintley produced a route via Carnforth and Kendal, with a long tunnel south of Haweswater, joining Locke's route some miles south of Carlisle. Locke disliked this, not only for some steep climbing which would be involved in getting out of Longsleddale, but the long tunnel also. Meanwhile, the people of Kendal disliked Locke's route because it left them off the railway.

In 1840 George Larmer, who had been Resident Engineer for the west end of the Newcastle & Carlisle Railway, 'discovered' a route up Grayrigg, which did not avoid Kendal altogether, and joined Locke's route south of Tebay. It was adopted, and an Act for the Lancaster & Carlisle Railway became law on 6 June 1844. Locke was appointed Engineer-in-chief, at a salary of £500 per annum for the two years that it was expected the line would take to build. J. E. Errington became Engineer, and Larmer and S. B. Worthington Resident Engineers for the sections north and south of Shap respectively. One of the assistants who laid out the line was Henry Robertson.

There may have been two first sods cut, one at Grayrigg and one north of Tebay, but however it was, work was swiftly under way, and the *Railway Times* reported on 25 January 1845 that 3,761 men and 367 horses were 'engaged on the line'. Brassey, partnered by Mackenzie and John Stephenson,

**Ex-LNWR Whale 4-6-0 as LMS No 8753 takes a curve on Grayrigg bank with a passenger train (despite the Class D freight headcode) on 6 June 1935. By this time these engines were already around 30 years old and had acquired a Belpaire firebox.** *H. C. Casserley*

had successfully tendered at £591,605, about £200,000 less than Locke's estimate of the cost. It was, at the time, the biggest single contract ever undertaken by a single group, a group that went on to

**Gradient profile, Grayrigg and Shap**

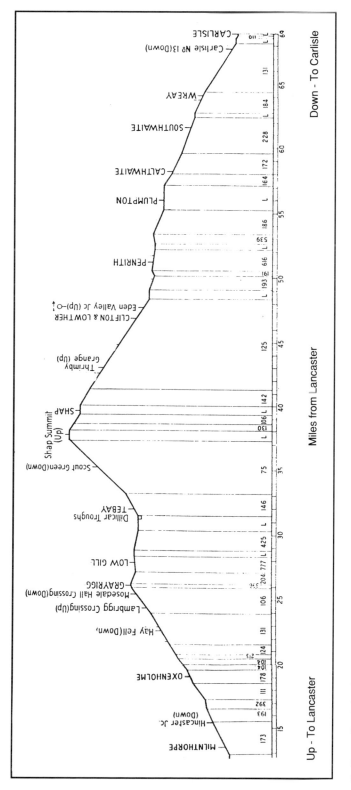

an even bigger one in 1846 when it began, also for Locke, the climb over Beattock. But the hoped for completion date of 1 July 1846 very quickly went by the board as difficulty was met in gaining possession of land near Wreay. There were labour troubles also, with frequent strikes, and, in February 1846, a riot near Penrith involving about 2,000 navvies. At the start of the contract the labourers received, on average, around 2s 6d per day, but by the time it was completed two and three-quarter years later this had risen to about 3s 6d.

There were 72 deaths during the course of the contract, a large number of them between Oxenholme and Shap, and mostly, in the opinion of the local press, due to carelessness on the part of the men. Up to 10,000 men were employed at any one time, though the average for the contract was nearer 2,000, who were assisted by 1,050 horses. In August 1845 the Directors were complaining that much of the work was behind, though, somewhat unreasonably, one of the items mentioned was Wreay cutting. Soon they were to give up their insistence on what was clearly becoming an impossible date.

Even so, by the time the men had been at work for two and a half years 70 miles of double track had been laid, really a quite remarkable effort in the circumstances. There were four viaducts, at Docker Garths and Borrow Beck to the south of Shap, and across the Rivers Lowther and Eamont on the north side of the summit, with two long deep cuttings, one at Shap, the other at Wreay.

Climbing proper begins at Milnthorpe, though there has been a two-mile pitch of 1 in 134 up from Carnforth. At Milnthorpe the rise is 1 in 173, continuing for a mile and a quarter beyond the station, where it eases to 1 in 193 for a mile and then still further to 1 in 392 for three-quarters of a mile. A mile and a quarter at 1 in 111 follows, to ease to 1 in 178 for a mile through Oxenholme, but to steepen to 1 in 104 some half a mile beyond the station.

This is really the start of Grayrigg bank, this slope continuing for a mile before easing first to 1 in 213, then 1 in 124. Two and a half miles at 1 in 131 follow, about halfway up which the line crosses beneath the A685 and swings sharply to the east. The pitch is succeeded by two miles of 1 in 106, which crosses Fiddlers Gill on a six-arch viaduct 50 feet high (Docker Garths) and brings the line almost, but not quite, to Grayrigg summit. A final few chains of 1 in 396 are still needed to take the line past the site of the station, named, as was the village, after a local squire, a Mr Gray Rigge.

There is then a mile-long downslope at 1 in 204, and as this changes to 1 in 777 the line swings north again, the majestic viaduct of Low Gill, relict of the

LNWR branch to Ingleton, still standing proudly to the south. The station here had a rather curious arrangement, with separate platforms on both main line and branch, with the actual junction just to the north of them. A short level stretch follows, then a one and a half mile downslope at 1 in 425.

The line is in the Lune Gorge now, as, close below the M6, it levels for the spot where Dillicar watertroughs used to be. Now swinging right, the line crosses the three-arch, 65-foot high Borrow Beck viaduct and hits the 1 in 146 which will take it past Tebay and out on to Shap Fell. Tebay, once the junction with a Stockton & Darlington Railway branch from Kirkby Stephen, lies at the mouth of the gorge, and was also home for the bankers that ascending trains once needed.

A mile beyond the station Shap bank proper begins, a shade over four miles of 1 in 75 across a windswept moor, with little shelter until the summit cutting is reached, 916 feet above sea level. The cutting here is up to 60 feet deep, cut mostly through hard whinstone, and was the most difficult part of the line to build; it took some 500 men several months of concentrated work to shift its 350,000 cubic yards of spoil.

The climb from the north is longer (21 miles against 15) but raises the line more in terms of vertical feet. Also, the steepest section is at 1 in 106, and that for less than a mile. Two lengths of level on leav-ing Carlisle are broken by a pitch of about 12 chains at 1 in 110, whereafter almost four miles at 1 in 131 take the line to within half a mile of Wreay. The cutting here has a maximum depth of 45 feet, and involved the removal of 410,000 cubic yards of spoil. It is bound by timber framing to counter the numerous slips which were experienced during its construction. One and three-quarter miles at 1 in 184 follows, and then a short level about 25 chains long. Three miles of 1 in 228 lift the line past the site of Southwaite station, and Calthwaite's site is passed on a slope of 1 in 172. An even steeper mile of 1 in 164 leads to a two-mile level past Plumpton, and two miles of 1 in 186 leads to an easier section which lasts until beyond Penrith.

An upgrade of 1 in 616 runs through the station, the only survivor between Carlisle and Oxenholme, and is succeeded by a sharp drop at 1 in 191 into the Eamont valley. The viaduct crossing the river is 70 feet high at its maximum, and has five arches of 50-foot span. That across the Lowther which soon follows is both longer and higher: it has six arches of 60-foot span, and stands 100 feet above the river. The

**BR Standard 'Clan' 'Pacific' No 72004 *Clan Macdonald* has only a few yards to travel to begin the formidable 1 in 75 to Shap summit, four miles of hard slogging on a mainly winding road. The 1 in 146 section, on which the crew of the 9.30 am Manchester-Glasgow on 27 May 1952 are trying to maintain as fast a pace as possible, stretches back one and a half miles south, to just beyond Tebay station.** *E. D. Bruton*

*Right* Stanier Class '5' No 45371 creates a fine smoke effect on 28 June 1952 as it heads past Shap Wells with a down Class E express freight. The banker is Tebay's Fowler 2-6-4T No 42404, and the driver of the train engine peers closely to see if he can identify the photographer. *E. D. Bruton*

*Below right* The same banker photographed from the back garden of a lengthman's cottage near Salterthwaite, assisting a Sunday morning parcels train on 25 May 1952. In remarkably clean BR lined black livery, the locomotive carries the duty number 93 on a board placed on the near lamp-iron. *E. D. Bruton*

line itself is on a gradient of 1 in 193 now, but this comes to a 60-chain-long level two and a half miles out of Penrith.

Now climbing begins 'for real', at 1 in 125 for no less than seven miles. There is a slight easing for a mile and a quarter to 1 in 142, then comes a 50-chain level past the erstwhile Shap station. All too soon drivers found themselves on the aforementioned 1 in 106, but it is short and from the end of it there is just half a mile of 1 in 130 to the summit level.

There were eight stations or stopping places between Oxenholme and Carlisle at first, Oxenholme itself being merely a changing point until 1847. They were Lambrigg (later supplanted by Grayrigg), Lops Fell (replaced by Tebay), Shap, Hackthorpe & Clifton, Penrith, Plumpton, Southwaite and Newbiggin & Wreay. A station three miles south of Penrith was built and named Brisco, but this vanished in 1852 to be replaced by Wreay, when, one assumes, Newbiggin & Wreay disappeared also.

In November 1897 a newspaper rumour was circulating that a 10-mile tunnel was to be built south of Carlisle - presumably it really meant Penrith - in order to avoid Shap, but in April the next year the *Railway Magazine* carried a rather more feasible suggestion of a deviation to ease the gradient to 1 in 135. But, as we know, nothing was done. Watertroughs were laid in at Dillicar, south of Tebay, in 1869.

The ten stations between Carlisle and Oxenholme have very nearly as many closing dates between them. The first to close to passengers, and the only one before the Second World War, was Clifton & Lowther on 4 July 1938, and the only wartime casualty, on 16 August 1943, was Wreay. Plumpton was the next to go, on 31 May 1948, and Calthwaite and Southwaite both followed on 7 April 1952. Grayrigg succumbed on 1 February 1954, which was the day when the Ingleton branch also closed, but, somewhat surprisingly perhaps, Low Gill station survived this event for just over six years, until 7 March 1960. The final closures, Tebay and Shap, took place on 1 July 1968.

Banking was frequent over the 1 in 75, and a stud of locomotives was shedded at Tebay for this purpose.

Stanier '4MT' 2-6-4T No 42544 of Carnforth MPD takes the curve through the 'birdcage bridge' cutting to Shap summit with the down 5.00 pm Oxenholme-Carlisle stopping train on 3 June 1950. The engine, in unlined black, still carries the letters 'LMS', and the train is comprised of Gresley stock, still in LNER varnished teak. *E. D. Bruton*

This became less important with the demise of steam, and soon after that electrification, completed in May 1974, made the idea laughable. It is greatly to the credit of Locke, Brassey and the rest that so little attention has been required to their trackbed, which now copes with weights and speeds far beyond their expectation or comprehension.

# Ais Gill

The line over Ais Gill, the one we know these days as the Settle & Carlisle line, was born of railway politics. The Midland Railway was dissatisfied with the service it was getting to the north by way of its own branch to Ingleton and the LNWR on to Low Gill and the West Coast line over Shap. So in 1866 it projected, at vast expense, its own independent line, which received Parliamentary Assent on 16 July.

Then the atmosphere changed. Relationships with the North Western improved, so the MR brought in a Bill to abandon its expensive offspring. The Lancashire & Yorkshire, which would connect with the new line at Hellifield, and the North British now became anxious that their own lines would suffer if the Ais Gill line was *not* built, and between them managed to scotch the Abandonment Bill. The MR was left holding a child it did not want, the building of which would cost money it could ill-afford.

But there was no alternative, and a first sod was cut at Anley, near Settle, in November 1870. The MR Engineer was John Sydney Crossley, who had been appointed in place of W. H. Barlow late in 1857, and it was he who staked out the route for work to begin.

Crossley, orphaned by the age of two, had been brought up by a Leicester architect. He assisted in the surveying of the Leicester & Swannington Railway, and then went to work, first for Vignoles, and then for Liddell, which led to his connection with the Midland Railway. The S&C was, no doubt, his masterpiece, and he died four years after its completion.

Inevitably there were numerous different contractors working on the 72 miles of railway, among whom were Eckersley & Baylis (Contract No 4, New Biggin/Petteril bridge), Firbank, for 14.5 miles south from New Biggin, Benton & Woodiwiss (Arten Gill/Kirkby Stephen) and John Ashwell, who beat Brassey in the tender for Blea Moor tunnel. Crossley's estimate for this had been £336,523, but the quotation accepted exceeded this at £349,226, Ashwell agreeing to take half the money during the sinking of the shafts at Blea Moor, and the other half when they were completed. The actual cost was near £1.25 million.

The men lived in shanty towns or in 110 buildings hurriedly erected in 1870. They had tiny compartments for family, cooking and lodgers, and 2,000 lived in such a settlement at Batty Green (Ribblehead). The conditions the men had to suffer were appalling, but pay was good by 1870 standards, labourers earning £1 5s per day and masons £1 15s. In time Sunday schools were established, and mission houses were also built, the MR employing two scripture readers, James Tiplady and William Fletcher. Day schools, too, were set up, the contractors financing a school for 43 children at Ribblehead. Many did not survive to reach school, however, for a page from the burial reg-

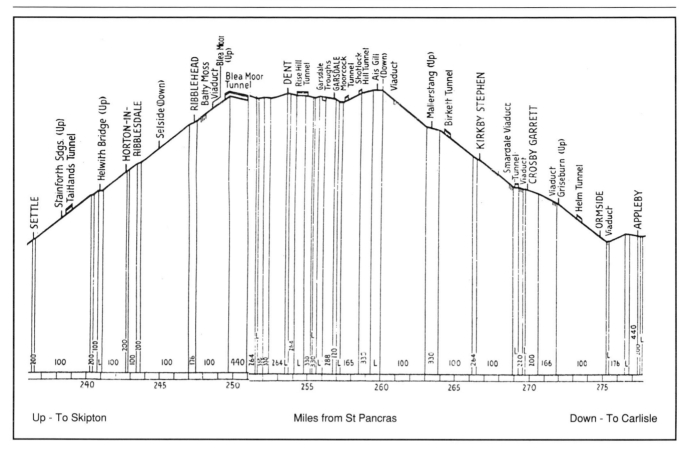

Up - To Skipton                    Miles from St Pancras                    Down - To Carlisle

**Gradient profile, Ais Gill**

ister of Chapel-le-Dale for 1871 shows eight burials between 22 January and 12 February, only one of which was of a person more than four years old.

By May 1870 work was going well on three contracts, but Ashwell was having trouble at Blea Moor. By July heavy rain had slowed things everywhere, and was, perhaps, a portent of things to come, though things had improved a little by September. There was a bitterly cold start to 1871 and more progress was made during that summer, until the rains came again in the autumn. But by September the company was ordering rails from the Barrow Haematite Iron Company.

At this time Ashwell had to hand the Blea Moor contract back to the Committee, who finished the job. Now also a smallpox epidemic claimed so many lives that the MR was asked to enlarge

Chapel-le-Dale churchyard. To this appeal the company contributed £20, and it gave a similar sum towards the enlargement of Cowgill school. Crossley, early in 1872, reckoned that the line would take at least another two years to complete - by the time two years had elapsed, Crossley was ill and the line was

**The up 'Thames-Clyde Express' heads through Kirkby Stephen West on 26 April 1954. The gradient is 1 in 100 here, and rebuilt 'Royal Scot' 4-6-0 No 46112** *Sherwood Forester* **still has some way to go to the summit.** *H. C. Casserley*

**Right at the top. 'WD' 2-8-0 No 90556 passes the Ais Gill summit marker board with a northbound Class E freight in 1963. Despite attempts to save it, the signal box on the right was destroyed by fire.** *P. H. Wells*

still nowhere near finished. Fine weather during the spring of 1875 helped things along, and at last, on 3 August that year, Crossley could write: 'I have pleasure to report that goods trains have this day travelled over the line'.

The final act in the construction of this line was made on 8 June 1875, when the Engineer's wife laid the final stone of Smardale viaduct, but it was still some way from opening. This took place, with muted celebrations, on 1 May 1876, after what, in his masterly history of the epic, Peter Baughan has aptly called 'Seven Years Hard'.

To list every change of gradient over the 72 miles of the line would be as tedious as it would be long-winded. Briefly though, the ruling grade is 1 in 100, and much of the line northwards from Settle to Ribblehead viaduct conforms to this. The slope across the viaduct is 1 in 101½ on a curve - it was begun on 12 October 1870 and completed in 1874, and its 440 yards consists of 24 arches, the highest 165 feet above the valley.

Blea Moor tunnel, which follows shortly, has a first summit within it. It is cut through boulder clay, and the deepest of its seven working shafts is 360 feet from top to rail level. The summit inside the tunnel is 1,151 feet above sea level, and the bore itself is 2,629 yards long.

After the downslope of 1 in 440 which follows the summit, the going is fairly level, across Dent Head

and Arten Gill viaducts, through Dent station and Rise Hill tunnel. This latter is built to the east of the original line, and was constructed between 1870 and 1874, using two working shafts, the deepest of which went down 147 feet. It is cut through the blue limestone forming the ridge between Dentdale and Garsdale, and is 1,213 yards long. The line falls to Garsdale now, curving left across Dandry Mire viaduct and into Moorcock tunnel, 227 feet long. Dandry Mire should have been an embankment, but the viaduct was substituted when the embankment failed to 'bind'. Gradients of 1 in 166 and 1 in 328 take the line up through Shotlock Hill tunnel, 106 yards long through boulder clay, to the summit at Ais Gill, 1,167 feet above sea level.

From the north one is climbing almost all the way from Carlisle, but the really arduous business does not begin until Appleby has been passed. Ormside viaduct spans the River Eden, and by the time the train reaches Ais Gill in 16 miles time, it will have climbed 667 vertical feet, at, again, a ruling grade of 1 in 100. Helm tunnel (571 feet, red marl) is on a gradient of 1 in 103, and Griseburn viaduct, which follows it, is at the summit of a mile of 1 in 100. This is 142 yards long, 74 feet high and has seven spans. Then come Crosby Garrett viaduct and tunnel, followed by Smardale viaduct, the last of the structures on the line to be completed - crossing 130 feet above Scandel Beck, it has 12 limestone spans and is 247 yards long.

It is 1 in 100 almost all the way to the top now, through Kirkby Stephen and Birkett tunnel. Work on

*Right* **Either the fireman miscalculated what his tender would take or he has been distracted by other matters. The front wagon of this southbound Class E freight, on 30 May 1951, gets a soaking from Garsdale troughs, as it travels behind Stanier Class 8 2-8-0 No 48401.** *H. C. Casserley*

*Below right* **Another southbound freight crosses Dent Head viaduct behind Stanier Class '8' No 48547. The short pitch of 1 in 264 which follows the viaduct leads to the final gradient to a summit in Blea Moor tunnel.** *H. C. Casserley*

this 424-foot bore began at the north end in November 1871 and finally reached the south end in January 1875, having encountered shale, lead ore, coal, slate, iron, grit, magnesian limestone and mountain limestone in that short distance. Two and a half miles of 1 in 100 lifts the line to Ais Gill viaduct (261 yards long, 75 feet high) and, shortly afterwards, the summit.

It was never an easy route to work, and there was much double-heading. It was never, therefore, a cheap route to work either, a legacy exacerbated by the infrastructure of viaduct and tunnel. The Midland used it because they had it, and often wished they didn't - one tends to feel that BR felt much the same. But politics created it, and it is not, perhaps, in view of activity from all sorts of bodies in recent years, too much to suggest that politics has ultimately kept it there. Now, thanks to sensible marketing, the route seems to be seeing more passengers than it has ever done, and it is to be hoped that this support will continue.

# Cockburnspath

'**N**o space in the whole drive is more beautifully romantic than that which the Company

must have felt the heaviest to deal with, viz the space leading to and from the celebrated pass or path called, from someone doubtless celebrated in his day, Cockburn or Cobor's Path (Cromwell, in his despatches to Parliament, wrote Copperspath). . .' (*Railway Times*, 27 June 1846)

An article about the East Coast Main Line in the *Railway Magazine* in 1897 does what so many similar ones have done before and since, and ignores almost completely that line's climb through the Lammermuir Hills. The Tweed and Tyne bridges are mentioned in passing, but other than that the problems of building the railway are completely ignored. And yet, so far as train working was concerned, the bank was the major difficulty.

Both the *Aberdeen Herald* and the *Newcastle Journal* reported a meeting in Dunbar on 9 July 1839 that favoured a rail link along the east coast between

The down 'Capitals Limited', headed by Class 'A4' No 60003 *Andrew K. McCosh*, passes the Border sign on 12 August 1950, with the climb to Cockburnspath summit and Penmanshiel tunnel still ahead of it. *E. R. Wethersett*

Negotiations were going on well before the granting of the Act; in March 1844 the company Chairman, John Learmonth, was writing to Sir George Sutton in connection with land and seeking support for the Bill. Sir George seems to have agreed, for the accounts show one payment for land, and another on 15 April 1845 of £765 for 'the relinquishment of a tunnel'. Sir John Hope was offered £7,000 for his land in March 1844, but evidently stuck out for more, since the account book shows a payment of £12,000 on 10 October 1845. Similarly, an offer to Lord Wemyss of £7,500 for 49.5 acres in May 1844 had become £9,451 2s 10d by the time it was paid in October and November.

Edinburgh and Newcastle, and during the 1840s there was much discussion, not only about which route should be used across the Border, but whether more than one was needed anyway. The Caledonian, in conjunction with the Lancaster & Carlisle, appeared to have control of the issue, but dithered about its route, allowing the North British to pip it at the post with a line between Edinburgh and Berwick. This was authorised on 4 July 1844, and opened on 22 June 1846, 14 months before the Caley route over Beattock.

Financial matters aside, the *Railway Times* announced on 24 August 1844 that advertisements for construction contracts for 20 miles of line had

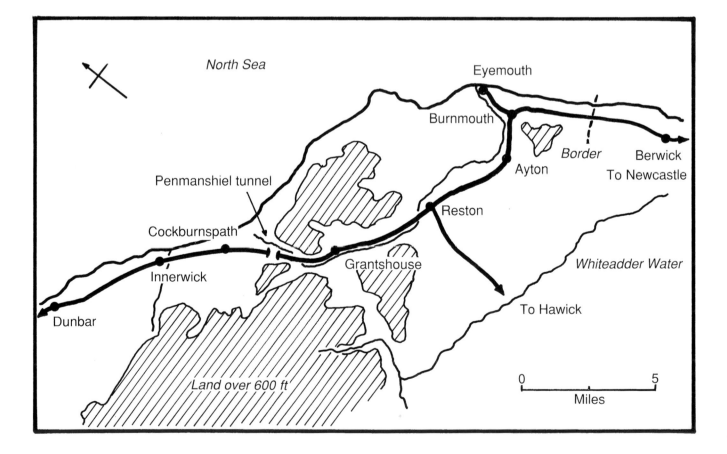

**Another 'A4', No 60009 *Union of South Africa*, near the summit of Cockburnspath bank on an up steam charter in 1966.** *Eric Aitchison*

been issued, and that some proprietors had already begun tree-felling along the route. In the report to shareholders of 3 September 1845 it was noted that much of the permanent way was laid, and that 'there was not any reasonable ground for doubting that the whole line would be completed and opened by the time originally proposed, viz May next'. Yet the Directors were, one feels, over-complacent, for no more than two or three days later the *Berwick Worker* was stating:

'On Monday morning last nearly 500 men in the Cockburnspath district, who have received from 14s to 16s per week, struck for an advance of wages to 20s.'

The demand was refused, and the men then walked down the line persuading others to join them, until a group of about 1,400 finally reached Berwick. The Berwick magistrates took fright, and arranged for a detachment of troops to be posted to the town. About 400 men then went back to work, and on Thursday morning 'the greatest number of Mr Evans's men also

returned. They have not received any advance of wages.'

Though the strike failed, it does seem to have prompted the Directors to some sort of action, however, since a committee visited the Cockburnspath area in the autumn of 1845 and found, to its horror, that the workforce seemed to be 'emerging from a state of mutiny, sullen and discontented'. The truck system was rife here, and in October 1845 there was a riot, when special constables were drafted in to control the navvies. In addition, the company set aside £100 for the services of a 'missionary', though there is no evidence of his appointment. Six months later there were more disturbances, and the Procurator Fiscal of Berwickshire called for extra constables, at a cost of £13 18s. Payments for equipment (batons, handcuffs, etc) were authorised also.

Notwithstanding all this, the Directors found themselves in a position to report to the shareholders on 17 February 1846:

'Several of the contracts on the main line are all but completed, and the others are in so forward a state as to give every reason to believe that they will be finished in time to admit of the line being opened in May next.'

Alas, it wasn't - or not quite. The line was inspected by Gen Pasley in May, and opened amid great rejoicing and a banquet at Dunbar on 18 June 1846. It might have been better had the Directors not been in so much of a hurry. Problems were to emerge all too soon, and the company minutes record the somewhat bland observation on 30 September that: 'Due to heavy rain since Monday last, certain of the bridges had fallen or were otherwise injured'. This was a distinct understatement. In fact, floodwater had washed away a length of embankment near Cockburnspath, where the Tower burn crossed beneath it, and caused the collapse of three bridges, two near Dunbar and the Tyne bridge at Linton. Six others were also damaged in some degree. It certainly raised questions about the workmanship (or lack of it) of those 'sullen and discontented' men, not to mention their supervision. The fallen bridges were replaced temporarily with timber structures, and later rebuilt in stone.

At a Special General Meeting on 30 October Learmonth made light of the disaster, remarking that the repair cost 'is very trifling indeed', and hoping that the line would re-open in ten to fourteen days. 'The bridges,' he then said, with an unconcern which almost takes one's breath away, 'would have fallen, whether or not the railway had been opened.'

So the line was open, albeit briefly, but many of the buildings were as yet incomplete. The *Scottish Railway Gazette* was optimistic, proclaiming that: 'Thursday the 18th of June will henceforth form an important epoch in the history of the Scottish railway system'. The *Railway Times* of 27 June was more pragmatic. 'Completion of the station-houses has been retarded from various causes,' it reported, 'chiefly on account of the difficulty of procuring workmen and materials - particularly iron.' One imagines that the imminent bridge repairs hardly improved this situation.

From an engine-driver's point of view the climb from Berwick, though much longer, is by no means the steepest. Half a mile north of Berwick there begins a four and a half mile pitch of 1 in 190, which lifts the line on to the cliffs and across the Border at Lamberton. This, it must be said, is not Cockburnspath bank proper, which does not begin for another five miles, but it is at least the start of the climb. Three miles beyond Lamberton, where Burnmouth Junction once was, the line turns sharply inland, and levels for a mile and a half past the site of Ayton station. A mile and three-quarters of downgrade and level follow this stretch, during which the line turns again through 90 degrees to a north-westerly direction, crossing on a viaduct a tributary of the Eye Water. Now the true bank begins, at 1 in 200, for two and a quarter miles past Reston, where, from 1862, the Berwickshire Railway once diverged inland

towards St Boswells and the Tweed valley. There is three-quarters of a mile of slightly easier going at 1 in 600 beyond Reston, but the gradient returns to 1 in 200 for the next three and a quarter miles. Then comes a mile-long pitch at 1 in 500, which lifts the line past Grantshouse (originally Grant's House) as the valley closes in on either side, and up to the short summit level, at 369 feet above sea level the lowest of the main-line Border crossings.

From the north the climb is steeper but easier to describe. It has begun before Dunbar, which is passed on a 1 in 300 gradient, and this steepens just south of the station to 1 in 200 for the best part of a mile and three-quarters. A level mile and a quarter follows, then a short down at 1 in 760, then another mile on the level. This ends at Innerwick, where the line begins to climb at 1 in 210, and continues to do so for a mile and three-quarters. Then, a mile north of the site of Cockburnspath station, the proper bank begins, four and a quarter miles at 1 in 96, crossing almost at once the biggest viaduct on the section, at Dunglass. This is 351 yards long and is built with six stone arches, three of 30-foot span, the main span with a throw of 135 feet and height above the Dunglass Burn of 111 feet, and then two more 30-foot spans. Cockburnspath station stood where the A1 trunk road crosses the line, and the long pull up ends with a brief 1 in 200, which brings the line to the summit.

Near the top of the 1 in 96 was Penmanshiel tunnel, 267 yards long. Of it, on 27 June 1846, the *Railway Times* had this to say:

'The tunnel at this place is 200 [sic] yards in length, and appears. . .to be furnished with the greatest care, a height of about 3 feet being of the rock, and the rest neatly cased with bricks, except where a more substantial arching may be required, and then it is, as usual, of well-dressed and perdurable stone.'

And so it remained until 17 March 1979, when part of it collapsed, trapping and killing two workmen. A diversion line was built through cutting to the west of the old course, and opened on 20 August, six weeks ahead of schedule. The work was done by Sir Robert McAlpine and Tractor Shovels, who began work on 8 May, and removed 200,000 cubic yards of rock and 133,000 yards 'soft dig'. Conditions, reported *The Railway Magazine* in October 1979, varied from 'being 12 inches deep in muddy slurry in wet weather, to "dust-bowl" conditions in dry weather. . . At night the site was as bright as a city street with a total of 18 high lighting towers in use.'

An attempt was made to obtain the new gradient

Grimy Class 'V2' 2-6-2 No 60812 leads a freight from Millerhill yard southwards through Cockburnspath station in 1963. *Eric Aitchison*

profile and details of the new summit height during the preparation of this book, but regrettably the Civil Engineer, Scotrail, was 'unable to provide' it. The *Railway Magazine* article quoted above, however, stated that the summit was now 'some four metres higher than it was originally'.

There were several stations between Berwick and Dunbar, none of which survives. They were (from the south) Burnmouth Junction, Ayton, Reston, Grantshouse, Cockburnspath and Innerwick - the last two named were the first to close for passengers, on 18 June 1951, and Reston and Grantshouse followed on 4 May 1954, Reston having lingered for three years after the demise of services along the St Boswells branch on 10 September 1951. Burnmouth Junction closed, along with the service on the branch to Eyemouth, on 5 February 1962, and Ayton succumbed on the same day. Now the route is electrified, and while the bank did not provide the problems that the steeper ones to the west did, there is now no noticeable difference, other than the scenery, in the ascent of Cockburnspath or Shap.

# Whitrope

**J**ohn Herepath, in his *Railway Magazine* of August 1839, reported a meeting in Edinburgh on 6 July which considered that one line would be sufficient to link Scotland with England, and that it should run, to a survey by a Mr Blackmore, from Edinburgh, through the counties of Mid-Lothian, Selkirk, Roxburgh and Northumberland, joining the Newcastle & Carlisle at Hexham, and 'admitting of a line diverging to Glasgow'.

This clearly foreshadowed the route that the North British was to take, but it was another 20 years before anything happened. The North British and the Caledonian companies were intense rivals, and the Caley cannot therefore have been overjoyed when

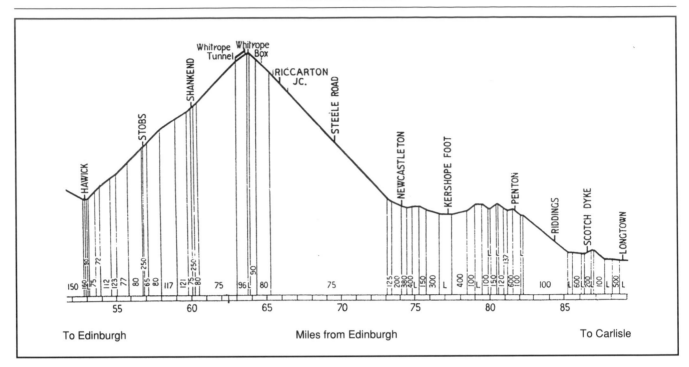

**Gradient profile, Whitrope**

the NBR, thinly disguised as the Border Union Railway, got powers on 21 July 1859 to build a line from Hawick to Carlisle. The CR, as we shall see, already had a direct route between Edinburgh and Carlisle, and had tried to counter the NBR's proposal by applying for a somewhat less elaborate line than the BUR had in mind. It failed.

The problem facing the North British was enormous. It had elected to build a main line 43 miles long through almost uninhabited (one almost wrote uninhabitable) countryside, for which substantial works would be required and very little intermediate traffic existed. But it set to work - if the Caley nose

**'A3' 4-6-2 No 4472** *Flying Scotsman* **climbs the 1 in 75 near Steele Road on a London to Aberdeen steam special in the mid-1960s. Note the SR rolling-stock.** *Eric Aitchison*

was to be bloodied, it could do no other - and even before the first sod was cut, building contracts, said *The Times* of 30 August 1859, had 'been let below the Parliamentary estimates'. Completion date was fixed at August 1861, and the line was to be double between Hawick and Riccarton, single thence to Langholm Junction, and double from there to Carlisle.

The first sod of the new line was cut at Hawick on 7 September 1859 by Mrs Hodgson, wife of the NBR Chairman. The company went to town in a big way over this, for on that day a banquet was given in honour of the event 'in a spacious marquee' (*The Times*, 9 September 1859). At about 2.30 pm 800 guests sat down in the marquee, while 300 to 400 working men dined in an adjoining tent, 'the communication being open between the two'. The festivities ended around 7.30 that evening.

Despite poor weather things appeared to be going well. *The Times* noted on 3 February 1860: 'The works on this line are progressing rapidly, and it is expected that a considerable length of it will soon be ready for the permanent way.' A month later the shareholders were told much the same thing at their half-yearly meeting. Six months later the southern section, from Carlisle to Scotch Dyke (11 miles), was expected to open shortly, and did so in October. All was not well in other parts of the line, however, and perhaps it is not greatly surprising that during the next twelve months *The Times* appears to have been left off the NBR's mailing list.

The weather was appalling almost throughout the entire construction period. Small wonder that the sentence 'Ritson [the contractor at Whitrope] is disheartened and will stop unless he is helped' crops up in a report to the Directors. Ritson was, in any case, the second contractor on this 4 mile 5 furlong length, for James Gow had worked the section at first. Ritson also had an adjoining 3 miles 3 furlongs at Riccarton. It was difficult enough to recruit men to work in that wilderness, and many of those who were prepared to sign on were not so prepared to stay. Add to this the hazard of

equipment becoming bogged down in marshy ground, subsidence of foundations and water everywhere, even in great quantities inside the three shafts of the tunnel, and the mind begins to boggle.

In his history of the North British Railway, the late John Thomas notes a visit to Slitrig viaduct in the spring of 1861 by one of the Directors, who observed that, since his last visit, a locomotive had passed over it. 'The appearance,' the Director wrote, 'of the soffit of the arch over the public road was not such as might be expected in a new bridge. It looked as if the engine had tested it rather severely.' Things were not much better by January 1862. Part of the Teviot viaduct had collapsed, and there had been a succession of landslips. Two contractors (Ritson was one of them) had their equipment sequestered and sold by the company.

Perhaps it is a wonder that the line opened at all, but open it did, on a day no better weatherwise than many of the others had been, for passengers on the first through train saw a snowy landscape - on 1 July! The line reportedly cost £400,000 more than the sum authorised for it by Parliament, but in spite of this the Directors celebrated again. *The Times*, 4 August 1862:

'The directors of this company on Friday [1 August] celebrated the opening of the new line from Carlisle to Edinburgh, at a banquet in Carlisle. About 600 shareholders inspected the line on Thursday, Friday and Saturday, and. . . availed themselves of the opportunity of passing through the picturesque scenery of the borders. Dinner was provided in the new engine sheds of the company, Mr R. Hodgson MP, Chairman of the amalgamated companies presided.'

The gable of land with Whitrope at its head gives a run of about 11.5 miles on each side, with very little difference between the vertical height climbed on

**Riccarton Junction was the most important place on the line over Whitrope, but it was also a bleak spot, at which the small community owed its existence entirely to the railway. There is no shortage of activity in this turn-of-the century picture - wagons being unloaded on the left, a full goods platform on the right, and, centre, a train, rear assisted, is about to leave for the south.** *Lens of Sutton*

either. From the south it began in earnest at Newcastleton, with a mile of 1 in 200, which then steepened to 1 in 125 for 25 chains. The main bank on this side was a continuous pull of seven and three-quarter miles at 1 in 75, taking in Steele Road and Riccarton Junction on the way. The gradient then eased, slightly, to 1 in 80 for a mile, and the last half-mile to the short summit level was at 1 in 90. Whitrope siding was about halfway up this last pitch, and the summit itself was 1,006 feet above sea level.

From the north it was more complicated. Hawick lay at the foot of a short 1 in 90 bank, which was succeeded by a rather shorter level. About 45 chains of 1 in 75 followed and then 40 chains of 1 in 72 led to three-quarters of a mile at 1 in 112. Half a mile of 1 in 123 came next, and this steepened sharply to 1 in 77 for the next three-quarters of a mile, before easing again to 1 in 80 for 70 chains. Short pitches of 1 in 260 and 1 in 65 took the line past Stobs - this was the steepest pitch on either side, but only a few chains long. Then came a mile of 1 in 80, a mile of 1 in 117 and three-quarters of a mile at 1 in 121, before 25 chains on 1 in 75 led to a short easing to 1 in 250 through Shankend station. It was brief relief only, for a short sharp pitch of 1 in 80 lay just beyond, leading to a two and a half mile length at 1 in 75. From the top of this it was another mile at 1 in 96, through the tunnel to the summit, which lay 300 yards beyond the southern portal.

The tunnel itself was 1,206 yards long, and, as has been hinted, was troublesome. It was cut through, from the north, 200 yards of old red sandstone on clay slate, then 700 yards of stratified sandstone, and finally shale beds alternating with thin bands of limestone and sandstone. Given this and the continuous deluge of water which poured down the shafts, one can understand poor Ritson's depression. Notably few Scots were employed among the miners on the Whitrope contract. Many of Ritson's men came from Wales - he had worked on a number of Welsh contracts, and had, no doubt, recruited these long-term employees there.

Financial results for the line were disappointing, though this should have surprised no one given the bleak countryside through which it passed. Like Ais Gill, its steep gradients required much double-heading, thus making it expensive to work, and it brought in little revenue. John Thomas shows that in 1920 Longtown, some nine miles north of Carlisle, generated £13,575, which was slightly under a half of the return for the whole line. In one of the line's best years Shankend could produce revenue of only £566 (£147 passenger, £419 goods), while the figure for Steele Road was even less - £381 passenger, £181 goods, total £562.

There were protests when the line closed on 6 January 1969, and the last train was held up for some time at Newcastleton, but in truth the writing had been on the wall long before that. A private scheme to save the line failed, and the track was removed with almost indecent haste.

# Falahill

'The North British Railway company,' proclaimed *The Times* of 23 December 1844, 'have been authorised by the shareholders to make an application in the ensueing (sic) session of Parliament for powers to form a line from the southern terminus of the Edinburgh and Dalkeith Railway to the town of Harwich [Hawick] and to raise additional capital.'

Ten days before Parliament approved the 'application' on 31 July 1845, an Act had been passed vesting the original company in the NBR. This also turned down a project extending the line even further south, to Carlisle. As we have seen, this had to wait until later, but it illustrates the urge of the NBR to stretch across the mountains towards the Border even then. It was estimated that the Hawick branch would cost £13,000 per mile, and it was said that there would be 'no heavy works to execute'.

It turned out to be the most expensive of the NBR branches, planned to climb through the valleys of the South Esk and Gore Water to a summit at Falahill, in a col between the Muirfoot and Lammermuir hills. Thence it would follow Gala Water, crossing it several times on cheaply built timber bridges. Put like that it doesn't sound too difficult, but the reality was to be otherwise, for it all but bankrupted the company.

In March 1845 the Chairman announced that '. . .a quantity of land has already been staked off at Dalhousie Mains south, and the engineer was going on by degrees, getting the more difficult parts of the line laid out'. Actual construction began late that year, and by the next February work was in hand on two ten-mile sections at Gorebridge and Borthwick. Two other contracts had just been let, and it was expected that the rest would be let by the end of the year. The Engineer, un-named in the report, was John Miller, with James Bell as Resident Engineer.

The Gorebridge section was being worked by Irish

navvies, while at Borthwick the workforce was a mixture of Scots and English. One Saturday the Irish, having received less pay than they considered appropriate thanks to the truck system in operation, were drowning their sorrows at an inn in Gorebridge. A pedlar tried to sell watches and then had to call the constabulary to recover samples which had 'gone missing'. Two Irishmen were arrested, then released by an Irish mob, which in a subsequent fracas so injured one of the policemen that he died next day. The English and Scots decided on reprisals, and destroyed the huts in which the Irish were living. Fortunately a force of Irish dragoons managed to dissuade a mob of their compatriots from wreaking further vengeance, and by the next Thursday all the men were back at work. Constable Richard Pace lies buried in the churchyard at Borthwick.

The Gorebridge/Borthwick/Tynehead section was, navvy rivalry apart, the most difficult section of the project, with a long, high embankment at Borthwick, considerable curvature and continuous cutting for just over two miles at Tynehead. The Chairman's autumn 1846 report, noted in the *Railway Times* of 5 September, remarked on how vigorously these were being pushed forward, but they were obviously costing more than anticipated, for before the line reached Galashiels a further loan of £35,000 was raised, and another £150,000 was being borrowed in December 1848. Freight trains were, however, by then running along the line as far as the unfinished tunnel at Bowshank, some five miles north of Galashiels. By the next November it had been decided not to proceed with any work south of St Boswells for the time being. The line eventually opened to Hawick on 1 November 1849.

The traveller faced fierce gradients in both directions, but that from the north was by far the toughest. It began shortly after Portobello, a shade over three miles from Waverley, with three-quarters of a mile at 1 in 80, and this was followed by 25 chains of 1 in 100 and a level of three-quarters of a mile. One mile and 25 chains then brought the line up to Millerhill, and three-quarters of a mile thereafter at 1 in 218 was succeeded by 25 chains of 1 in 250. A mile at 1 in 228 took the line past Eskbank, and just beyond Hardengreen Junction (for the Peebles Railway, opened 4 July 1855) the line took off at 1 in 70 and stayed that way for the next three and a quarter miles. There was a quarter mile or so of level at Gorebridge, which was followed by successive half-miles at 1 in 70 and 1 in 111. This ended at the now vanished settlement of Fushiebridge, and the next three and three-quarter miles reverted to 1 in 70, round the numerous curves through Borthwick and Tynehead. This pitch finished at the end of the previously noted long cutting, when the line contoured along the escarpment

for a while at 1 in 100. Before long, however, it turned south, still at 1 in 100, into the col and up to the watershed at Falahill. There was a brief level at Falahill box, a bleak spot 900 feet above sea level, the line having been raised around 800 feet in ten miles.

From the south the rise was both less and longer. It began half a mile south of Galashiels with a mile-long pitch of 1 in 120 through the station. There were then almost two miles slightly steeper at 1 in 110, to be followed by an easier pitch of 1 in 155 for three-quarters of a mile. Just under a mile at 1 in 99 took the line through Bowland, and was succeeded by a pitch at 1 in 175, almost three miles long. This carried the line through Bowshank tunnel, straight and

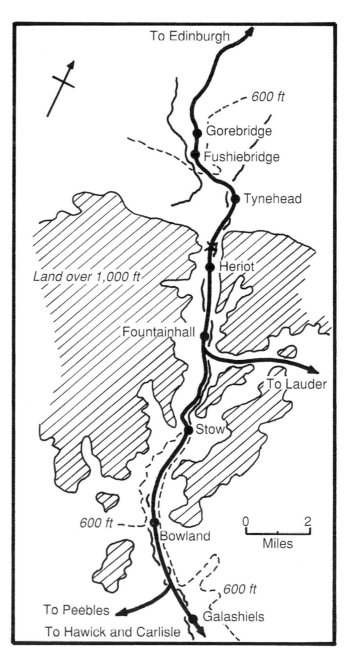

about 200 yards long. The station at Stow lay at the top of this pitch, and the line levelled for about 25 chains before a mile and a quarter of 1 in 200. There was then a brief level across the most substantial of several Gala Water crossings, near Watherston, succeeded by a mile and a quarter at 1 in 150. Then

came another level for a little less than half a mile, before another section at 1 in 150, this time for a mile and a half, lifted the line past Fountainhall Junction. This was where the Lauder Light Railway, opened on 2 July 1901, climbed steeply away to the east towards a destination in the next valley. Another brief level was followed by another mile of 1 in 150, but this steepened to 1 in 100, then eased to 1 in 110 at Heriot. A final 70 chains of 1 in 132 brought the line to the summit level after a climb of 16 miles and 500 feet.

*Left* Tynehead station was situated on the southbound climb to Falahill, in a deep cutting and on a slope of 1 in 70, two miles below the summit. The station building lay on the eastern side - note the advertisement for the *Evening Dispatch* hung beneath the station nameboard. *Lens of Sutton*

*Below* 'A3' 'Pacific' No 60093 *Coronach* takes a light goods from Millerhill yard to Carlisle over a snowbound summit at Falahill during January 1960. *Eric Aitchison*

The North British timetable of 1850 shows three passenger trains daily in each direction between Edinburgh and Hawick, with two each way on Sundays. The 53-mile journey took two and a half hours, for which the 1st class fare was 11 shillings, the 4th class 4s 5d, but passengers could only travel 4th class on the early morning train in each direction. There was a certain amount of goods traffic as the line opened up the tweed mills of Hawick, and coal was carried of course. The line became used more when the through line to Carlisle was open, but double-heading was normal, and this, with the resultant light engine mileage, meant that by no means could it ever have been the nice little earner the NBR had no doubt hoped for.

The stations originally authorised between Glenesk Junction (Eskbank) and Galashiels were, listed from the north, Tynehead, Heriot, Fountainhall and Stow. These were later supplemented by Eskbank, Dalhousie, Gorebridge, Fushiebridge, Falahill (Goods), and Bowland. Most survived until the Edinburgh/Galashiels services ceased on 10 September 1962, the only exceptions being Fushiebridge, which was a wartime casualty on 4 October 1943, and Bowland, which lasted ten years more, until 7 December 1953. Passenger services on the Lauder Light Railway ceased as early as 12 September 1932, but goods traffic, with a break between 1948 and 1950, lasted until 1 October 1958.

# Beattock

Which was to be *the* route to Scotland? It was a burning question in the early 1840s, and Locke, given the task of advising in the matter, investigated two. One, following Annandale and involving a steep ascent through Elvanfoot, with very little in the way of population on its course, he did not favour. The other suggested route went up Nithsdale, where not only were the gradients easier, but the towns of Dumfries and Kilmarnock could also be served.

The MP for Dumfries-shire, Mr J. J. Hope-Johnstone, strongly favoured Annandale, and asked Locke to think again. Locke began to see that it could be done, though the reason for his reservations was way ahead of his time. He was not so much worried

about getting up the bank; 'In the descent there is more danger,' he wrote, 'and this is a question of importance.' But it was another 30 years before engineers gave serious thought to the problem of braking power.

The Caledonian Railway obtained its Act for a line between Carlisle and Glasgow, using the Annandale route, on 31 July 1845. Locke was Engineer, assisted by John Errington; Brassey undertook the construction contract, and was to commit no fewer than 20,000 men to it. The first sod was cut by Lady Jane Johnstone Douglas on 11 October 1845, and work was swiftly under way.

It was not without its problems, for in June 1846 the *Dumfries Courier* was noting a series of 'melancholy and fatal accidents', observing sadly that 'several of these unfortunate men were natives of Dumfriesshire'. Rather worse, a year later, was an outbreak of black-spotted typhus in the Ecclefechan/Crawford area. The *North British Mail* attributed it to 'almost entire want of vegetables', and commented that many navvies were living in huts built of wet turf or damp, mossy soil. 'The fever,' wrote that journal's correspondent, 'has assumed the most alarming aspect about the highest summit level, and the contagion has spread to a considerable extent among the regular inhabitants of the district'. Land for a special cemetery was acquired at Elvanfoot, and 29 victims had been buried there by 9 July 1847, with others elsewhere.

Nevertheless, the work progressed. In May 1847 the *Dumfries Courier* sent a representative to the site, who, in the course of a flowery article - far too long, regrettably, to quote in full here - told readers of the newspaper that '. . .upwards of three miles of permanent rails have been laid, and [an]other two miles [are] in a state of forwardness to admit of the plate and sleepers being. . .put down'. Masonry works and about two-thirds of the cutting at Greskine were completed. The report closed:

'The summit. . .is beginning to own the might that slumbers in a 'navy's' [sic] arm, and, ere six months elapse, will present a less formidable front to the invasion, by the giants of steam, of these mountain solitudes, where erst the genius of retirement held undisputed domain.'

Caledonian shareholders were told on Wednesday 28 July 1847 that the southern portion of their line, 40 miles from Carlisle, was nearly completed, and would be opened for traffic in the course of the next five or six weeks. On 28 August Locke wrote to Hope-Johnstone:

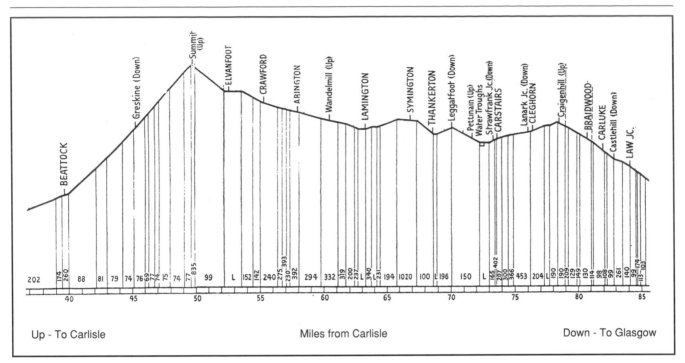

Up - To Carlisle          Miles from Carlisle          Down - To Glasgow

**Gradient profile, Beattock**

'The Line from Beattock to Carlisle is now laid, and prodigious efforts have been made by the contractor during the last fortnight when I saw it, in order to have it ready by the end of the month. A few works remain to be finished off but the Road, Ballasting, Bridges (the operational parts of the line) are well and substantially executed and I have no fear of any examination by the Inspector. You may open the Line whenever you think proper with perfect safety.'

On 2 September *The Times* reported that an inspection date had been fixed, and that although some buildings were unfinished, there was no anticipation of problems. A ceremonial opening of the Carlisle to Beattock section was held on 9 September, and it became open to the public next day.

Locke's letter also held promise of an early opening for the rest of the line. 'The Contractors,' he wrote, 'are now pushing the works so as to open throughout in November next. . . It is perfectly practicable, but it will be necessary to use Temporary stations at Glasgow and perhaps at Edinburgh.'

Considerable work still needed to be done, however. 'The time of opening,' reported *The Times* of 2 September, 'awaits the completion of the summit cutting, which originally contained 430,000 cubic yards and is now reduced to 20,000 cubic yards of rock; it will take about two months to complete.' There were more employee problems, too, before all was ready, for a dispute blew up between a contractor, Stephenson & Co, and labourers, who claimed they had been paid short. This, reported the *Railway Times* (22 January 1848), was settled in the navvies' favour, since the magistrates held that it could

'WD' 2-8-0 No 90152 tackles the climb to Beattock summit on 1 June 1951 just north of the station that gives the bank its name. *H. C. Casserley*

This view looks north from the same spot on the same day as an ex-Caledonian Railway 0-4-4T No 55237 with stove-pipe chimney assists an express up the hill. The only survivor of this class, CR No 419, can now be seen on the Bo'ness & Kinniel Railway. On the right the single-coach Moffat 'auto-train' heads out along the short branch. *H. C. Casserley*

not be proved that they had been informed that their wages were to be cut.

As for the statistics of the route, the gradient profile is formidable from whichever side one looks at it. The steeper slopes are on the south side, however, though things are comparatively easy until a hump north of Ecclefechan has been crossed, and another smaller one a mile south of Wamphrey. There is then a mile-long level before the line begins to rise at 1 in 202 for three and a quarter miles. Half-miles of 1 in 174 and 260 bring the line past the site of

Beattock station, closed on 3 January 1972, after which climbing begins with a vengeance. A shade over two miles at 1 in 88 is followed by a shade under a mile of 1 in 81. A mile and a quarter of 1 in 79 steepens to 1 in 74 for the next 70 chains, with another 70 chains at 1 in 76 succeeding that to take the line past Greskine. The 25 chains of 1 in 69

Bankers in repose: Beattock shed houses Fowler 2-6-4T No 42414 and Fairburn 2-6-4T No 42110 awaiting their next duties. The last of this class, No 42141, also survives, on the Keighley & Worth Valley Railway. *Eric Sawford*

which follow are the steepest on the bank, and then come half a mile of 1 in 77 and 30 chains of 1 in 74. Seventy chains at 1 in 75 are succeeded by a little over a mile at 1 in 74, with 50 chains at 1 in 77 leading to the final, easier, slope of 1 in 835 for a quarter of a mile. The line has reached its 1,015-foot summit, having risen 675 feet in the ten and a quarter miles from Beattock.

Approaching the summit from the north is no pushover either. Climbing begins at Uddingston, after the Clyde has been crossed, with a short pitch of 1 in 107, followed by slightly under two miles at 1 in 135. Then comes a 70-chain pitch at 1 in 115, followed by a series of short, quarter-mile or so bursts at 1 in 178, 132, level, 146 and 143, the last of which takes the line through Motherwell. Three-quarters of a mile at 1 in 116 lifts the railway to Flemington, where a mile and a quarter of 1 in 137 and two miles of 1 in 102 bring it past Wishaw South. Now comes another succession of short pitches: 1 in 103, 113, 174, with half a mile of 1 in 99 up to Law Junction.

Then a sequence of half miles at 1 in 140, 261 and 99, and 10 chains at 1 in 108 bring the line through Carluke on the steepest gradient this side, a mile of 1 in 98. There are 10 chains of 1 in 114 before a mile of 1 in 139 through Braidwood, after which a quarter-mile at 1 in 149, three-quarters of a mile at 1 in 129, a quarter at 1 in 209 and half a mile of 1 in 190 lifts the line to a summit at Craigenhill.

The steepest part is now over, and a steady descent at nothing steeper than 1 in 190 leads to Carstairs. There is a brief down of 1 in 165 to Strawfrank Junction, and a three-quarter mile level before a pull up at 1 in 1560 over two and a quarter miles to Leggatfoot. Over this hump, and another through Symington, and the line falls away again towards Lamington. There is a half-mile level beyond the station site (closed on 4 January 1965), then a quarter mile up at 1 in 237. Following half-miles are graded at 1 in 200 and 1 in 319, and a mile and a half of 1 in 332 is succeeded by a mile and three-quarters at 1 in 294. Three-quarters of a mile at 1 in 392 is followed by three short pitches of 1 in 230, 393 and 275, and the site of Crawford station (also closed on 4 January 1965) is passed on a 1 mile 25 chain pitch of 1 in 240. Crawford was near the top of this stretch, which steepens to 1 in 142 for 50 chains and then becomes 1 in 152 for a similar distance. A mile and a quarter on the level brings the line through Elvanfoot, after which a final pitch at 1 in 99, two and a quarter miles long, leads to the summit.

Though it did not occur specifically on Beattock bank, one cannot, perhaps, pass by without mentioning the appalling smash which occurred on 22 May 1915 at Quintinshill, on the 1 in 200 up from Gretna

Junction. It was a signalman's error rather than the bank that was to blame, but it was the worst railway accident that has occurred in the UK, claiming the lives of 227 and injuring 246.

# Polquhap

The line south from Kilmarnock to Dumfries had its beginnings when the Glasgow, Paisley, Kilmarnock & Ayr Railway decided to try to reach England. It arranged with the Glasgow, Dumfries & Carlisle company that it would build a branch south from Kilmarnock to Horsecleugh, near New Cumnock, to meet that undertaking's line coming north from Carlisle via Dumfries.

This was only feasible, of course, after Locke had been persuaded by Caledonian interests to abandon the Nithsdale route, and great must have been the relief in GPK&AR circles when he did so. Many in Glasgow regarded this withdrawal as an English betrayal, and support from that quarter for the Dumfries project was therefore good. The Horsecleugh branch was authorised on 21 July 1845, and though, unfortunately, the Dumfries line was rejected in that session, it gained Royal Assent on 16 July 1846.

Despite the Glasgow support, however, finance was still short, and it was 31 August 1847 before *The Times* could report:

'That portion of the main line from Gretna to Sanquhar, a distance of 51 miles, has been let to respectable contractors at a fair price and the works in general are progressing satisfactorily. Of the main line there only remains about 14 miles, from Sanquhar to Cumnock, unlet, which is of easy construction, and can without difficulty be completed at the same time with the rest of the line. . . The portion between Dumfries and Sanquhar has been let in three contracts of 11, 6 and 4 miles respectively, and are to be completed in March 1849.'

Only six months later however, owing to a trade depression, the half-yearly meeting of 15 February 1848 extended the completion dates of some contracts. Then, six months after that, there were more problems. The shareholders were told in the Directors' report that:

'With regard to the line north of Dumfries, circumstances have occurred to retard its progress. The contractors for the Drumlanrig contract, on which the tunnel, one of the heaviest works on the line, is situated, have found it expedient to make arrangements with another party of skill and experience in such undertakings, to relieve them of its execution.'

The contractors, one surmises, had gone bankrupt, though a more cheerful note was sounded with the news that twelve miles of line between Dumfries and Thornhill might be ready in six months, this giving a continuous line of 36 miles from Gretna to Dumfries. This, with the Cumnock extension, which was now open, left 'only about 30 miles to complete the direct communication with England'.

The considerable money troubles were still unsolved, however. For some weeks the workmen were unpaid, and roamed the countryside seeking, as it were, what they might devour. Needless to say this was of much annoyance to the populace in general, and the farmers in particular. Despite efforts to raise a loan, there was a point in January 1849 at which the only funds available to the Directors was a sum of £114. But the spring of that year saw an improvement, and on 1 September 1849 the *Railway Times* could report that:

'The new contractor for the Drumlanrig tunnel

is proceeding vigorously with its construction, and has bound himself to complete it by 1st October 1850. . . The Board recently contracted the unlet portion of the line between Sanquhar and Old Cumnock. This has been divided into four contracts, and the execution of the works has been undertaken by able and responsible contractors for an aggregate sum of about £67,000, being greatly under the estimate previously given.'

The tunnel was finished in the summer of 1850 and the contractor probably achieved his 1 October target, since the line opened throughout on 28 October.

It involves little in the way of hard work to trains travelling north, a fact which no doubt prompted Locke's original plan. There are easy gradients as far as Portrack viaduct, which crosses the River Nith five miles beyond Dumfries, to the north of Holywood. It was the only Glasgow & South Western viaduct originally built of timber, though a wrought iron superstructure was later substituted. It was designed and built under the direction of John Miller, of Grainger & Miller, Edinburgh.

Beyond Portrack the line rises at 1 in 200 for four and a half miles, after which comes a three-quarter mile level followed by a short 1 in 400, and, for a while, a general steepening. A mile of 1 in 200 takes the line past Closeburn and is succeeded by a quarter of a mile at 1 in 180 and a mile and three-quarters of 1 in 150. Half a mile of 1 in 155 is then followed by another half-mile at 1 in 150 and three-quarters of a mile of 1 in 148. A mile and a half at 1 in 150 comes before a very brief level and the final pitch, at 1 in

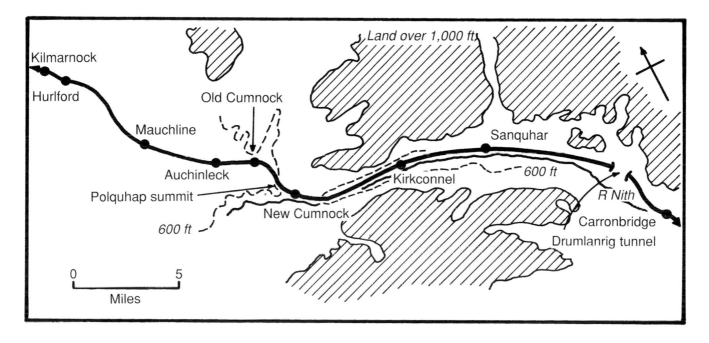

150, for a mile through Carronbridge and ending at the south portal of Drumlanrig tunnel.

The tunnel is, however, not the summit of the climb, which still lies twenty and a half miles on. Drumlanrig is 1,395 yards long, is the longest on the G&SW system and the second longest main-line tunnel in Scotland. It was built for double track, and, like all the major works on this line, was designed by John Miller. North of the tunnel the line continues on a falling gradient, and from now on the steepest section on the run to the summit at Polquhap is two and three-quarter miles at 1 in 180 on the approach to Sanquhar.

From the north side, however, it is a very different kettle of fish. Climbing begins just north of Hurlford with a fairly easy quarter-mile at 1 in 480. This is followed by three-quarters of a mile at 1 in 210 through Hurlford itself, and then two miles at 1 in 100. A minimal steepening to 1 in 99 takes care of the next mile and a quarter, after which is another pitch of 1 in 100 for three-quarters of a mile. Garrochburn, at the top of this, is taken at 1 in 105, there is a short easing to 1 in 190, and an further easing for 25 chains of 1 in 215. Halfway along the next pitch, 30 chains of 1 in 380, is the north portal of Mossgiel tunnel - it is short, 683 yards long, and the gradient changes to 1 in 400 down about a quarter of a mile inside. Easy slopes follow through Mauchline. Half a mile south of the town there begins a quarter-mile gradient of 1 in 180, which steepens to 1 in 160 for half a mile. Towards the end of this pitch the line crosses what is often regarded as the finest viaduct in the UK - Ballochmyle.

In hard statistics, which really do not do it justice, Ballochmyle viaduct is built of masonry, has three 50-foot approach spans at either end and a central span of 181 feet. The River Ayr passes 163 feet below the rails, and it was for some time the biggest bridge in Europe: it is still the highest railway bridge in the UK. Its designer was John Miller, who was born not far away, in Ayr, in 1805. He went to Edinburgh University, and made such a success of his civil engineering business that he could retire in 1849, to an estate at Innerleithen. His partnership with Grainger had a great influence on railways in Scotland. Grainger concentrated on English work after 1840, leaving his native country to Miller.

Beyond the viaduct the gradient increases still further, to 1 in 150, for a mile. Short lengths at 1 in 380, 200 and 150 follow, and then comes a longer pitch, of 1 in 180, for a little under a mile. A small hump at Auchinleck, with a short 1 in 300 on either side of the level south of the station, brings the line to 50 chains of 1 in 200. This is followed by three-quarters of a mile of level, preparatory for the final assault.

This begins with three-quarters of a mile at 1 in 146, which carries the line across Templand viaduct, built of masonry with 14 arches and passing 145 feet above Lugar Water. Curving south through Old Cumnock, the slope steepens infinitesimally to 1 in 145 for the next three-quarters of a mile, after which comes a half-mile easing to 1 in 150. A very brief level leads to three-quarters of a mile at 1 in 175, and the final few yards to the summit level are at 1 in 200. This is 616 feet above sea level, and from here a southbound journey is almost all downhill until the 1 in 200 up to Drumlanrig tunnel.

Through trains to the Midland Railway began using this route on 1 May 1876, and by 1908 five up and six down such expresses ran daily. After that a decline began, but in LMS days it became a useful diversionary route, and since the closure of the Port Road via Newton Stewart has taken Stranraer traffic, albeit a long way round. After rationalisation just Auchinleck and Kirkconnel remain as passenger stations between Kilmarnock and Dumfries. Holywood (called Killylung until renamed on 28 October 1850) was the first to go, on 26 September 1949, and Auldgirth followed on 3 November 1952. Carron Bridge was so spelled to begin with, but by 1860 had become the single word by which it is better known; it closed on 7 February 1953. Hurlford, the first at that end of the line, closed on 7 March 1955. Closeburn lost its passenger service on 11 September 1961, and the remainder, Mauchline, New Cumnock, Old Cumnock (plain Cumnock until 10 January 1955), Sanquhar and Thornhill, all succumbed on 6 December 1965.

# Cowlairs

**B**y the late 1840s the coalfield in the isthmus between the Rivers Forth and Clyde had already been opened up, and there was a new need for a direct railway between Glasgow and Edinburgh, using a valley previously considered too roundabout, which lay to the north of the coalfield. Two long viaducts were required, but the main problem lay at the Glasgow end, where the Forth & Clyde Canal Company refused to sanction a bridge across its property. Locke and Rastrick advised that differences in levels could

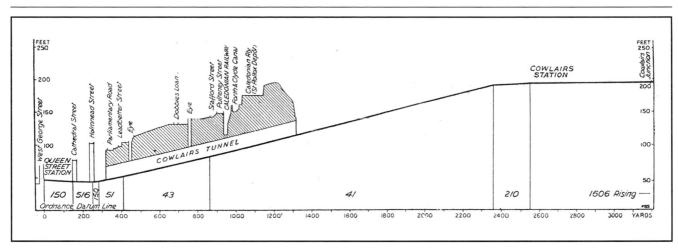

be overcome by 'an inclined plane. . .two miles of 1 in 40, with a tunnel after the manner of the Euston Square incline. . .' This course was adopted, the approach to Queen Street station from Cowlairs running by way of a steep tunnel, which passed beneath the canal at Port Dundas. It was to be worked by a stationary engine.

The Edinburgh & Glasgow Railway Company obtained its Act on 4 July 1838. Joseph Mitchell, later to become an eminent civil engineer himself, was involved in the work and wrote in his *Reminiscences*:

'John Miller was appointed consulting engineer, and Mr Locke. . .was appointed conjointly with

**Gradient profile, Cowlairs**

Mr Rastrick; but Mr Miller informed me that he did not require the extraneous help of either.'

The contract for the Cowlairs section was let by 18 February 1839, and in June of that year the *Glasgow Journal* observed that, 'Messrs Marshall are busy at the Glasgow terminus, and are burrowing in the earth at various places to facilitate the execution of the tunnel'.

**Ex-GCR 'Director' 4-4-0 (LNER Class 'D11') No 62687 *Lord James of Douglas*, rear-assisted, nears the top of Cowlairs bank on 1 August 1953. On the right a light engine makes its way down the hill towards Glasgow Queen Street.** *Peter Hay*

Whishaw visited the site too, commenting on an incline at Cowlairs of '1 mile 14.6 chains at 1 in 43'. He makes no other reference to it except to note three tunnels of 476, 292 and 272 yards, each with a span of 26 feet, a height of 22 feet, with sidewalls 21 inches thick and arches 18 inches thick. Work was obviously proceeding during his visit, because he also says:

'The works of this railway have been carried into execution under the general direction of Mr Miller, of Edinburgh, and are expected to be completed in 1841. The principal contracts are let to Messrs Gibb and Son, Messrs Forbes, Ross and Mitchell, and Mr N. Marshall.'

Despite Whishaw and a review of the North British Railway banks in an 1898 issue of *The Railway Magazine* which gives the gradient as one and a quarter miles at 1 in 45, another version, illustrated here, has a short 1 in 51, a quarter-mile of 1 in 43 and 1,500 yards of 1 in 41. The official gradient profile lists it as 1 in 46 for the first 25 chains, 1 in 41 for the next three-quarters of a mile, and 1 in 210 for the final few chains. You pays your money. . .

The stationary winding engine at the summit was built by Kerr, Neilson & Co for £2,900, and the original hemp rope was replaced by wire cable in 1847. This did not prevent the incline's worst accident, on 1 August 1850, when a grossly overloaded Scottish Central train set back without authority at Cowlairs and was run into by an oncoming E&G train. Five passengers were killed, and a number of others injured. Rope working continued under the NBR (which absorbed the E&GR in 1865) until new regulations came into force in December 1907, and heavy tank engines began to help trains up the hill.

It had been ten years before that when *The Railway Magazine* of October 1897 noted: '. . .a rumour that it is proposed to work the Cowlairs incline without the stationary engine is again in circulation. This time it is stated that the gradient will be improved.' But nothing was done, and even after 1907 the assisting tank engines were still attached to a cable; authority to remove this was not given until 26 August 1909, and the following month the stationary engine went for scrap.

In more recent years, continuous welded rail has been laid through the tunnel, and there is now headroom for electrification. Class '47' push-pull units took over the services on 3 May 1970, and have now themselves been supplanted by the Class '158' Super Sprinters. The line is now, perhaps, busier than it has ever been, so that, whatever its operating disadvantages, the incline at Cowlairs seems destined to be with us for some time to come.

A wider view of the top of the incline, as Thompson 'A1' 'Pacific' No 60152 *Holyrood* breasts the climb on the same day as the previous shot. Behind the train is Pinkston North goods station, with the line to Craighall leading away to the right. *Peter Hay*

140

# 7
# NORTH OF FORTH

## Glenoglehead

**E**ven by the early 1860s, when railway development in the less well-populated parts of England was advancing quickly, plans for railways to the remoter parts of Scotland were only just beginning to come together. Indeed, as we shall shortly see, even the important town of Inverness was not connected to the south by rail until 1865. Both the North British and Caledonian companies were anxious to extend their fields of influence, however, and when a scheme to link Callander and Oban was promoted in 1864, the Caledonian's ally, the Scottish Central Railway, agreed to work it when completed. Despite its ambitions, the Caledonian was not enthusiastic, its shareholders having, as John Thomas remarked in his history of the line, 'no stomach for squandering cash among the Perthshire hills'. On 5 July 1865, with little

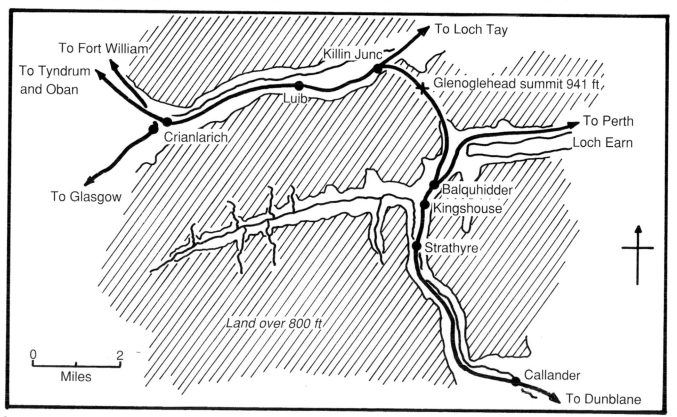

*Above* **Stanier Class '5' No 45400 approaches Glenoglehead summit with a goods train from Oban during June 1960.** *Eric Aitchison*

*Left* **Near Glenoglehead summit, also in June 1960, a pair of Stanier '5s', led by No 45049, head an Oban/Glasgow passenger train.** *Eric Aitchison*

Dunblane, Doune and Callander Railway, about One and a Half Furlongs Eastward from the Booking Office of the Callander Station of the Railway.'

When the scheme had been promoted, Brassey had offered to build the line. By the time construction was set to begin, however, he was struggling with his own financial problems. Of the ten tenders received, the award went to John MacKay at a price of £124,218, and a first sod was cut on 29 October 1866. MacKay based camps between Callander and Lochearnhead, and found that though there were no difficulties with the light sandy soil, there was a dearth of building stone - until, that is, he got to Glen Ogle.

trouble, the Callander & Oban Railway gained authority to build

'. . .a Railway commencing about Five Furlongs South-westwards from the Schoolhouse in the Town of Oban called the Oban Industrial School, and terminating by a Junction with the

His men were well-behaved, by the lights of the time, and were paid monthly at their working sites. Only one constable was necessary for policing, and there were protests when a second was suggested. Money was short, however, and the work went slowly. Rails, 2,250 tons of them, were delivered during the summer of 1867; they varied in length, and were laid on locally made larch sleepers. Then, in November 1867, the CR decided that work should cease for the winter. This would, of course, have involved the company in a large compensation payment to MacKay, but an arrangement was reached by which he would phase the work over as long a time as he could.

By March 1868 three-fifths of the cuttings and three-quarters of the masonry were finished. But 1868 became 1869 and the line seemed no nearer completion - the antis in the CR wanted an abandonment beyond Tyndrum, and a Bill was prepared. But 17.5 miles of the line were finished, and under its agreement the SCR had said it would work the line if 20 miles were complete. After some persuasion the CR agreed to work what there was. Timber station buildings were erected at Callander, Killin, Strathyre and Lochearnhead, and Capt Tyler inspected the line on 18-19 May 1870. It was opened on 1 June.

From Callander the line headed north-west, following the valley of the River Leny. It fell for the first half-mile or so, before 25 chains of 1 in 102 led into a mile and three-quarters of 1 in 60; this climbed the Pass of Leny, and was topped by 15 chains of 1 in 92. Now the line followed the shore of Loch Lubnaig with little notable variation in gradient. Strathyre station lay at the head of the Loch, and the line then bore right by Kingshouse towards the head of Loch Earn.

Just before Kingshouse, however, the climb began in earnest, with three-quarters of a mile at 1 in 139 carrying it past the platform installed there. This then steepened to 1 in 58 for about 50 chains before easing slightly to 1 in 201 through Balquhidder station. Five miles at 1 in 60 lifted the line high above the head of Loch Earn, giving a view said by many to have been the finest from any British train, and into Glen Ogle, where a final short pitch of 1 in 384 brought the line to its summit, 941 feet above sea level. This was the site of Killin station at first, but later, when Killin Junction was opened lower down, its name was changed to Glenoglehead.

In the autumn of 1870 there came a rumour that the North British was projecting a railway through the Trossachs. To protect itself, and against the wishes of some shareholders, the Caledonian let the 17-mile Glenoglehead/Tyndrum building contract to Easton Gibb, of Cardiff, for £69,261. It gave no engineering problems, and was opened in August 1873.

The climb up to Glenoglehead from this side began at Luib, in Glen Dochart, with 25 chains of 1 in 119, and continued with two and a half miles at 1 in 69. Then the gradients eased a little, with short pitches at 1 in 98, 58 and 138, at the foot of which the line passed Killin Junction. This station, from where the 5.25-mile branch to Killin and Loch Tay dropped down at 1 in 50 for almost four of them, was two and a quarter miles from Glenoglehead summit. Two miles of this distance was graded at 1 in 70, and two final, very short, pitches were at 1 in 84 and 1 in 491.

The line did good tourist business, and many were the excursions run in connection with steamers at Oban and in other causes; in 1911 the CR listed 32 involving the route. In 1923 the C&O, still independent, became a part of the LMS, though it retained its individuality and much traffic up to the Second World War. Sunday excursions were not resumed after 1945, and from the early 1950s a decline set it.

There were special regulations for traffic in Glenoglehead. Drivers were required to descend slowly enough to be able to stop in the event of a sudden rockfall, and it was one such that killed the line, albeit only shortly before its already decided execution date. A massive landslide near Balquhidder on the morning of 27 September 1965 was not thought at first to be serious, but closer inspection showed otherwise - it would take a month to repair, said the engineer's report, and would cost £30,000. The line was due to close in five weeks anyway, so it was abandoned forthwith - no doubt there are still rails beneath the rubble.

# County March (West Highland) and Corrour

**T**he North British Railway's counter to the Callandar & Oban was a line north from Glasgow via Loch Lomond to Crianlarich, where it crossed the C&O, then going further north across Rannoch Moor and by Lochaber to Fort William. The Highland, now firmly ensconced in Inverness, was not best pleased by this interloper at the other end of the Great Glen, but there was, in truth, little it could do about it. There were worries about how the line would disturb the deer-forests too, but an Act was passed on 12 August 1889 and a first sod cut at Fort William later that year.

The engineers for the line were Formans & McCall of Glasgow, and the contractors Lucas & Aird, a Westminster firm with Scottish connections. The job was split into two sections: Craigendoran to Crianlarich, and from there to Fort William. It is, of course, the latter which concerns us here, but the Resident Engineer for both sections was G. M. Tarry.

Building began at five points - Fort William, of course, plus Tyndrum, Crianlarich, Arrochar and Helensburgh. Many of the men were itinerant Irish navvies, a large number of whom absconded after a few weeks, unable to stand the conditions. North of Ardlui their weekly wage was 21 shillings, though part of this was paid in basic foodstuffs, apparently in an attempt to prevent them from spending *all* of their pay on drink!

The most difficult section, predictably, was Rannoch Moor, and it would have bankrupted the company had not one of the Directors, J. H. Renton, devoted a large part of his fortune to bailing it out. The method used for overcoming the 20 miles of boggy ground was one we shall meet again in the Druimuachdar and Dava sections, but a 20-foot-deep morass north of Rannoch could not be conquered even by this technique. A viaduct 684 feet long was substituted, the granite for the piers coming from Cruach cutting nearby.

Loch Treig was used to ferry supplies and materials to the men working at the sites at Corrour and on the moor. Many of the men who built the line were local crofters and fishermen, whose travel between home and site was paid for by the contractors, who also built, in the words of the *North British Daily Mail*, 'clusters of substantial and comfortable huts' for them.

The line opened on 7 August 1894, and gave its passengers (as indeed it still does) an almost continuous climb for 15.5 miles from Ardlui. The break comes at Crianlarich, which is actually on a falling gradient, but at the foot of the 1 in 64 which drops from the end of the platform the climb begins with 1 in 78 for about 25 chains and then 50 chains of 1 in 60. The slope on this side is laid out quite symmetrically, with short levels of easier grades at intervals, and it is a short level the traveller comes to now. The line is contouring up the east flank of Strath Fillan, and the level is followed first by a mile of 1 in 60, then by 10 chains at 1 in 114 and another 50 chains of 1 in 60.

The next respite is 10 chains level, which is succeeded by a little over a mile at 1 in 66 and a shade under half a mile of 1 in 60. Tyndrum station provides a breather of 1 in 260 for about ten chains, then comes another mile of 1 in 60. There is then a slight easing to 1 in 84 for 30 chains, but the slope is back to 1 in 63 for the last 30 chains, County March summit (1,024 feet) being reached at milepost 43 from Craigendoran Junction.

It is all downhill to Bridge of Orchy now, where climbing begins again - two and a half miles of it being at 1 in 66 - to a summit at Gorton, after which the line descends to Rannoch. A mile south of the station is the viaduct, of nine arches, and, like Glenfinnan, further to the west, built on a curve of 12

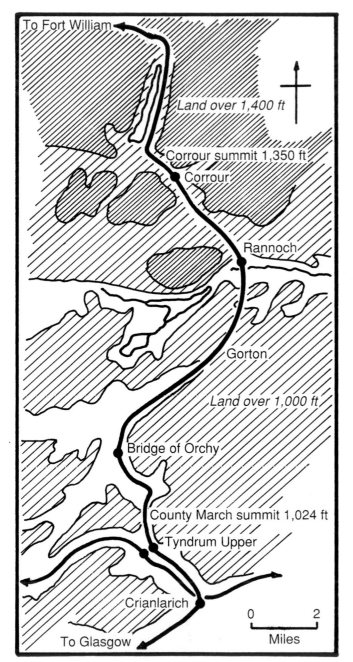

To Fort William

*Land over 1,400 ft*

Corrour summit 1,350 ft

Corrour

Rannoch

Gorton

*Land over 1,000 ft*

Bridge of Orchy

County March summit 1,024 ft

Tyndrum Upper

Crianlarich

To Glasgow

0    2
Miles

**A pair of Stanier Class '5s', led by No 44975, forge north about half a mile beyond the Tyndrum County March summit in 1960.** *Eric Aitchison*

chains radius. From Rannoch a little under one and three-quarters of a mile at 1 in 53 leads to a brief down at 1 in 100 and a level, where the rock cutting (Cruach) is graced with a protective snowshed. After another hump comes 50 chains of 1 in 79, a short 1 in 264 and then another 50 chains of 1 in 86. An easing to 1 in 300 leads to a 30-chain downslope at 1 in 83, but this is followed by a sharp up-pitch at 1 in 63, three-quarters of a mile at 1 in 191 and a quarter mile at 1 in 64. A short level, a quarter of a mile up at 1 in 61, and the worst of the climbing on this side is over. There are 25 chains of 1 in 428, 12 chains of 1 in 295, three-quarters

of a mile at 1 in 140, at the top of which is Corrour station, and the final quarter mile is taken at 1 in 380. The summit is 1,350 feet above sea level, a few yards over 72 miles from Craigendoran, and one can scarcely imagine a bleaker spot for a railway.

The climb to this point from the north side is defi-

**BR Standard Class '5' 4-6-0 No 73109 double-heads an ex-LNER Class 'B1' 4-6-0 on a morning Fort William to Glasgow train near the County March summit in 1961.** *Eric Aitchison*

**A pair of ex-NBR 4-4-0s, Nos 9407 and 9307, nearing Tulloch as they blast towards the summit at Corrour on 19 June 1937.** *H. C. Casserley*

nitely more arduous. It really begins at Spean Bridge, climbing steadily through Lochaber, past Roy Bridge, after which there are pitches at 1 in 80, 64, 59 and 65. At Tulloch, however, the line turns abruptly south, climbing for almost two miles at 1 in 59, this burst of energy bringing it to Fersit, where there is a short tunnel of 150 yards and a slightly easier section - a quarter mile of 1 in 1280, and three-quarters of a mile at 1 in 444. The next five and three-quarter miles is graded at 1 in 67, along the eastern slope Chno Dearg, with the waters of Loch Treig becoming further and further below on the right. Towards the top of this pitch the line turns away from the loch into a col, and a mile below the summit the gradient eases to 1 in 745 briefly before resolving into 1 in 59 for the rest of the way.

This is not all, of course, and the steepest slope on the hill is yet to come. There are short, steep pitches up to Gorton, but thereafter steadily downhill to Bridge of Orchy. Then 25 chains of 1 in 75 take the line south from the station, with a similar length of 1 in 350 to follow and a short pitch at 1 in 166. Half a mile of 1 in 77 comes next, then 30 chains of 1 in 61 and 50 chains at 1 in 132. This steepens to 1 in 91 for half a mile and then there are 50 chains of 1 in 254

before the final two and a quarter miles of 1 in 55 which lift the line to the County March summit. This begins about halfway round the famous horseshoe curve, a nine-mile detour necessary to gain height by contouring around and across the mouth of a wide side valley.

The line has been single throughout its life, and there are passing places at all the stations on the section discussed, Tyndrum Upper, Bridge of Orchy, Rannoch, Corrour and Tulloch, with an extra one at Gorton. The 1991/2 timetable shows four trains each way on Monday to Friday, four down and three up on Saturdays, and one down and two up on Sundays.

# Druimuachdar

**T**he southern section of the Inverness & Perth Junction Railway's line reached the highest mainline summit in the UK, at 1,484 feet. On 29 October

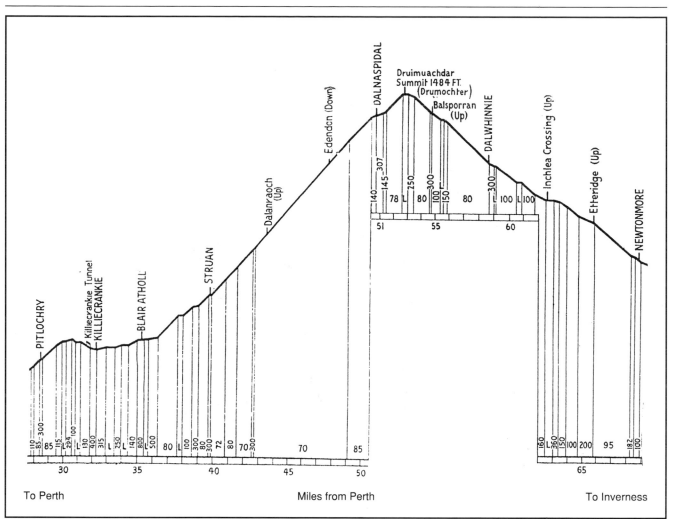

PITLOCHRY
Killiecrankie Tunnel
KILLIECRANKIE
BLAIR ATHOLL
STRUAN
Dalanraoch (Up)
Edendon (Down)
DALNASPIDAL
Druimuachdar
Summit 1484 FT.
(Drumochter)
Balsporran (Up)
DALWHINNIE
Inchlea Crossing (Up)
Etteridge (Up)
NEWTONMORE

110 | 85 | 300 | 85 | 115 | 294 | 100 | L | 130 | 400 | 315 | L | 250 | L | 140 | 800 | 500 | 80 | L | 100 | 300 | 80 | 300 | 72 | 80 | L | 300 | 70 | 85

140 | 145 | 307 | 78 | L | 250 | 80 | 300 | L | 150 | 80 | 300 | L | 100 | L | 100

51 | 55 | 60

160 | L | 360 | 150 | 100 | 200 | 95 | 182 | 100

30 | 35 | 40 | 45 | 50 | 65

To Perth | Miles from Perth | To Inverness

1862, a year after the first sod for the project had been cut, *The Times* noted:

'The report of the Directors states that the works along the whole line are making satisfactory progress. The last portion of the works, about 28 miles in length, was contracted for in May last and since that time the utmost activity has prevailed at all points in pushing on operations'.

Joseph Mitchell was the Engineer. He was born in Forres on 3 November 1803, a son of John M. Mitchell, who had worked with Thomas Telford. Joseph was himself a pupil of Telford for three years, was elected MICE in 1837, and later worked on several Scottish railways. He was struck

**Gradient profile, Druimuachdar**

**The 4-6-0 goods engines designed by David Jones for the Highland Railway were built specifically to cope with the gradients between Perth and Inverness. Here one of them, as LMS No 17924, tops the summit at Druimuachdar with a northbound freight on 15 May 1928.** *H. C. Casserley*

147

*Above* A southbound mixed train passes the large summit board at Druimuachdar, and a slightly swivelled gradient post. It is 1936, so we are still in LMS days, and the Stanier Class '5' is No 5173. Doubling the track eased the snow problem at this altitude, but no doubt the fence behind the train helped in this regard too. *H. C. Casserley*

*Left* The summit board at Druimuachdar. *A. G. Ellis*

'Another difficulty was crossing the river Garry at Struan, four miles from Blair, where there were waterfalls and plantations, through which there were pleasure walks to view the falls. This interesting spot he [the Duke of Atholl] objected to have touched, and I got over this difficulty by spanning the road and river obliquely at the narrow point by a three-arch bridge, thus not interfering with either his plantations or walks. The railway bridge was, in fact, an ornament to the falls, and he was much pleased with what he considered the ingenuity of the arrangement.'

down by a paralytic disease in 1862, but slowly recovered to reach a ripe old age, dying at Inverness just 23 days after his 80th birthday.

He chose his Druimuachdar contractors with care, and this paid off handsomely in the speed and efficiency with which the line was built. There were several engineering problems, not least the crossing of the River Garry, which Mitchell was later to recall in his *Reminiscences*:

It took Mitchell a deal of tact to persuade the Duke that the railway need not spoil his property, and he notes that, in the end, the 'Duke of Athole [sic] took great interest in the works, which seemed to give him a new pleasure'.

This was not the only problem, for a substantial amount of breastwork was needed in the Pass of Killiecrankie, where the gorge was so narrow at one point that a ten-arch viaduct 54 feet high and a short tunnel (128 yards) had to be built to get the line through. A girder bridge 515 feet long and 67 feet high carries the line across the Tay at Dalguise - this uses two iron trellis girders, one of 210-foot span and the other of 141 feet. There is another short tunnel at Inver, and a third, 310 yards long, near Dunkeld, but this last had been built in the mid-1850s by the Perth & Dunkeld Railway.

The Directors were optimistic about an opening the following summer; it was, however, not to be, but in truth they did not underestimate by much, for *The Times* reported on 2 September 1863 that 'this important line, 100 miles in length, is now ready for the inspection of the Government Officer. . .' Soon afterwards Capt Tyler RE went over the line accompanied by the Hon T. C. Bruce, Chairman of the company, and other Directors. He found the arrangements to his liking, and *The Times* was thus able to note on 11 September 1863:

'The line was opened throughout for public traffic on Wednesday [9 September]. Four trains run each way on weekdays, and one Parliamentary train each way on Sundays.'

The section from Pitlochry to Dunkeld had opened on 1 June, and the Forres/Aviemore part on 3 August. The Directors' report of 26 October observed that 'the traffic in every way exceeded the expectations of the directors'.

The steepest climb is from the south, and though there are pitches of 1 in 190 and 1 in 85 either side of Pitlochry, the bank proper does not really begin until about a mile beyond Blair Atholl, with a mile and a half of 1 in 80. There is then a short level 'step' before 50 chains or so of 1 in 100, again followed by a level 'step'. Another 50 chains, this time at 1 in 80, another, shorter step and then about 70 chains of 1 in 72 bring the line past Struan, or, these days, where Struan station used to be, just beyond the three-arch bridge mentioned above. There are no more reliefs - 70 chains of 1 in 80 steepen to a mile of 1 in 70 and then 10 chains at 1 in 300 lead on to the main slope, six and a half miles of 1 in 70.

Only in such circumstances, one supposes, can the ensuing mile and a half at 1 in 85 be called easier. Twenty-five chains of 1 in 140 lift the line to Dalnaspidal (or the site thereof) and a half-mile easing to 1 in 307. Then comes a quarter mile of 1 in 145, before, finally, a one and a quarter mile pitch reaches the summit level, about 1,200 feet above Blair, and some 17.25 miles on.

From the north there is nothing like so much footage to climb, and, while by no means easy, it is at least easier. The gradient begins, effectively, a mile north of Newtonmore with three-quarters of a mile of 1 in 304, steepening to 1 in 100 for 25 chains through the station. A short easing thereafter to 1 in 182 leads to two and a half miles of 1 in 95, as the line bears left and climbs out of Strathspey and into Glen Truim. Now comes a mile and ten chains of 1 in 200 and 70 chains of 1 in 100, succeeded by half a mile of 1 in 150 and 25 chains of 1 in 360. A level stretch follows, lasting for half a mile and taking the line over Inchlea Crossing. Three-quarters of a mile of 1 in 160 and 70 chains of 1 in 100 herald another half-mile level 'step', which is followed by a mile and a quarter of 1 in 100. Ten chains of level, 25 chains of 1 in 300, and the line reaches Dalwhinnie, set at the foot of Loch Ericht.

The line bears to the left across the tail of the loch and enters another side valley, the prelude for another steep climb, this time for two and three-quarter miles at 1 in 80. A short 1 in 150, a short level, half a mile of 1 in 100 and a short 1 in 300 bring the line to the foot of the last pitch of note. This is a mile of 1 in 80, from the end of which half a mile of 1 in 250 leads to the summit level. On this side of the summit the line has climbed about 500 feet in 15.75 miles.

Banking was very much a part of operations over this section of line, so that special siding facilities were required at appropriate places such as Inchlea. It was to solve this highly uneconomical method of working that David Jones developed his famous six-coupled goods engines of 1894, the first locomotives of the 4-6-0 wheel arrangement in the UK.

The Highland very soon found that the single track originally laid was proving to be a bottleneck - in the 144 miles between Perth and Inverness only about 15 were double, and this sometimes led to lengthy delays. The train staff and tablet system was introduced in 1890, as a substitute for the telegraph, and in 1897 authority was given for doubling, within two years, 17.5 miles north of Blair Atholl. John Best, the contractor who did the work, was later to build the Strome Ferry to Kyleakin line for the HR in 1897. The doubling went some way to solving the snow problem in cuttings too, for the wider space between the cutting sides now gave the snow less chance to drift.

The doubling programme had topped the summit by 1901, and was extended to Dalwhinnie in 1909. Extra passing loops had been added too in the years from 1896 and 1911, though some were removed again during a 1930s economy drive. The track was singled throughout in 1966, but was re-doubled between Blair Atholl and Dalwhinnie 12 years later. Stations have been rationalised too, but only Struan and Killiecrankie have closed, on 3 May 1965.

# Dava Moor

'The works on the Inverness and Perth Junction Railway have been commenced,' announced *The Times* on 29 October 1861, 'and will be vigorously prosecuted.'

How often have we met similar statements before in these pages, but this time for once it was true. Less than two years later the line, about 100 miles in length, and across two major summits, one of them the highest in the UK at the time, was open. This was largely due to the company's Engineer, Joseph Mitchell.

The reason for the line was simply that the people of Inverness had, they felt, been let down by the Great North of Scotland Railway, which had promised them a link with the south via Aberdeen and failed to provide it. The scheme that the I&PJR came up with left the Caledonian Railway at Stanley Junction, north of Perth, and headed for the mountains by way of the already built Perth & Dunkeld Railway, which it would take over. Through Pitlochry, Blair Atholl and the pass of Druimuachdar it went, and came to Strathspey at Newtonmore. This it followed for a while before climbing out of the strath to cross Dava Moor to Forres, where it joined the Inverness & Aberdeen Junction Railway.

All this makes it sound a good deal easier than it actually was. Mitchell was way ahead of the thinking of his time, and the first Bill was ridiculed in Parliament. Influential people were involved, however - Sir Alexander MacKintosh was an active promoter, and James, Earl of Macduff, Bt, took £30,000 worth of shares, subscribing in the early days to get the project off the ground. And persistence paid off; the line was authorised on 22 July 1861 and a first sod was cut near Forres on 17 October. 'Lady Seafield,' says Mitchell in his *Reminiscences*, 'was kind enough to perform this duty.'

The good progress was maintained, and six months later the Directors were talking of an opening between Forres and Grantown towards the end of 1862. This was over-optimism, and was not cured by harsh reality, because the Directors' report of 29 October 1862 expected that: 'about 40 miles at the north end. . .will be ready for opening early in the spring. . .' The line wasn't ready then either; there

had been problems with drainage in the peat bogs near the summit. Deep ditches were cut 50 feet apart to drain the surface water, then a 15-foot wide strip between them was layered with turf and heather, though even this did not solve the problem completely, extra sleepers having to be inserted in some places for stability where the peat was more than 20 feet

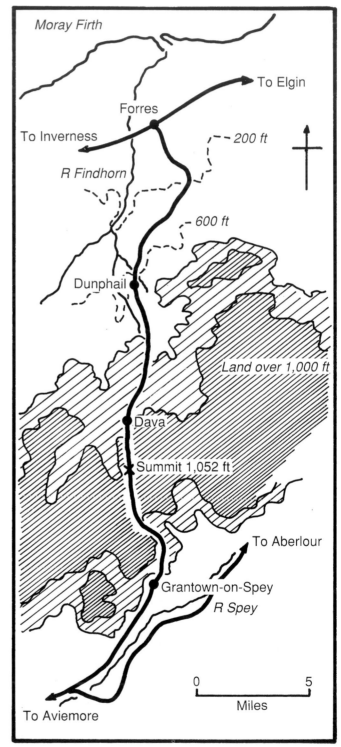

thick. As the peat dried it shrank, and ballast had to be inserted periodically to maintain the level. By the end there was almost 30 feet of it in some places. This drainage technique was also used at the watershed around Druimuachdar.

So it was another ten months before, on 3 August 1863, the section between Forres and Aviemore was opened. *The Times* seems, actually, to have got itself in a muddle over the opening date - it announces, correctly, on 8 September 1863 that the opening of the line throughout will take place next day, only to backtrack two days later to say that just the 36.5 miles (it was actually 35.5) between Forres and Aviemore had in fact opened on the 9th. Next day it contradicts itself again to state that the line 'opened throughout for public traffic on Wednesday. . .' - ie 9 September. 'The summit level,' it said on 10 August, 'is about halfway between those places, and its elevation is 1,000 feet [official height was 1,052 feet], forming on the average an ascending gradient from Forres of about 1 in 100.'

The longer and steeper haul to the summit at Dava Moor was from the north. It began almost off the platform end at Forres with a dozen chains of 1 in 150, but this soon became a mile of 1 in 70. Half a mile of 1 in 100 was followed by another half mile at 1 in 75, and 10 chains at 1 in 300. Then it was back to 1 in 75 again for the next six miles, as the line turned first east and then curved sharply back to a general south-westerly direction through Newtyle Forest. The 1 in 75 ended at Dunphail, where the line ran parallel with the old military road, now the A940, for a while. There was a short pitch of 1 in 300 through the station, then 1 in 125 for about ten chains before half a mile of 1 in 150 led to a minor summit, followed by a quarter mile down at 1 in 300 to cross the River Divie. This crossing formed the major civil engineering work on the section, and was a masonry viaduct 477 feet long standing 105 feet above the river

Now the line emerged above the tree-line, climbing first at 1 in 100, then 1 in 70, then for a little over a mile at 1 in 74. A two-mile pitch of 1 in 70 followed, there was a short respite of 1 in 200 and another three-quarters of a mile at 1 in 76, the conical slopes of the Knock of Braemoray rising steeply to the right. Then came two 25-chain lengths of 1 in 160 and 100 before 50 chains of 1 in 160 led past Dava station, which served very little in the way of a settlement, but which was sometimes the inhabitants' only contact with the outside world. Three-quarters of a mile of 1 in 100 and half a mile at 1 in 200 led to the first summit, beyond which the line descended at 1 in 160 for three-quarters of a mile. A similar length of 1 in 130 led to the real summit, 17.75 miles from

Forres and 1,012 feet higher.

From the south the climb began two miles north of Broomhill, with half a mile of 1 in 110 followed by three-quarters of a mile at 1 in 80. There was a short easing to 1 in 300 through Grantown-on-Spey station, after which things got tough again: three-quarters of a mile at 1 in 84 and then three and a half miles of 1 in 80, which took the line over the A939 and past Castle Grant Halt. Then came a sharp curve to the west and the line came out of the woodlands on to the moor. It straightened, too, for the final 25 chains at 1 in 100 and three-quarters of a mile of 1 in 350 which brought it to the summit.

This line was particularly prone to the ravages of the weather, and trains stuck in snow up here were not uncommon. But the Highland Railway (as the I&PJR became two years after the line opened) kept as abreast as it could of the weather's vagaries and usually managed to get traffic through. The route took a long way round, but it was a big improvement on nothing, and served the Highland well for over 30 years, when it was supplanted by the shorter alternative over Slochd Mhuic. It then became a secondary link, but was no less valuable for that.

There were three intermediate stations and one halt on the bank to begin with - Rafford (between Dunphail and Forres), Dunphail, Dava and Castle Grant Halt. Rafford survived only until 1865, but the others remained in use for another century, until the passenger service over the line was withdrawn on 18 October 1965.

# Slochd Mhuic

**W**hen railway journey times began to reduce, the Highland Railway began to look for a way to cut the time that had to be taken in travelling between Perth and Inverness. That was the ostensible reason given, anyway, but another anxiety may have been a possible incursion up the Great Glen by the NBR, which was working the West Highland Railway and was thus at Fort William. So in an effort to protect its position the Highland devised a 'cut-off' from Aviemore through the Monadhlaidh mountains and down to Inverness via Daviot and Culloden. From Aviemore, though steep, the climb is not so long, but

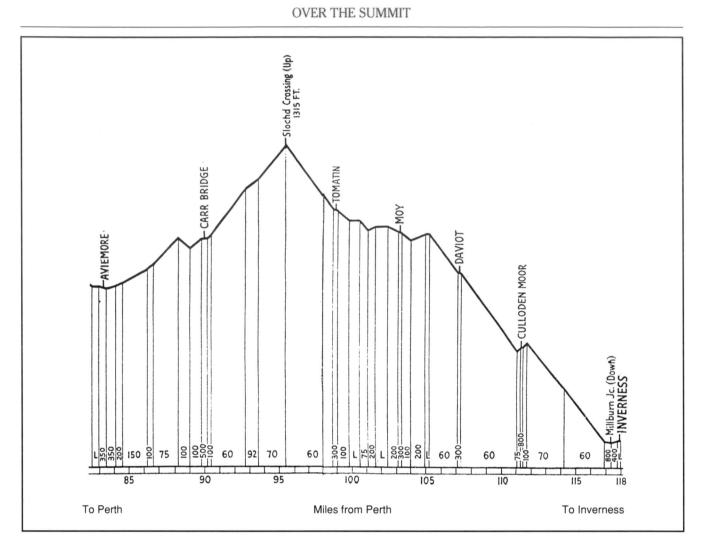

To Perth                    Miles from Perth                    To Inverness

**Gradient profile, Slochd Mhuic**

from the Inverness side it presented the enginemen with a formidable obstacle.

Powers for the line were obtained on 28 July 1884, but the completion of the work was by no means so quickly achieved as the original main line had been 30 years earlier. Still, it could equally be said that the civil engineering involved was more complex - a viaduct and deep cutting at Slochd, and two long viaducts over the Rivers Findhorn and Nairn. The line was engineered by Murdoch Paterson, who, sadly, died at Culloden three months before it was completed. It opened on 1 November 1898, and an article that appeared in the *The Times* the following day gives a flavour of the period and the problems involved:

'The new railway, which was opened yesterday, is only 34 miles in length, but in constructing it many serious difficulties have had to be overcome. In fact the line is in some respects a triumph of engineering skill. Deep cuttings have had to be made, enormous embankments built up, and numerous mosses, river and mountain gorges crossed. There are over 150 bridges, some of them immense structures. The work has also had to be carried out under adverse conditions. Thus, at the Drumbain cutting, which is the largest on the line and is situated over 1,300 feet above sea level, the weather is so severe during the winter that the work had to be suspended for four months or so at a time. The line begins at Aviemore Junction, and the first station is a Carrbridge, a village which is rapidly gaining a reputation as a health-resort, and is recommended as specially suitable for asthmatical persons. As far as Carrbridge the railway has been open and used for traffic for the past six years. This part of the line, extending to six and a half miles, was the most easy to construct, the only difficulty which the engineers encountered being a peat moss in Crannich Wood. Beyond Carrbridge the line crosses the River Dulnan [sic] on a bridge having a span of 180 feet and standing 56 feet above the bed of the stream. Then comes an

Fowler 'Mogul' No 13105 nears the summit at Slochd Mhuic with a ten-coach southbound express, marshalled in a notable variety of stock, on 20 July 1931. From here it is two miles to the summit, all at 1 in 60. *H. C. Casserley*

embankment 45 feet high, followed by a long cutting 50 feet deep and immediately thereafter a huge viaduct across the desolate gorge named the Slochd Muick [sic]. This viaduct is 400 yards long, and is supported on eight arches of 37 feet span each. The height is 105 feet, and there is a rising gradient of 1 in 70. A solid-looking structure, it is built of natural granite and is in keeping (so far as such a thing can be) with its gloomy surroundings.

'At Carrbridge the line is 914 feet above sea level and about five miles further on the summit level of the line (1,320 feet) [sic] is attained. It is here that the Drumbain cutting already mentioned is situated. The largest on the line, the depth of a considerable portion of it is 56 feet. To carry the line across the Findhorn valley and river there are two viaducts. The first, 445 yards long, is of steel built on granite pillars, while the second, which is much shorter, is of stone. Near these is Tomatin station, distant from Carrbridge some nine miles, and four miles further on is Moy station, in the vicinity of Moy-hall, the residence of Mackintosh of Mackintosh. The next station, Daviot, is perched on a high limb on a spur of the Monadhliath [sic] Mountains, and from here a magnificent view is obtained of the surrounding country. . .

'The magnificent scenery opened up along the route was greatly admired, and the well-finished, substantial appearance of the railway was a matter of special comment.'

The climb really begins at Aviemore, with about 50 chains at 1 in 350 a little beyond the platform. This increases to 1 in 200 for half a mile, after which comes a pitch of a mile and three-quarters at 1 in 150. Half a mile of 1 in 100 comes then, and, still increasing, a mile and a half of 1 in 75. Now the line falls for three-quarters of a mile at 1 in 100 before rising for the same distance and inclination to a short stretch of 1 in 500 that includes the station at Carr Bridge. From the platform the line rises for 10 chains at 1 in 100, then for a little over two miles at 1 in 60, followed by an easing to 1 in 92 for just under a mile. Two miles at 1 in 70 bring the line to its 1,315-foot summit, in, as *The Times* correspondent noted, a deep cutting. Because of the need for staff to be here, a small settlement grew up, and

Other than the Culloden viaduct, the one that crosses the Findhorn river is the major work on the Sloch line. This is how it looked in August 1989. *Allan Mott*

153

special trains were run down into Inverness so that the inhabitants could shop.

Those shoppers, or rather the drivers who conveyed them, had no easy task. Milburn Junction is the point at which the Slochd line leaves the coast route, and for half a mile the gradient is only 1 in 600. The next two and a half miles are at 1 in 60, and a similar distance after that at 1 in 70, as the line contours along the north side of Culloden Moor, gaining height in order to be able to take a wide loop across it. There are downgrades past the site of Culloden Moor station, and soon afterwards the line swings out high above the Nairn valley on a viaduct of 28 50-foot spans and one of 100 feet. Built of red sandstone, the viaduct is 600 yards long and stands 130 feet above the river. Then, exactly seven miles out from Inverness, three and three-quarter miles of 1 in 60 begin, the line climbing along the hillside in order to be able to enter the valley of the Craggie Burn. The pitch ends as the line turns towards the mountains, and becomes a 10-chain easing at 1 in 300 past the site of Daviot station.

Another 1 in 60 pitch follows, but only for two miles this time, at the top of which is a short level and a mile downhill at 1 in 200. A 50-chain pitch at 1 in 100 brings the line to a short section at 1 in 300 through Moy, and this is followed by three-quarters of a mile at 1 in 200, and a similar distance on the level, with Loch Moy lying below on the left. A brief down at 1 in 200 leads to half a mile up at 1 in 75, a three-quarter mile level and the same distance up at 1 in 100. The River Findhorn comes into view on the left, and Tomatin station stood on an easing of 1 in 300. The final three and a quarter miles to the summit is graded at 1 in 60, including, immediately south of Tomatin, the viaduct across the River Findhorn. This consists of nine steel lattice girders each 132 feet long, the viaduct's total length being 445 yards, and standing 143 feet above the river. At the summit the line has risen more than 1,100 feet in just under 22 miles, or 50 feet per mile, an average of 1 in 105 over the entire distance.

There was a bad accident at Baddenden Burn, about one and a half miles north of Carrbridge, on 18 June 1914, when a bridge across a tributary of the River Dulnain collapsed beneath the 11.35 am train from Perth to Inverness. Maj Druitt held an enquiry at Carrbridge station on 23 June, whereat the crew of the train said, according to *The Times* of the next day, that 'they felt the train swerve as it crossed the bridge, but by the time they had brought the train to a standstill the bridge was gone'.

The verdict confirmed a theory propounded in a colourful account of the accident printed in *The Times* of 20 June, that a flash-flood caused by a recent cloudburst was the culprit. Five passengers died, but thanks to a remarkably swift piece of work by Sir Robert MacAlpine a new bridge was opened for traffic only three weeks later.

All the intermediate stations except Carrbridge are now closed. The line is double from Inverness to Culloden Moor, but on the single section crossing places are retained at Slochd, Tomatin, and Moy. A dozen or so passenger trains use the line daily in each direction during the week, and about half that number on Sundays.

# Raven's Rock, Corriemuillie and Luib

'**I**f the people of these districts,' said the Chairman of the Inverness & Perth Junction Railway Company at Inverness on 27 October 1863, 'could subscribe capital to make those lines, the company would offer them all reasonable assistance and encouragement.'

'These districts' referred to Strome Ferry and the west coast, and the I&PJR was as good as the chairman's word. Support was promised, and an Act for the Dingwall & Skye Railway was obtained on 5 July 1865. It served a predominantly agricultural area, and provided the first rail link between the fishing villages of the west coast and the markets of the east. Yet not everyone wanted it. Sir William Mackenzie of Coul and the local populace of Strathpeffer did not, and a new Act (dated 29 May 1868) was needed before work could begin, avoiding that town by making a deviation to the north, and limiting to Attadale the railway's extent, at least for the time being. 'Strathpeffer saved a little capital,' commented Joseph Mitchell, 'but lost much business.'

The D&SR's Engineer was Murdoch Paterson, an associate of Mitchell. Paterson had been born in Inverness in September 1826 and was apprenticed to Mitchell at the age of 20. He moved to a firm of contractors in 1851, but returned to Mitchell three years later, to be taken into partnership in 1857. Ten years later Mitchell retired, and, though Mitchell had

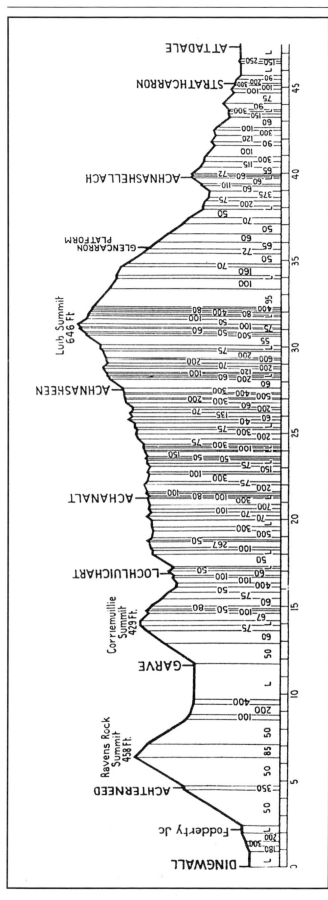

**Gradient profile, Raven's Rock, Corriemuillie and Luib**

already laid out the Strome Ferry line, Paterson was actually responsible for building it.

The construction contract for the 21.5 miles between Dingwall and Achanalt was let to Messrs Granger, while Messrs Macdonald became responsible for the line from there to Attadale, 25.5 miles. The completion date was fixed at 1 July 1870. There seem to have been no notable problems, for shareholders were told on 29 October 1869 that there was every reason to expect the line to open on time. By now the contract for the remaining five miles to Strome Ferry, and the works there, had been let to a Mr Macgregor. In fact the line was just over a month late in opening, for goods on 5 August 1870 and for passengers on 19 August. Its 53 miles had cost the company £4,284 10s 11d per mile, remarkably cheap when compared with the cost of, say, Gresford 24 years earlier. Land here was no doubt cheaper, but the going must have been a good deal harder.

The first two and a half miles out of Dingwall are unexceptional, but beyond the site of Fodderty Junction (of which more anon) the train moves straight from level on to a long embankment across the valley, graded at 1 in 50, for two miles. There is a brief easing to 1 in 350 past where Achterneed station once stood, and then the line takes off at 1 in 50 again, for slightly over one and a half miles this time, to the summit at Raven's Rock. It is perhaps interesting to reflect that this 458-foot peak, reached after three and three-quarter miles of hard climbing, was only necessary because the folk of Strathpeffer prevented the line from taking the easier way through the town. That these views were shortsighted was soon shown when the little town became known for its chalybeate water and a branch to it was opened from Fodderty Junction on 3 June 1885. Perhaps the crowning irony was provided when the daughter of Sir William Mackenzie, one of the main objectors, welcomed the inaugural train, while his son rode on the footplate of the engine. In fact, the place eventually became so busy that the railway company was encouraged to build its own hotel.

Raven's Rock has an equally steep drop down the other side, which is followed by a long level section along the lochside to Garve. A little over a mile of 1 in 50 begins at the platform end, and three-quarters of a mile at 1 in 60 follows it, easing to 1 in 75 for the last quarter of a mile to the next summit. This is Corriemuillie, slightly lower than Raven's Rock at 429 feet, and only half as long in terms of actual climbing. There is now a two-mile descent, which then rises again for a short distance to a small peak at Lochluichart. From here to the next summit, at Luib, the gradient profile looks more like a saw-edge than anything else. Suffice then perhaps to say that other than for three-quarters of a mile leading out of Lochluichart, much climbing and descending is at 1 in 75; there are also a number of pitches between that gradient and 1 in 50, though none of them is long. The trend is upward, past Achanalt to Achnasheen, where there is half a mile of 1 in 60 off the platform end as the line bears south towards Loch Gowan. Then comes another group of very short pitches that end in a down of 1 in 70 for a quarter of a mile, followed by a climb of 1 in 200, broken by a short pitch of 1 in 300. The line is climbing along the south shore of Loch Gowan now, where ten chains of 1 in 75 and a quarter mile level bring the line to a half mile pitch at 1 in 55. This is topped by a brief level, and short lengths of 1 in 50, 60, 75 and 100 finally lift the line to Luib summit, 646 feet above sea level.

From the western side the climb is a good deal easier to describe. From Strathcarron to Achnashellach is a rising sawtooth, and beyond the latter place the line drops steeply for a mile or so through Achnashellach Forest. A mile further on comes half a mile of 1 in 50, followed by similar distances of 1 in 70, 50, 60 and 65, which brings the line to Glencarron. The next mile is at 1 in 72, 50 and 70, after which there is an easing to 1 in 160 for half a mile and a short level. Fifty chains of 1 in 100 come then, steepening to a mile of 1 in 95. Very short lengths at 1 in 400, 80, 400, 80, 100 and finally a quarter mile of 1 in 50 bring the railway to the summit.

Down the saw-edge to Lochluichart now, from where Corriemuillie is attained by way of short pitches of 1 in 50, 75, 60, 80 and 50, with a final half-mile of 1 in 67 to the summit level. The climb to Raven's Rock from this side begins two miles west of Garve with quarter of a mile of 1 in 400, steepening for the next half-mile to 1 in 200, then still further to 1 in 100 for a quarter of a mile. One and a half miles of 1 in 50 comes next, and the climb ends with a last three-quarters of a mile at 1 in 85.

The *Inverness Courier* reported very heavy traffic at the opening, with some double-heading and a monster train of 49 vehicles. This was due at Inverness at 10.00 pm but was late. 'We need not wonder,' commented the newspaper, 'it was long past the hour before it arrived here.'

The line did well from the start, showing what was described as a 'satisfactory return for the first year of working', that working being done, incidentally, by the Highland Railway. Sheep traffic in particular was noticed as being on the increase. In 1874 the shareholders were told that though tourist traffic was slow to build up, but was improving, and there were good prospects for fish from Lochmaddy and the Outer

Hebrides. By now the company was carrying mails under the Act of 1873 which allowed it to do so.

The Highland Railway obtained re-authorisation for the extra ten miles from Strome Ferry to Kyle of Lochalsh on 29 June 1893, and this was opened on 2 November four years later. The line has lost none of its tourist popularity, and since 1983 BR has run a (hired) observation car regularly along the route during the summer months. Most stations have survived, the only casualties being Achterneed, Glencarron and Fodderty Junction, which lost its passenger service to Strathpeffer on 23 February 1946 and its freight traffic on 26 March 1951. The line has been single throughout its life, and passing places remain at Garve, Achnasheen and Strathcarron. Trains - three each way on weekdays are shown in the Winter 1991/2 timetable, but none on Sundays - are controlled by radio telephone.

# Lairg

From Inverness to Wick is but 80 miles as the seagull (or perhaps raven) flies, but to travel between the two by rail involves a roundabout journey of twice that distance. The route is made up of lines built by four separate companies over a period of 14 years, the third of which built the first summit, at Lairg.

The Inverness & Ross-shire Railway began things, and its line, authorised on 30 July 1860, was to cover 31 miles between Inverness and Invergordon, on the north shore of the Cromarty Firth. It travelled due east at first, along the south shore of the Beauly Firth, turning sharp north at Beauly and then going via Dingwall. A more direct route across the firths was scotched by Sir Alexander Matheson, who had estates at Ardross. He was, after all, the company chairman. . .

Having reached Invergordon on 23 March 1863, the railway was extended northward by the Inverness & Aberdeen Junction Railway. The route skirted the high ground to Tain, but then declined to bridge the Dornoch Firth at that point in favour of a course along the southern shore of the firth. A mile-long bridge towards Skibo looks feasible, and it would have saved an awful lot of mileage (not to mention journey time), but it was not to be. Again the gentry had a hand - the Duke of Sutherland made a large subscrip-

One of the reasons for the continued existence of the line over Lairg summit are the oil installations. This is Lairg's oil terminal in June 1987. *Allan Mott*

tion on the understanding that the line would go by Ardgay, and having done that there was then no logical alternative to a route via Lairg.

The line was continued by the Sutherland Railway, which obtained Parliamentary approval on 29 June 1865 to build 32.75 miles from Bonar Bridge (Ardgay) to Brora. Work began the next month, the contractor being Messrs Brand & Son, an Aberdeen firm, which had tendered £111,949 for three contracts. 'The works,' the Chairman told the shareholders in October 1865, 'on that portion of line extending from Ardgay station of the Highland Railway to Kirkton, near Golspie, a distance of 25 miles, has been let to Messrs Brand and Son, contractors, and are in active progress. . . The works of the line are going on satisfactorily. . .and [the contractor] no doubt will be able to complete it to your satisfaction.'

A year later *The Times*, reporting the shareholders meeting on 30 October 1866, reported that they had been told that the foundations of the Oykell viaduct had been secured and that they would be ready to receive the ironwork next spring. But optimism about an opening of the first 27 miles to Golspie in the autumn of 1867 had declined by that October to a hope 'that the line would be ready for traffic early in January'. One reason for delay was the rock cutting at Lairg, which proved more arduous than had been anticipated, but there was another reason too. 'Messrs Brand & Son. . .have been greatly hindered in their working operations by delay in the delivery of the patent rails which were supplied by an English firm.' No doubt some readers of that February issue of *The Scotsman* enjoyed that.

The line finally did open, to great rejoicing and probably some relief, on 13 April 1868. A banquet, presided over by General Matheson, was given at the Golspie Hotel for the Duke of Sutherland and the Directors - it was no secret that without His Grace the line would have failed to get even this far. Before this event the *London Scotsman* noted on 3 February, in an article about the line, that:

'The gradients are somewhat severe. From the Oykell there is an ascent of 1 in 72 to 75 for about eight miles to the summit, which is upwards of 500 feet above sea level. There are several very heavy rock cuttings. The scenery at some parts of the line is almost equal to the finest of the many picturesque views on the Highland Railway, by which company the traffic is to be worked.'

One can almost see the grudging expression on the HR press-release writer's face as he squeezes that 'almost equal' in, largely, one guesses, to drag the Highland Railway logically into the piece too.

The climb to Lairg summit begins a little over two miles north of Bonar Bridge, fairly unobtrusively, with a pitch of just less than a mile of 1 in 150. Just below

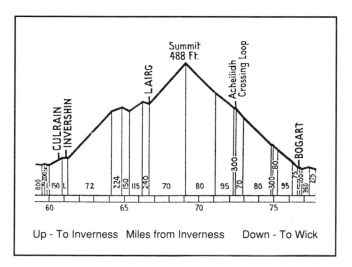

Gradient profile, Lairg

the top is Culrain, beyond which the line curves right, levels to cross the River Shin, and swings left into Invershin station. Now the proper bank starts, with a shade under three miles at 1 in 72, which eases for three-quarters of a mile to 1 in 224, and then falls for half a mile at 1 in 150. Three-quarters of a mile at 1 in 115 raises the line again, only for it to fall for half a mile at 1 in 240. Lairg station lies at the foot of the dip, and off the platform end begins two and a half miles of 1 in 70. During this section the line curves gradually southwards, the final tweak bringing it to its summit, in the rock cutting which so delayed things in the building.

Heading towards Inverness from Bogart the south-bound train is actually travelling north-west! There is a short length of 1 in 75 off the platform, and this is succeeded by a mile of 1 in 95. It eases briefly to 1 in 80 and even more briefly to 1 in 300 before steepening for a mile and ten chains to 1 in 80, and 50 chains of 1 in 70. There is then a short (10 chains) pitch of 1 in 300 and a mile of 1 in 95, steepening for the last time to 1 in 80 for the run to the top, 488 feet above sea level, whatever press-releases from the Highland Railway might pretend.

# County March

**T**he County March summit lies some hour and twenty-five minutes' journey-time (60.5 miles) from that at Lairg. The stretch of railway on which it lies was built by the Caithness & Sutherland Railway, to link a failed project for a line between Wick and Thurso with the railhead slowly pushing north from Golspie. This line had by then, and thanks once again to the Duke of Sutherland who built it, reached Helmsdale, where, if it was going any further, it would have to turn inland. A 'numerously attended meeting' was held in Wick on 2 February 1871, at which a rather disappointing return by way of subscriptions was a mere £1,000. A committee was appointed to canvas for more and must have been successful, for the new line was accepted by Parliament on 13 July 1871, to run from Georgemas Junction to Helmsdale, 46 miles, with a large proportion of it across some of the bleakest countryside in the United Kingdom.

Murdoch Paterson, who was to be appointed

Engineer to the Highland Railway in 1874, was in charge of this new project, with W. Baxter as Resident Engineer. In the end, Paterson seems to have dealt with the northern half, from the summit northwards, leaving the rest to Baxter.

The work began with little delay. In November it was reported that Paterson had marked out the line 'from the County boundary to Wick and Thurso respectively', and it was resolved to start work at once. The Directors also noted gratefully that many landowners and tenants on the course of the line had 'met the company in a liberal spirit in regard to the compensation to be paid to them'.

In such country it was essential to provide decent accommodation for the navvies, and they were housed in groups of about 60 in barracks spaced out along the route. Each evening a locomotive would collect the labourers from their sites and carry them to the yellow-painted timber houses, which are said to have been comfortable and well-furnished - a far remove from the almost contemporaneous conditions at Ais Gill! But by September 1872 the work was far enough advanced for *The Scotsman* to be able to report a visit by the Duke of Sutherland, when he ran his private locomotive and carriage over the first few miles of line at the Helmsdale end. He was accompanied by Mr Baxter, and the report concluded by remarking that 'the line is making great progress throughout both counties'.

There had been delays, nevertheless. Work on the Caithness side had begun on 1 April 1872 and Paterson reported that in spite of disruptions by the weather a quarter of the excavations had been completed, together with all the cross-drains and ditches over three-quarters of the line. 'The masonry of the two viaducts over the Thurso river,' he told the shareholders, 'is ready for the girders, and the foundations for the Wick river viaduct is being proceeded with.'

On the southern section Baxter reported that the small workforce engaged during the winter had been increased in the spring, and progress had been steady. The wet summer had caused delays here too, but these had been overcome, and 'upwards of four miles' of permanent way had been laid and was now being ballasted.

The next winter was appalling too, but the navvies battled on and twelve months later 50 miles of the total 66 (including the Wick and Thurso branches) had been laid. Only about 60,000 cubic yards of earthworks were left to be excavated in the Altnabreac area, and the Directors hoped for an opening early the following summer. Six months later the six-mile stretch immediately north of the summit was all that remained to be completed, and Paterson was confident of an opening on 1 July. Yet something must have gone wrong, for Col Rich did not inspect